American Protestants and TV in the 1950s

Religion/Culture/Critique
Series Editor: Elizabeth A. Castelli

AMERICAN PROTESTANTS AND TV IN THE 1950S

RESPONSES TO A NEW MEDIUM

MICHELE ROSENTHAL

palgrave
macmillan

AMERICAN PROTESTANTS AND TV IN THE 1950S
Copyright © Michele Rosenthal, 2007.

First published in 2007 by
PALGRAVE MACMILLAN™
175 Fifth Avenue, New York, N.Y. 10010 and
Houndmills, Basingstoke, Hampshire, England RG21 6XS
Companies and representatives throughout the world.

PALGRAVE MACMILLAN is the global academic imprint of the Palgrave Macmillan division of St. Martin's Press, LLC and of Palgrave Macmillan Ltd. Macmillan® is a registered trademark in the United States, United Kingdom and other countries. Palgrave is a registered trademark in the European Union and other countries.

ISBN-13: 978–1–4039–6573–8
ISBN-10: 1–4039–6573–0

Library of Congress Cataloging-in-Publication Data is available from the Library of Congress.

A catalogue record for this book is available from the British Library.

Design by Newgen Imaging Systems (P) Ltd., Chennai, India.

First edition: October 2007

10 9 8 7 6 5 4 3 2 1

Printed in the United States of America.

to the memory of my father
Ralph N. Rosenthal
(1931–1990)

Contents

Preface

RELIGION/CULTURE/CRITIQUE is a series devoted to publishing work that addresses religion's centrality to a wide range of settings and debates, both contemporary and historical, and that critically engages the category of "religion" itself. This series is conceived as a place where readers will be invited to explore how "religion"—whether embedded in texts, practices, communities, or ideologies—intersects with social and political interests, institutions, and identities.

In her monograph, *American Protestants and TV in the 1950s: Responses to a New Medium*, Michele Rosenthal challenges readers to think in new ways about the relationships between religion and technology, between religion and media. Even the most casual observer of contemporary American religious culture understands the savvy with which evangelical Protestant broadcasters have capitalized on the power of the televisual and other mass media forms. Rosenthal historicizes the success of this cultural investment by placing it alongside the less-well-known story: the failure of mainline (liberal) Protestantism to engage with technologically mediated formats with similar canniness or ease. Presenting several concrete case studies that ground the argument, Rosenthal raises broader theoretical questions about religion and mediation, about the role of purportedly secular forms in the translation of religious messages and the construction of virtual religious communities in the U.S. As an important contribution to the growing field of religion and media, *American Protestants and TV in the 1950s* is a welcome addition to the RELIGION/CULTURE/CRITIQUE series.

ELIZABETH A. CASTELLI
Religion/Culture/Critique Series Editor
New York City
September 2006

Acknowledgments

American Protestants and TV in the 1950s could not have been written without the invaluable support and guidance I received from Martin E. Marty, Wendy Griswold, and Martin Riesebrodt during my time as a student at the University of Chicago. Martin E. Marty has been a never-ending source of citations and suggestions, and I continue to be grateful for his kindness and friendship. Over the years, my colleagues in the field of religion, media, and culture have offered insights, encouragement, and important critiques of this work. Specifically, I would like to thank Lynn Schofield Clark, Stewart Hoover, David Morgan, and Diane Winston for their friendship and collegiality.

Even in the electronic age, I have relied upon the kindness and skill of archivists at the Billy Graham Center in Wheaton and the Presbyterian Historical Society in Philadelphia who aided me in my search for source materials. The Louisville Center for the Study of Protestantism provided funding at a crucial stage. The Center for Religion at Princeton graciously allowed me to present one of the early chapters, for which I received important feedback. An earlier version of chapter two appeared in a collection entitled *Practicing Religion in the Age of the Media: Explorations in Media, Religion, and Culture*, edited by Stewart M. Hoover and Lynn Schofield Clark. (New York: Columbia University, 2002). An earlier version of chapter three, "This Nation Under God: Mainline Protestant Responses to the New Medium of Television," appeared in *The Communication Review*, 4(2001): 353–377, and is reproduced with permission of the Taylor & Francis Group, LLC., http://www.taylorandfrancis.com.

My colleagues and students in the Department of Communication at the University of Haifa have provided me with an important context for intellectual pursuits and have enriched my thinking about communication beyond the American Protestant boundaries of this book. I am especially grateful to Tamar Katriel, Yael Maschler, and Rivka Ribak for their friendship and guidance.

In Israel, I feel I have been especially lucky to join a wonderful extended family. My mother-in-law, Ruth Nevo, continues to inspire me with her day-to-day enthusiasm for art, literature, and family. I appreciate her living example, her generosity and kindness toward me, more than these words might convey. Special thanks likewise go to Ilana Pardes and Itamar Lurie for their unending patience, positivity and encouragement.

Despite the fact that they are geographically remote, my brother Michael Rosenthal and his wife, Janelle S. Taylor, have remained close and I am thankful for their friendship and intellectual camaraderie. Likewise, I am grateful for close friends, thanks particularly to The Zimmers—Terese, Bob, David, Benjamin and Alex; Sarah E. Hodges and Stephen P. Hughes; Leora Batnitzky, Haya and Erez Birk; and Netta Cohen.

And lastly, and most importantly, my family deserves the greatest acknowledgement: Amos Nevo, my husband and partner, for his love and care and our children Naomi, Netta, and Ilan for our daily life together.

This book is dedicated to the memory of my father, Ralph N. Rosenthal, whose quirky curiosity about the past, and fascination with old technologies (clocks, music boxes, scientific instruments) accompanied me through childhood and provided the backdrop to my own historical interests.

Introduction: The Triumph of Televangelism and the Decline of Mainline Religious Broadcasting

In March 1987, Televangelism became headline news.[1] Stories of sexual and fiscal impropriety turned ministers Jim Bakker and later Jimmy Swaggart into household names. Journalists played their part as well, relying upon the well-known historical trope—the hypocritical minister—to outline and shape their reports.[2] Yet despite the cultural familiarity of this Elmer Gantry type of narrative, journalists and arguably their readers, remained "surprised" by the depth and the strength of the subculture these ministers represented, and their extensive and effective use of the television medium. They were not alone: throughout the 1970s and much of the 1980s, sociologists and scholars of religion largely ignored the beliefs and practices of these media savvy ministers and discounted the potential effects of religious broadcasting. In the wake of the scandals, both reporters and scholars tried their hand at explaining this strikingly American phenomenon that was coming to be known as the electric or electronic church.[3]

But just as compelling, for both journalists and scholars, was the relationship of the televangelists to what was called "The New Christian Right," a group that was first recognized and patronized by presidential candidate Ronald Reagan in 1980 and that later gained momentum during his 1984 reelection campaign. This politically conservative coalition of evangelicals, fundamentalists, and charismatics challenged the received consensus concerning the role of religion in the public sphere. In the post-Scopes trial era, the modernist liberal version of Protestantism, a version that was often designated as mainline, had confidently dominated the public sphere and largely disregarded the potential strength of their evangelical and fundamentalist counterparts.[4] The fear of secularization was far more tangible to mainline leaders than the slight possibility of an evangelical revival.[5] The appearance of the New Christian Right in the 1980s suggested the contrary: religion could survive and adapt to the demands of the modern world and, despite previous predictions of extinction, evangelical or conservative Protestantism could potentially thrive, perhaps more so than its liberal counterpart.[6]

Televangelism (even in its scandalous state) provided a vibrant illustration of this possibility. Television, the quintessentially modern communications medium, could be used to promote an old-time Gospel religion, which at face value seemed to negate the very modernity that bore such a technology. Mainline Protestant leaders, whose epistemological positions allowed for far greater tolerance of science and its technological fruits, nonetheless remained reticent about television, and reluctant to use this new communications technology to promote their agenda. In contrast, evangelical and fundamentalist leaders who remained committed to a conservative theology embraced the television as a means to spread the word of God. Mainline Protestant leaders did not anticipate the growing importance of television in American culture—both as entertainment and in the public sphere.[7] Evangelical and fundamentalist leaders likewise may not have understood the implications of their decisions—but their relative success in religious broadcasting, particularly as regards the creation of an active audience would serve their cause culturally and politically in very important ways.

While sociologists of religion in mid-twentieth century America prophesied the decline of religion in general, they ignored the stalwart quality of conservative antimodernist Protestantism. By the end of the 1980s and early 1990s, numerous books on fundamentalism, the Christian right, and religion in twentieth-century America, all suggested that not only was religion here to stay, but that the sort of religion that might best survive in modern or postmodern society (depending on the commentator) might precisely be that kind that was epistemologically antithetical to it, yet culturally flexible.[8] Mainline religion, particularly in its Protestant guise, which remained modernist but decidedly culturally conservative, may or may not have a fighting chance. The jury is still out.

In 1950s America, however, when television emerged as the newest and most innovative communications medium, mainline Protestantism was in its heyday. Mainline Protestant leaders along with sociologists and historians of American religion (and there was some overlap in these categories—between the religious and the academic) tended to view evangelical Protestantism as a withered branch of a hearty healthy tree. Confident that their hegemonic position within Protestantism itself and in the broader public sphere would continue, mainline leaders largely ignored and dismissed evangelical and fundamentalist efforts to utilize the new medium of television. At the same time, they were often at a loss with how to respond to this new medium. As beneficiaries of free airtime on the major networks (as a public service), mainline Protestant leaders negotiated the television from its earliest days. Despite this clear economic advantage (their evangelical and fundamentalist counterparts had to purchase airtime), by the 1980s, televangelists largely dominated the airwaves, and mainline Protestant broadcasting was largely an experiment of the past.

This book compares the different ways in which mainline and evangelical Protestant leaders responded to the new medium of television. These particular case studies provide an important vantage for viewing the changes within American Protestantism over the last fifty years. Fueled by the aphorism that we live in an age dominated by media, particularly of a visual orientation, this study seeks to integrate the insights of communication studies, particularly the social construction of technology approach, with the history of American Protestantism. The aim of this volume is to further our knowledge and understanding of the ways in which conservative Protestantism has managed to negotiate and thrive in the modern mediated public sphere, and to suggest and explain why liberal or mainline Protestantism has not.

These are the very issues that have dominated the public discussion in the aftermath of the 2004 elections: what happened to liberal religion? The popularity of Jim Wallis' book *God's Politics: Why the Right Gets it Wrong and the Left Doesn't Get it: A New Vision for Faith and Politics in America* and other similar pleas for the return of faith and spirituality to the Democratic party suggest that the secularism touted by the Democratic party alienates a large number of voters, and that the lack of a liberal religious voice in the public sphere provides the conservative or evangelical Protestant voice far too much leeway to be the "religious" voice of the American people. The Christian Right, Wallis argues, is the product of "secular fundamentalism" and the mistakes made by

> liberal elites who seem to have an allergy to spirituality and a disdain for anything religious. In particular they have such a visceral reaction to the formulations of the religious Right that they make the mistake over and over again, of throwing all people of faith into the category of the right-wing conservative religion. That mistaken practice has further polarized the debate over religion and public life in America and has even deepened the impression among many Christians that the real battle is between belief and secularism.[9]

And Wallis continues in his conclusion with fifty predictions for the new millennium. Of these, at least eight deal explicitly with the media and condemn its present state. Yet, nowhere in his book does Wallis locate the importance of the media in creating this imbalance between the religious Right and what he defines as "better religion" (some kind of syncretic mix of prophetic Protestantism and liberal religion). And, while he is acutely aware of the power of the media to shape the agenda in the next millennium, he remains reactive and critical rather than proactive and positive.[10] Although the religious Right has provided a critique of the mainstream media, it has at the same time provided a rich alternative media for its constituency.[11] The difference in the liberal and conservative approaches to media is crucial for understanding their relative standing in the contemporary public sphere.

To understand how the Christian right managed to master the media and not only survive the predictions of doom and gloom but thrive, we need to understand how the mainline liberal Protestant leadership failed under seemingly favorable economic, social, and cultural circumstances and to examine the reasons for its public decline. In other words, comparative research provides a necessary corrective in a field that has been far too dominated by theologically informed, and often politically charged, rhetoric. *American Protestants and TV in the 1950s* reframes the historical narrative of religious broadcasting in America by adopting a comparative approach that examines both mainline and evangelical responses to the new medium of television. Unlike previous studies of televangelism that have either ignored the medium per se, or have granted far too much importance to it,[12] this study rests upon a dialogical understanding of technology and society.[13] From this perspective, new technologies are grounded within particular social and cultural contexts, which in return shape their reception, uses, and functions. While a particular technology (or communication medium in this case) might have certain given characteristics, the meaning and shape of these characteristics are formed within a historical moment and social location. The process of mediation that inevitably accompanies the rise of a new technology has social and cultural implications. Writing about the telephone in America, Claude Fischer observed: "As much as people adapt their lives to the changed circumstances created by a new technology, they also adapt that technology to their lives."[14] From this perspective, as Raymond Williams wrote, the "moment of any new technology is a choice."[15]

To understand the different ways in which mainline and evangelical Protestant leaders *chose* to respond to television during its first two decades (~1946–1966, the critical period during which the contours of the new medium were negotiated and shaped), we examine the rhetoric of key organizations and journals. While the television today is an almost taken-for-granted object, Americans in the 1950s faced the challenge of negotiating the new medium's place and form in the American home and in the culture at large.[16] American Protestant leaders likewise were faced with a similar task—negotiating the new medium for their communities. The content and shape of that negotiation form the basis for the historical narrative in *American Protestants and TV in the 1950s*.

More precisely, *American Protestants and TV in the 1950s* examines the rhetoric of mainline and evangelical leaders concerned with television and suggests the ways in which that rhetoric informed their choices concerning the reception, use, and criticism of the new medium. This emphasis upon the medium itself and the ways in which the users shaped the medium suggest that to truly understand both the "failure" of mainline religious broadcasting and the "success" of televangelism we have to look beyond economic and structural explanations,[17] as well as explanations that rely upon variations of technological determinism, toward a more interactive, dialogical understanding of the relationship between a technology, a specific community, and the broader cultural context. Just as evangelical Protestants turned out to be far more "modernist" in their pragmatic approach to technology than their theological rhetoric would indicate, mainline self-defined liberal Protestants were far more ambivalent about modernity than has been previously suggested.

Chapter 1 approaches the television from an historical perspective, suggesting that understanding the ambivalence with which mainline Protestant leaders approached television is as important as understanding the ways in which evangelical leaders embraced the new medium. The following chapters focus upon four case studies; each examines a slightly different set of Protestant negotiations with the new medium of television. In conclusion, this volume reexamines a central paradox in American religious history: why the form of Protestantism that designates itself and is publicly conceived as "old-time religion" has regularly been the innovator in the area of media. In stark contrast, its more staid establishment counterpart has tended to be antagonistic to these new media, dismissing them with harsh theological and aesthetic judgments.

Chapter 1

American Protestantism and the Television: A Paradoxical Relationship

And this gospel of the Kingdom will be proclaimed throughout the earth as a testimony to all nations; and then the end will come.

(Matthew 24:14)

Go therefore and make all nations my disciples; baptize men everywhere in the name of the Father and the Son and the Holy Spirit, and teach them to observe all that I have commanded you.

(Matthew 28:19–20)

Evangelism lies at the heart of Protestant conceptions of communication.[1] For the evangelist, time and space are obstacles to be overcome and any invention that might aid in that process has often been perceived or even publicly acknowledged as divinely inspired. Martin Luther, for example, called the press an act of grace.[2] The history of communications in America testifies to the perseverance of this theological understanding of new media. At the opening of the first telegraph line in 1844, Morse took little credit for his years of labor, fundraising, perseverance, or ingenuity (his plan for the telegraph was conceived in 1832), sending instead a short message: "What hath God wrought?"[3] Simultaneously expressing the fear of potential change wrought by the telegraph and attributing divine authorship to that change, Morse's ambivalent message probably resounded well with his contemporaries. If the impetus behind the device was divine, public use of the new medium could be considered not only as legitimate, but also necessary. Fear of the changes created by new electric inventions such as the telegraph, telephone, and the light bulb were alleviated partially by the hope that the heathens would soon be saved as a result. This "electric theology," as Carolyn Marvin calls it, cautioned prudent use of the new technologies, lest one's beliefs be called into question either through a flagrant display of earthly affluence or by wasting time that could be devoted to the Bible.[4] Nineteenth-century religious leaders, notes Marvin, found it far easier to extol the virtues of the new technologies for extending "the Gospel to the barbarous savages . . . while the electric distribution of the Word to their own parishioners filled them with unease."[5]

How are we to understand such an ambivalent and mixed endorsement of these new communications technologies? James Carey, in his essay "A Cultural Approach to Communication," suggested that we distinguish between two coexistent conceptions of communication: transmission and ritual. A transmission view of communication grows out of an evangelistic paradigm: "communication is a process whereby messages are transmitted and distributed in space for the control of distance and people."[6] In other words, the Gospel is preached in order to expand the Kingdom of God. This model of communication is based on transportation or conquest metaphors, which subsequently informed scholars' research in the areas of influence and persuasion. The evangelistic paradigm suggests that the message is relayed in order to convince its recipient to change their opinion. Communication is a means to a specific desired end: conversion.

In contrast, the ritual view of communication does not emphasize expansion or persuasion, but rather "the maintenance of society over time."[7] Scholars of communication more interested in this quality of communication have examined the important ways in which "media events" act to express and solidify common sentiments or how rituals and the media are intertwined in the contemporary context.[8] Through communication, the community unites and coheres and reinforces its self-understanding. If the evangelistic Gospel informs the transmission view, the repetitive nature of the mass on Sundays embodies the ritual view. In Carolyn Marvin's example, nineteenth-century religious leaders were ready to endorse new inventions that could transmit messages across distances in the name of God but were more fearful of how these same communications devices would affect the nature of the community at home or in the church. In other words, they felt at ease with the ways in which greater distances might be overcome through the use of the new medium and they identified with the aim of transmitting the gospel, but at the same time they were more fearful of the ways in which their local communities might be affected by that same invention.

Similarly, Protestant leaders in 1950s America often adopted paradoxical approaches toward the television. Carey's conceptualization of communication as embodying both transmission and ritual models help us to understand the ironic outcomes of such approaches. While the rhetoric of leaders might justify the use of new communications technologies by calling upon the transmission model of communication, the communication produced might primarily serve a ritual function. Televangelists, for example, claim to be using the airwaves to convert the heathens across America, but research has convincingly shown that televangelism largely functions in a ritual capacity for homebound (by choice or necessity) believers, providing an electronic community of sorts, and that very few nonbelievers are actually converted through the television broadcasts.[9] In contrast, mainline Protestant leaders often legitimate their critique of mass media in terms of a transmission model of communication, citing its potential to damage the existent community. At the same time, they ignore the potential contribution of mass media to community building. Television, in some forms, can provide the means for social cohesion—not just dissolution.[10]

These paradoxical approaches to media appear throughout the history of American Protestantism. This is perhaps not surprising given the fundamental role that the newly invented printing press played in the success of the Reformation. In her landmark study, *The Printing Press as an Agent of Change: Communications and Cultural Transformations in Early-Modern Europe*, Elizabeth Eisenstein convincingly argued that the printing press was both a "precondition" and a "precipitant" for the Reformation, without which the "priesthood of all believers" would not have been possible.[11] While the causal formulation of this thesis has been called into question, the close relationship between Protestantism and the emergent print culture remains indisputable.[12] For example, Protestant pamphlets published in the 1520s and 1530s constituted the second mass printing in history[13] and provided what Steven Ozment called a "blueprint" for the Reformation.[14]

The consequences of such a relationship have been far from straightforward, instead the preferred adjectives might be paradoxical or ironic. Eisenstein claimed that the innovation of printing should be viewed in these terms:

> The many changes introduced by the new technology far from synchronizing smoothly or pointing in one direction, contributed to disjunctions, worked at cross-purposes and operated out of phase with each other.[15]

The advent of the press may have contributed to the success of the Reformation, or forwarded the Weberian march toward rationalization and secularization, but it also helped to rekindle and/or preserve interest in more esoteric forms of religion. The occult, astrology, and *Kabbalah* gained in popularity thanks to newly printed versions of older texts.[16] Likewise, the affects of the press upon the nascent Protestant movement also seems to have been mixed and far from uniform.

While the press played a formative role in the Reformation fight against the Roman Catholic Church, it also may have contributed to the fragmentation of the new movement. In so far as the press aided the Reformers' by allowing for the widespread circulation of their ideas, it simultaneously subverted their potential authority. As Mark Edwards has argued:

> paradoxically, printing also undermined central authority because it encouraged the recipients of the printed message to think for themselves about the issues in dispute, and it provided the means—printed Bibles especially—by which each person could become his or her own theologian.[17]

In the American context, the tension between individualism and authority that was expressed through issues of printing and literacy remained an important theme. Martin E. Marty has suggested that in the colonial period Protestant leaders promoted literacy in order to encourage community, not realizing that in doing so they would be partially responsible for building the voluntaryistic, denominational system of American Protestantism. More Bible readers meant more Bible interpreters and subsequently the potential for consequential, even schismatic differences of opinion also grew.[18] The trend toward individualism was thus reinforced through the promotion of biblical literacy.[19]

Throughout the history of American revivalism, preachers legitimated the innovative adaptation of new communications media by emphasizing the overwhelming importance of converting the individual. Using new techniques to reach larger and larger audiences, these media entrepreneurs would nonetheless defend their ventures by stressing how individual members of the audience were converted. In the process, these communication innovators often built impressive communities (if not traditional churches), much to the chagrin of those who opposed their newfangled techniques.

George Whitefield, the man that Harry S. Stout has defined as the first modern religious celebrity, innovatively adapted newspaper publicity for revivalist ends.[20] Whitefield regularly created news events, exaggerated the numbers of the crowds, published paid advertisements as if they were objective accounts written by a third party, and used his own magazine *Weekly History* to promote his revivals on both sides of the Atlantic Ocean.[21] Whitefield adapted the rhetoric and techniques of the secular marketplace to preach the "new birth."[22] Such creative tactics proved to be extraordinarily effective and would later be considered the forerunners of modern trends such as parachurch organizations, and institutionalized revivalism.[23]

The number of souls reached with the message may have increased with these new techniques, but so did the emphasis of individual experience over family, creed, and community.[24] Commercial uses of print might have been effective but they were also transformative. Harry S. Stout and Frank Lambert have both suggested (in separate studies) that the roots of modern evangelism and its particular relationship to mass media and market culture can be traced to Whitefield's career. Frank Lambert points to one of the greatest ironies of the Great Awakening: the Calvinist Whitefield embracing mass marketing. While Chauncey and the other proto-Unitarians rejected Whitefield's Calvinism as narrow and decidedly unenlightened, they also denounced his innovative, rational adaptations of the latest commercial means to propagate his message to vast audiences.[25]

In the post-Revolutionary period, itinerant preachers of all stripes would duplicate Whitefield's efforts. Never before had there been so much access to popular printed material of all kinds, and never before had preachers been so shrewd about their uses.[26] Nathan Hatch partially attributes the success of the Second Great Awakening to this new approach in communications:

> Despite their wide diversity, Methodists, Baptists, Universalists, Disciples, Mormons and Millerites were all communication entrepreneurs, and their movements were crusades for broadcasting the truth. Each was wedded to the transforming power of the word, spoken, written and sung; each was passionate about short-circuiting a hierarchical flow of information; each was supremely confident that the vernacular and the colloquial were the most fitting channels for religious expression; and each was content to measure the success of individual and movements by their ability to persuade. By systematically employing lay preachers, by new forms of religious folk music, they ensured the forceful delivery of their message.[27]

This pattern, whereby the successful revivalist would embrace the latest media technology, while those less friendly to the revival would reject this form of adaptation as problematic, would repeat itself in the late nineteenth and twentieth centuries.[28] In the process, the history of communications was wedded to the history of American Protestantism. Protestant responses to television must therefore be viewed as an episode in this longer story.

The Literature on Televangelism

Not surprisingly, most scholarly literature on religion and television in America has focused upon one side of the story, namely the rapid rise of televangelism.[29] In a pioneering study of televangelism, Peter G. Horsfield described several interactive elements that produced an environment conducive to the televangelists' success: changes in government regulations, the growth of conservative churches and the decline of mainline churches, the advent of new computer technologies, the adaptability of evangelical theology to television, and the changing economic considerations of television stations in the 1960s and 1970s.[30] With basic variations in emphasis, this account soon became the standard historical explanation for understanding the rise of televangelism.

Scholars who followed Horsfield focused more and more on understanding the audience. As the new Christian right became active and visible in the political and public sphere, gaining an accurate count of televangelist viewers and estimating the percentage of active supporters became important foci of research.[31] Debates about audience size soon led to further debates about the true efficacy of televangelist preaching upon the viewers. Despite a conversionist rhetoric that theoretically legitimated the large sums that the televangelists requested from their viewers, scholars soon concluded that the TV worked far better to reinforce audience members' preexistent opinions rather than to convert them to new ones.[32] The importance (and potential threat) of televangelism was not that it would convert millions of American viewers to its political and religious causes, but that it had acted powerfully and effectively to unite and reinforce the existent opinions of millions of Americans of evangelical background.[33] In the process, the balance between the private and the public dimensions of religion had noticeably shifted.[34] As the religious television program entered the home directly (and, as its detractors noted, therefore discouraged churchgoing in favor of a more private worship), it also simultaneously made more public those issues that had heretofore been part of the private realm (issues such as the moral failings of Jimmy Swaggart).[35] In other words, televangelism's effects turned out to be neither simple nor one-dimensional, but most often contradictory or paradoxical.

Subsequently, scholars have increasingly turned away from "effects" models of explanation toward a more interactive model of religious television. In this newer model the audience occupied center stage as scholars placed emphasis on understanding the role of the viewers in the construction of the Electronic Church. The "meaning" of the programs was no longer understood to be located within their contents but could be found lurking in the interstices between the individual viewer, the community constructed out of those viewers, and the society at large.[36] The viewers were not just Christian couch potatoes, but humans actively in search of ritual and community (notably traditional reasons for practicing religion).[37] Still, a fundamental question remained unanswered: why was conservative Protestantism so successful in utilizing this new medium?

Pursuing the historical angle, Quentin J. Schultze identified several important elements within the evangelical tradition that promoted an affinity with the media culture: "a disinterest in tradition, a faith in technology, a drive to popularize and a spirit of individualism."[38] From Schultze's perspective, the embrace of radio and television by segments of the evangelical population was rooted within particular theological and cultural traditions. The "successful" use of new communications technologies by evangelicals was therefore a natural consequence of their *weltanschauung*. In contrast to Schultze, Janice Peck adopted a broader sociological framework of explanation. The Electronic Church, in Peck's eyes, must be viewed and examined as one of the possible strategies (liberal Protestantism, for example, offers a competing strategy) for coping with the "crisis of meaning" left in the wake of modernization.[39] Importantly, she noted that each evangelist offers a distinctive appeal, ultimately aimed at different audiences. Although collapsed under the category of "televangelism," Jimmy Swaggart and Pat Robertson each offers different answers to the quandaries posed by modernity.[40]

These studies have helped us to understand something about the ways in which the "conservatives" become innovative, media-savvy evangelicals and to understand the meaning of that process, but we know far less about the ways in which the adaptive mainline "liberals" became cultural conservatives.[41] Ann Swidler has argued that to explain a particular cultural outcome (in this case, the rise of televangelism and the decline of mainline broadcasting), one must not only understand the relationship between a particular ideology and the action under study, but also suggest why that ideology and not another succeeded under those circumstances.[42] Studies of religion and television in America have heretofore largely ignored this latter task. Why was mainline Protestant broadcasting such a failure?

Most historians and sociologists have given much of the credit to a series of Federal Communications Commission (FCC) rulings, most particularly a 1960 decision that claimed that no public interest was served by the differentiation of sustaining and commercial time.[43] In other words, to fulfill their "public interest" obligation, the stations no longer were required to give away time on television but could meet this obligation through commercial television programming. Under these new market conditions, the evangelicals were better equipped than the mainliners to compete for time, and thus, the Electronic Church, as we know it today, was born.

From this account, we understand the practical means whereby the televangelists came to dominate the airwaves, but we gain little insight into the decline of mainline Protestant broadcasting. As the representative of twenty-nine denominations (143, 000 congregations, 33 million members), the Broadcast and Film Commission of the National Council of Churches of Christ (the BFC of the NCCC) potentially had far greater financial resources to call upon than most of the conservative one-man-band shows such as Oral Roberts and Rex Humbard.[44] If lack of potential resources does not explain the declining mainline Protestant involvement in television, there must have been internal factors contributing to that decline. Why, then, did the mainline essentially opt out of the television business?

From an insiders' perspective, the mainline responses to the television in particular and the mass media in general were formed out of necessity.[45] In other words, the relative failure of religious broadcasting is perceived to be the result of theological integrity. From this perspective, mainline Protestantism *chose/chooses* to elide the mass media. The onus is therefore placed on the *nature* of mass media, which are seen to be in direct contradiction to the true Christian ethos.[46] The true Christian message in all its complexity, it is claimed, cannot be transmitted through the mass media without distortion.[47] Basing their claim firmly on the foundations of medium theory, these (mostly) mainline scholars/theologians have been quick to suggest how well conservative theology, with its clear and unambiguous messages, translates into TV sound bites.[48] The complicated abstract nature of liberal theology, this argument usually adds, was less adaptable to the television's requirements. Likewise, the mainline emphasis on cooperation was viewed as being directly in contradiction to the television industry's ethos, which was noted to be far more similar to the evangelical emphasis on competitiveness.[49]

While these types of explanations legitimate the course of action adopted by the leadership to their mainline constituencies, ultimately they fall short when scrutinized under the historical and sociological gaze. The observation of theological simplicity seems to be polemically based. Just as there are simpler variations of liberal modernist theology, some variations of conservative theology are complex. The television's constraints as a medium, particularly as it developed in the context of U.S. commercial broadcasting, may have limited the kinds or types of messages that can be successfully transmitted to a mass audience, but that still does not explain either the willingness of evangelicals or the resistance of the mainline to adapt to these constraints.[50] Liberal Protestantism, particularly (although not solely) in its modernist variety, throughout the nineteenth century, embraced a strategy of conscious cultural adaptation.[51] At the basis of this optimistic theology, lay the assumption that Protestant accommodation to the changes in modern society was not only possible, but also desirable.[52] Why then did the liberal Protestant leadership draw the theological line at the mass media in general and television in particular?

I suggest that the theological claims of both mainline and evangelical leaders should be treated as primary source material to be unpacked and understood, rather than as operative explanations. These theologically informed responses to television offer a window for viewing the *construction* of Protestant responses to television. Mainline and evangelical leaders adapted different strategies for coping with the advent of the television (and the radio before it). To understand the historical outcome, we need to understand the sources of these differences, and the ways in which these differences affected how each group actually approached the medium.[53] How did their specific cultural repertoires shape the different kinds of television strategies pursued by evangelical and mainline leaders?[54]

Similarly, the medium of television has been far too often conceived by historians of religion as a static object whose use is determined through its invention. The television, as a medium and as a cultural construct, has been shaped both by its users and nonusers as much as its creators and marketers. In other words, the television is a socially constructed medium whose uses are *at least* as culturally determined as they are technologically influenced. As Raymond Williams insightfully observed:

> We have now become used to a situation in which broadcasting is a major social institution, about which there is always controversy but which, in its familiar form, seems to have been predestined by technology. This predestination, however, when closely examined, proves to be no more than a set of particular social decisions, in particular circumstances, which were then so widely if imperfectly ratified that it is now difficult to see them as decisions rather than as (retrospectively) inevitable results.[55]

Studies by Lynn Spigel and Cecilia Tichi on the introduction of television into American life reveal the *process* whereby this new medium was assimilated into the American home, and how TV culture came to be constructed.[56] Preexistent ideas about leisure and work and the nature of domestic life shaped the ways in which Americans received the television into their homes, and the ways in which television practices evolved.[57] Contemporary concerns, such as the cold war, sexual politics, or the debates on mass culture, have likewise played a formative role in determining the nature of television. As Cecilia Tichi notes: "no matter how strikingly new a technology may be, once introduced into society it becomes deeply enmeshed in long-term cultural traditions and conflicts."[58]

Tracing the ways in which Protestant leaders negotiated the television, then, requires a broader understanding of the cultural meaning of commercial forms of entertainment or mass media in 1950s America. The word "negotiation" here refers generally to the ways in which Protestant leaders perceived of television (as that perception is reflected in their writings), used the television (both symbolically and practically), and attempted to influence the shape of television and the culture it spawned.[59] Televangelism was only one possible response to the rise of this new medium and should be contextualized as such.[60]

Television reception in America was partially shaped by concerns of cultural hierarchy and the maintenance or disruption of cultural boundaries. Paul DiMaggio and Lawrence Levine have shown how cultural classifications are anything *but* static over time, although they might seem that way at first glance.[61] In nineteenth-century America, Mozart and Shakespeare belonged to both the popular and the elite realms. As the century progressed, this kind of mixed audience would become an anachronism, as art and symphony followed by opera, dance, and theater came to be canonized as "high culture" and were structurally incorporated in nonprofit institutions such as the Chicago Art Institute and the Metropolitan Opera Company.[62] In America, this history of cultural hierarchy has a Protestant dimension. As forms of culture were elevated to the status of high culture, they underwent a process of "sacralization."[63] Art, for example, (somewhat surprisingly considering the seemingly long tradition of proclaimed iconoclasm in Protestantism) came to be considered and described in religious terms.[64] To be considered as "true art," painting or sculpture had to elevate the viewer *above* the mundane, reflecting the divine impulse behind such artistic endeavors.[65] Fine art museums thus were often conceived as modern day (Protestant) cathedrals.[66]

At the other end of the cultural hierarchy, Protestantism, as Laurence Moore, has shown, was equally influential. While dime novels and P. T. Barnum's museum would never be considered to be as elevated and sacred as opera or theater, they were eventually grudgingly accepted as wholesome forms of entertainment.[67] Thus, Protestant evaluations and practices shaped the ways in which Americans defined art (and high culture) as well as commercial forms of entertainment and leisure (low- and middle-brow culture). In the process, art was elevated to a sacred status while certain forms of commercial entertainment were certified as wholesome or moral (if rather base).

In the 1950s, debates over cultural hierarchy focused on the potentially manipulative effects of mass culture.[68] This public discourse intersected with the advent of television and may have affected the different Protestant responses to television. Evangelical or mainline responses to television may be considered as a question of "taste."[69] Mainline leaders may have deemed television as essentially a middle- or low-brow medium and subsequently viewed association with such a form of entertainment as "improper," or disadvantageous.[70] They feared how TV might affect their cultural standing. In one of the early studies of television, mainline Protestants were the only group in which television ownership was inverse to economic class. In other words, the richer the mainline Protestant the less likely s/he was to own a television.[71] In contrast, for evangelicals, one of the television's attractions may have been its association with technology and science. Evangelical acceptance and use of television might have been perceived as an opportunity to increase the cultural respectability of "old-time religion," which had been so recently humiliated in the Scopes Trial.[72] In rejecting or embracing the new medium, Protestant leaders of both camps erected social boundaries that distinguished one from the other and, in doing so, identified with specific segments of the broader culture.

The Study of Mass Communication as an Academic Discipline and as a Resource for Protestant Leaders

Like its object of study, the study of mass communications is a relatively young academic discipline. The advent of television in America coincided with the end of World War II, the time when the first departments of communication were founded.[73] Research on radio had already been conducted for commercial purposes, but throughout the war, mass communication research had been of great interest to the government who wished to assess the effects of propaganda upon the enemy, and to devise effective morale-boosting campaigns for the American public.[74] The ruling paradigm of this early research seems to have been formulated by Harold D. Lasswell: "Who says *what*, to *whom* via what channels with what *effects?*"[75] The fear of fascism—and after the war, a growing fear of communism—shaped not only the academic research agenda, but also the popular understanding of mass communications. Could governments or organizations (particularly those hostile to American ideals) use mass communications to wage a war on the minds of the average citizen? In this context, understanding the effects of mass media was essential. Could a radio program or television broadcast determine an individual's attitude, opinion, or behavior? How did this process of persuasion work? These were central questions that plagued researchers and were likewise reflected in the popular discourse about media. The metaphor used here (and at least attributed to Lasswell) is the media as hypodermic needle that injected content directly into the passive audience.[76] This construction of an all-powerful media and the complete lack of will among audience members would be called into question by empirical communication research. By 1955, P.F. Lazarsfeld and E. Katz published a volume entitled *Personal Influence: The Part Played by People in the Flow of Mass Communication*, devoted to describing and understanding the limited effects of the media. Nonetheless, popular accounts of the media still (and to this day) tended to construct its influence as unmediated and absolute.[77]

For Protestant leaders in pre-television America, their preconceptions of the mass media, particularly radio, provided an important frame for understanding the new medium of television. Still, there were many unanswered questions: was television a tool given by God for evangelism or a deceit designed by Satan to distract the viewer from more important matters? How did the visual dimension of television differentiate it from its predecessor the radio? What would be its cultural role in post–World War II America? These and other unanswered questions shaped the Protestant leaderships' understandings of television in the early years.

In all acts of cultural production, there are both intentional and unintentional consequences, leading in some cases to ironic outcomes.[78] In the process of negotiating their ideals into everyday practices, self-proclaimed liberals *acted* as cultural conservators while self-proclaimed conservatives *acted* as cultural innovators.

Toward a Dialogical Approach to Media, Religion and Culture

Research in the social construction of technology (often referred to as the SCOT approach) has suggested that users' responses are an essential part of the constitution and construction of new technologies. Most importantly, the SCOT approach demonstrated how social and cultural differences in the users not only lead to different interpretations and uses of the same technology, but to actual modifications of the original technology. The "safety bicycle," for example, was manufactured in response to the construction of the high-wheeled bicycle as dangerous.[79]

Scholars in cultural and communication studies have complimented this approach through their examination of the ways in which technological objects are "domesticated" into the home. Roger Silverstone et al. have used this metaphor of domestication to describe the phases that a household goes through when acquiring a new technology. First, the object—the television, for example—is possessed or obtained, that is, through purchase or as a gift. Next, the television is objectified and is displayed in the household, that is, a place is found for it in the family room. Then, the television is used in the domestic context, that is, the children gather every day after school to watch their favorite program. Lastly, the television can be understood in symbolic terms, i.e., as a status item that differentiates them from their neighbor who is TV-less.[80] In other words, although new technologies often seem invisible and natural within a very short period, at the time of adoption users go through a process—they *domesticate* the object for home use.

More recent research likewise suggests that nonusers and resisters of technologies also make an important contribution in the development of technology.[81] In his studies of new technologies and rural life in America, Ronald Kline suggests, "resistance is a common means of negotiations between producers, mediators and users that helps to create socio-technical change."[82] In other words, when individuals or communities oppose a particular technology in their community or don't purchase it or refuse to use it in the way in which manufacturers designate its use then they are considered to be resisting the new technology. Sally Wyatt, in her essay, "Non-Users also matter," suggests that there are different kinds of nonusers of the internet: those that resist using the new technology, the rejecters—those who tried it but then rejected it, and those who don't have access—and each subgroup requires consideration. She suggests that previous explanations of nonusers have usually focused almost exclusively upon economic considerations, and have not adequately analyzed the motivations of the nonusers that might be quite varied depending upon their particular circumstance.[83]

In other words, this approach to technology suggests that users and nonusers have an important role in the cultural and *actual* construction of new technologies. There is, what might be called, a dialogic aspect to the user(or nonuser)/technology relationship.[84] In the case studies delineated below, I examine how both users (evangelical Protestants) and nonusers (mainline Protestants) engaged with and formulated their responses to the new medium of television. Heretofore much of the scholarship concerned with religion and media has not examined how different subcultures of users and nonusers respond, resist and adapt to new media. Just as individual households have to go through a process of domestication, mainline and evangelical Protestant leaders had to go through a parallel process—deciding how the medium would be treated in the institutional context (i.e., should services be rescheduled to accommodate sports events?) and suggesting how individuals affiliated with their communities should likewise address this issue—e.g., should their be a ban on televisions or a ban on watching certain programming, etc. The case studies below document this process, comparing how different groups of users and nonusers approached this new medium, and the possible consequences of these approaches.

Chapter 2

"Turn It Off!": The Liberal Protestant Critique of Television

In May 1960, Elvis Presley, newly released from the army, appeared on television. After his performance, an editorial in *The Christian Century* declared the program to be "pernicious," a sign of the "depth of decadence into which our scale of values has sunk." Elvis's wiggling pelvis was dismissed as "revolting exhibitionism," which most unfortunately was accessible "at the twist of the youngest wrist." Even worse, this performance had earned Elvis a whopping US$125,000, a sum that could have been spent on the yearly salaries of twenty-five teachers or forty-two ministers, or sixty-three farm hands. If Americans were willing to allow such "distasteful" programs into their homes, they could expect nothing more than the "ruin which awaits such a people."[1]

Exorbitance was Presley's main crime. The idea that Americans would spend leisure time passively watching a wriggling pelvis, indirectly paying large sums to do so, conflicted with older ideals—namely, the Protestant work ethic and the correlative understanding of leisure (mostly Victorian in origin). For *The Christian Century* editors, television viewing was at best a waste of time, and at worst a direct assault on the American (that is, Protestant) way of life. Subsequently, television never received much attention in *The Christian Century*'s pages. During the early years of commercial television, there were a few articles by guest writers who argued that the church (i.e., liberal Protestantism) must confront and harness this new medium for both missionary and educational purposes. These pleas for practical involvement in television, however, were largely overshadowed by negative evaluations of programming content. For the editors, little on television warranted positive praise or even critical evaluation. Even religious television was largely ignored by *The Christian Century*. True to its rather highbrow, intellectual character, the magazine was reluctant to cede to this new medium its due cultural weight. For the most part, readers were counseled simply to "turn it off!"[2]

Despite their relative scarcity, the articles and editorials that do mention television provide an opportunity to understand the ways in which this new medium was received and acculturated by a segment of the liberal Protestant leadership.[3] Throughout the nineteenth century, liberal Protestant leaders played an active role in creating and defining acceptably wholesome forms of commercial culture. By the post–World War II era, however, Laurence Moore has argued that this "ambition receded and ended in the tasteful packaging of a commercial product that still sold but did not arouse much consumer enthusiasm."[4] Notably, this so-called liberal Protestant lack of "inventiveness" is dated (more or less) to the era that coincides with the rise of broadcasting. While the theater, fiction, and sports were eventually "reformed" enough to be considered moral forms of entertainment, the movies, the radio, and the television proved to be far more problematic.[5] This critical approach toward broadcasting shares something in common with the secular post–World War II critique of mass culture and fear of technology's (mis)uses. At the same time it indicates a broader shift in the liberal Protestant leadership's approach to commercial culture.[6]

Why at that particular moment in history were liberal Protestant leaders incapable of reinventing the wheel? The new medium of broadcasting may have made that task more difficult or less inviting. Perhaps the social meanings attributed to the radio or television were somehow different than those attributed to the nineteenth-century forms of commercial culture. This chapter argues that it is not enough to claim that liberal Protestantism was "worn out" or that it had become theologically bankrupt and therefore incapable of effectively transforming yet another form of commercial culture.[7] Likewise, accounts that emphasize structural developments in broadcasting, and innovations in computer technologies that eventually favored conservative Protestant approaches to media, do not adequately explain why mainline Protestants refused to adapt to those changes.

Why did liberal Protestants give up the cultural battle, leaving the task to their more conservative counterparts?[8] The reasons for this transition are far from self-evident. To understand the relationship between the decline of liberal Protestant interest in the creation and production of acceptable forms of culture and the subsequent rise of interest amongst their more conservative counterparts, this chapter traces how part of the liberal Protestant leadership responded to the introduction of the television and places these responses in their theological, historical, social, and cultural contexts.

In the changing social context of post–World War II America, mainline Protestant hegemony was increasingly called into question, both by its own leaders and by the voices of a more pluralist America that had heretofore been mute. In this context, the strategy of Christianization (the efforts to reform and shape cultural life according to mainline Protestant norms), which had been so effective in the nineteenth century, could no longer be maintained. The new strategy was one of (almost calculated) disregard, the articles and editorials in *The Christian Century* offers an important resource for illustrating how this disregard was constructed and legitimated as a viable approach to this new medium of communications.

The Christian Century's response to television was shaped by older cultural and theological assumptions—such as iconoclasm, anti-Catholicism, asceticism—and by fears of changes in the cultural status quo (e.g., increasing pluralism, the transformation of the American Victorian home and domestic piety, the rise of the leisure society and decline of the work ethic). In the post–World War II period, as hegemony became harder to maintain, thicker cultural boundaries would need to be drawn. If the culture at large could no longer be assumed to be reflective of Protestant values, mainline Protestant leaders would have to delineate what *did* reflect Protestant values. In doing so, they would reconfigure the relationship between mainline Protestantism and American culture. Practically speaking this meant that high culture would increasingly be identified as the sole bearer of mainline Protestant values.

This chapter examines some of the different ways television was portrayed, described and discussed in *The Christian Century* during the first fifteen years or so of commercial broadcasting (approximately between 1946 and 1960). By drawing out some of the cultural and theological assumptions that shaped this discourse, this chapter suggests why television was rarely considered worthy of serious consideration by *The Christian Century*, then takes a closer look at the ways in which television *is* described on the pages of *The Christian Century*, and shows how the editors understood the affect of television on the audience, the role of government in the regulation of this new medium, and the ethical dilemmas posed by television for liberal Protestants. The conclusion discusses the broader ramifications of this case for our understanding of the relationship between American Protestantism and the television.

"Can Protestantism Win America?"[9]

Founded in 1884, *The Christian Oracle* was optimistically renamed as *The Christian Century* in 1900 and then subsequently purchased by Charles Clayton Morrison in 1908. For forty years, Morrison worked as editor, turning the previously Disciples of Christ–affiliated magazine into the preeminent, ecumenical mainline religious weekly that it eventually became. As such the influence of *The Christian Century* is measured more accurately by the nature of its readership—many of whom would count themselves among the religious and lay leaders of mainline or liberal Protestantism—rather than by its rather small circulation of 40,000.[10]

Early references to television in *The Christian Century* can be characterized by their moralistic tone, a tone born of an assumption of cultural hegemony. Despite its relatively small circulation, the editors wrote with an assurance that they were the rightful and historical guardians of American culture.[11] For the first ten years of commercial television, this self-perception seemed well warranted. Church attendance and church construction reached their peak just as television became accessible to most of the population.[12] For a brief moment, Protestantism (or "religion in general," as it was called by those who came to oppose the superficial nature of the revival) seemed to be (re)winning America.[13] While there was some reason to worry that the faith of Protestant America was being challenged by Roman Catholicism and secularism, overall the mood was one of triumphalism, tempered only by the fear of imminent cultural change.

In 1946, the first year that Radio Corporation of America (RCA) and DuMont offered their black-white sets for sale to the public; Charles Clayton Morrison, the founder and editor of *The Christian Century*, published a thirteen-part series of articles entitled "Can Protestantism Win America?" This series, written as a follow up to Harold Fey's controversial set of articles "Can Catholicism Win America?" published in *The Christian Century* a year before, was both a lament on the state of Protestantism in America and a strategy to preserve Protestant cultural prominence.[14] In the fifth article, "Protestantism and Commercialized Entertainment," Morrison argued that along with a "secularized educational system and the widespread acceptance of the messianic pretensions of science" (subjects of earlier articles), overexposure to commercialized entertainment was making the "culture . . . removed farther out of reach of the appeal of Protestant Christianity."[15] Commercialized entertainment was not just morally deplorable (that was too obvious to deserve comment) but had affected the content and balance of the American mind: "This incessant bombardment of the mind with sensuous stimuli has subtly, but profoundly, changed the quality of the mentality of our generation."[16] While the Puritans may have overemphasized the mind over the senses, the contemporary generation had tipped the scale toward sensations to the point where all standards had been undermined, and tastes corrupted.[17] For Morrison, the new emphasis on technique over subject matter illustrated the "complete inversion of aesthetic values and moral standards," a process that testified to the high degree of "cultural decadence."[18] To save America from the fate of Rome, the church needed to actively intervene: "The task of saving America from the enervating influence of the commercial exploitation of the people's leisure, rests uniquely upon the shoulders of Protestantism. It must assume this responsibility if it is to save itself and win America."[19]

In this context, the decline of Protestant influence in America is explicitly linked to the rise of commercial entertainment. Despite the fact that television has yet to appear on his mental horizon, it is clear that Morrison would judge it to be irredeemable. As another example of a sensuous medium that stresses technique over content, and image over idea, the television could not play a positive role in American culture (at least not in a Protestant America). No number of sustaining or public service hours for religious programming on radio or television could offset the destructive influence of everyday commercial entertainment. For Morrison, the aesthetic resulted from his ascetic, inner-worldly Protestantism. The post–World War II leisure society, as it was coming to be known, was at odds with the work ethic. There was no "elective affinity" between this new America and ascetic Protestantism. If Protestantism (as Morrison understood it) was to survive these cultural shifts, it would need to convince Americans to reject the hedonistic comforts of the armchair for the hardwood pew on Sunday. Only a united Protestantism could "win America" from the Catholics and secularists and prevent America from sliding down a decadent and slippery slope.

Morrison's critique of commercial entertainment rested on an older discourse that rejected play as "the devil's work."[20] Despite the efforts of nineteenth-century liberal Protestant leaders such as Frederick Sawyer, Horace Bushnell, and James Leonard Corning to elevate and control play, there were those who continued to condemn all forms of leisure, and to oppose Protestantism's entrance into the marketplace of culture.[21] As Moore notes, "A prejudice of this strength does not simply disappear. What happens first is a shift in its terms and tone."[22] Shying away from a blanket condemnation of play, Morrison focused his attention on its twentieth-century incarnation: commercialized entertainment. A new cultural boundary was in the process of being drawn. The enemy was not play but its commodified cousins, leisure and entertainment, whose main crime was their contribution to the secularization of society. In the end, however, Morrison avoided positively defining moral leisure, entertainment, or art.

Unlike the nineteenth-century leaders who strove to Christianize and reform new forms of culture, and who struggled with areas of the fine arts (such as painting), twentieth-century liberal Protestant leaders largely rejected and/or ignored the newer forms of commercial culture. As the fear of losing Protestant America to the Catholics and secularists grew, the cultural confidence of liberal Protestant leaders declined. In such a climate it was increasingly difficult not to see commercial culture as a threat, rather than a potential ally in the fight to maintain hegemony.[23] Echoing the views of their secular contemporaries who were increasingly critical and fearful of mass culture, liberal Protestant leaders increasingly looked toward the sacralized world of high art to provide a sanctuary for religious culture.[24]

This general approach to culture provides a context for viewing the early reception of television in *The Christian Century*. Although Morrison's traditionally triumphalist (but pacifist) liberal Protestantism was being challenged by a younger generation of Christian realists who were more accepting of (and maybe even embracing of) pluralist America, they remained equally suspicious of commercial entertainment and the new leisure society.[25] These suspicions often came to be vocalized as a fear of depersonalization in an age of conformity. If the older generation of liberals (represented here by Morrison) and the younger generation of realists (Niebuhr et al.) found little to agree about the role of the church in society (or the depravity of man), they could find common ground in their rejection of commercial entertainment, albeit for different reasons. By the early 1960s, the TV was still a rare item on the pages of *The Christian Century*; by the time it did begin to get coverage, the content of the criticism had shifted away from personal moral considerations (e.g., alcohol, gambling, etc.) to larger public concerns, particularly the civil rights movement. The early years of television, 1946 through 1960, however, was a transitional period for TV and for *The Christian Century*, as first Paul Hutchison (1947–1956) and then Harold Fey (1956–1964) took over the mantle of editor from Morrison.

"TV—a Giant for Good or Ill"[26]

Understanding the liberal Protestant's leadership's rejection or lukewarm reception of broadcasting media also gives us an opportunity to explore the ambivalent side of American popular discursive conventions concerning communications technologies. Scholars have documented the double-sided, utopic-dystopic discourse that seems to accompany the introduction of new technologies from the nineteenth century until today. Religious leaders have tended to speak this mixed language as well. Electricity, for example, was both celebrated as the best way to reach the savages with the Gospel and equally feared for its social affects on the local church body.[27] The radio church service was promoted as the ideal substitute for those physically unable to go to their local churches, but it was considered to have a potentially detrimental affect on church attendance.[28] In both its optimistic and pessimistic variations, this discourse notably shares an assumption of audience passivity as well as a didactic understanding of broadcasting.[29]

In addition to editorials, *The Christian Century* also published articles by guest writers about television, particularly religious television. Both the editorials and articles by guest writers concerning television were equally ambivalent about the potential affects of this new medium on the audience. If television really was as effective in convincing its viewers as advertisers seemed to think, then the church had "a miraculous opportunity for witnessing."[30] Advertising strategies were considered to provide a potential model for religious broadcasting. "Television missionaries," argued J. Edward Carothers, "must profit by the discovery of the beer manufacturers; namely, that a regularly appearing personality is the best way to hold a regularly listening audience."[31] Other guest writers, however, were more cautious. If television could be such an effective minister/salesman, left in the wrong hands it could be lethal. A. Gordon Nasby in a 1949 article warned that "Hitler did his job in Germany in the space of a few years because he had modern techniques and methods of communication at his disposal. Today with television at hand, the time in which men's minds can be molded has been frightfully shortened."[32] Two years later Alton M. Motter reiterated this fear: "This constant flood of words, sounds and pictures is doing something to the American mind."[33]

Notably, the fear of mass propaganda and its political effects seems to have been far greater than the fear of television's affects on liberal Protestantism itself. Motter was one of the few contemporary critics who understood that the television was transforming the American home, and domestic piety right along with it: "Grace at the table or family devotions must compete with Charlie McArthy. And in many homes Charlie wins out!"[34] If the television replaced the hearth, symbolically and physically, then television rituals might also came to replace what Colleen McDannell has labeled "rituals of the hearth."[35] Throughout the nineteenth century, the Protestant home had been the center of a domestic religion that had been promoted and accepted as a legitimate and effective means for preserving the Christian nature of the nation.[36] Centered around the Bible, both physically and verbally, family worship marked both the beginning and the end of the day.[37] The physical home itself, both in terms of its layout (the parlor) and the articles displayed within, likewise reflected the central role of domestic religion. What happened to domestic religion in the twentieth century? How was it transformed in its transition to Levittown and the hundreds of other new suburbs that popped up in post–World War II America? While the history of twentieth- century domestic religion has yet to be written, it is clear that the TV must be seen as one of the important additions to the post–World War II household. As Cecilia Tichi and Lynn Spigel have documented, the advent of the television required Americans to reconfigure many aspects of domestic life: the structure of the living room, the way in which women's work was perceived, and other such aspects. Clearly, domestic religion too was transformed in the process. In this respect, the advent of the television would prove to be far more threatening to Protestant hegemony than most liberal Protestant leaders could foresee.

In contrast to the guest writers, the editors tended to be even more critical of television as a medium and were largely uninterested in the compensatory potential of religious television. Television first made its appearance on *The Christian Century*'s editorial pages while there was still some public discussion over its potential format. Two of the earliest columns that mention TV refer to the possibility of an "advertising-free" version of the medium. Listening to radio advertisements had been annoying, but the visual dimension of television made advertising seem almost obscene: "Will we have to stop in the midst of one news commentary *to see* the commentator rub tonic into his hair, or another down a fizzy hangover pill, or another lather his face with brushless cream?"[38] If iconoclastic Protestants had largely come to accept painting as morally permissible, visual images used for commercial ends were far more problematic.[39] Reaching into the heart of the Christian home, television advertisements promised daily exposure to a wide variety of random and potentially problematic images. Thinking in a futuristic manner, the editors asked if a "pay per view" system could not be installed that would bill individuals for programs much like a telephone bill and thus bypass commercial advertising.[40]

Once the format of commercial TV had been established, editorials refocused the cause on public interest television, backing suggestions that the Federal Communications Commission (FCC) set aside a channel in each community,[41] and that each channel be forced to provide public service time, part of which should be devoted to religious programming.[42] The hope was that the sustained-time system, which had been established in radio and gave the mainline federal (and then national) council of churches almost complete control over public service Protestant programming, would be duplicated in the new medium.[43] Despite this stated editorial position, however, efforts by mainline religious broadcasters were largely ignored by *The Christian Century*. Until 1960, mainline Protestants continued to receive free air time on television as a public service by the broadcasters, but the programs coproduced by the National Council of Churches Broadcast and Film Commission with the networks during this time were generally not reviewed in *The Christian Century*. With the exception of the 1952 editorial "This is the Life," which enthusiastically praised a program produced by the Missouri Synod Lutherans (notably a denomination outside of the National Council of Churches), no religious television program received endorsement by *The Christian Century* during these years.[44]

In the eyes of the editors, TV's potential contribution (however limited) lay in the realms of politics and education (and notably not entertainment). Observing Governor Thomas E. Dewey's 1950 political campaign, the editors were hopeful that television could bring the "town-meeting" to America's living rooms. These fleeting hopes that the TV could create a new public sphere or that the TV could act as an alternative educator in remote areas were soon dashed. The editors soon questioned whether any public service programming would or could have much effect on viewers. A campaign encouraging parents to use the Salk vaccine was considered to be a failure: "Could we have overestimated people's responsiveness to propaganda?"[45] If the audience was not really paying attention, the television's potential both for good and evil was far more limited than previously thought. Despite this growing awareness of the limitations of television, the editors nonetheless remained committed to challenging the networks to use television in as productive and as responsible a manner as possible. This included broadcasting political campaigns, debates within congress, speeches by the president, as well as educational courses.[46]

The Catholic Threat

Overall, the editors paid far more attention to what they perceived as the misuse of television by the Roman Catholic Church and outsider, old-time Protestants such as Billy Graham and Oral Roberts. Faith healing made good television, and the editors noted that no mainline programming was on the air "to offset this travesty on Christian teaching."[47] Even Graham's evangelical crusades were considered to embody a particularistic theology and tactic from which "official Protestantism" should keep a distance.[48] The Roman Catholic use of television provoked even greater controversy on the pages of *The Christian Century*. There was a general fear that the opulent ritual of Catholicism was far more televisable than ascetic Protestantism,[49] and that Catholics would use this advantage to sway America to their cause. Catholics were also not afraid to be doctrinally specific on television, and the editors were afraid that Protestant viewers would be exposed to heresies such as the doctrine of the Virgin Mary, especially on TV holiday specials at

Easter and Christmas.[50] Bishop Fulton Sheen, the most recognized and popular religious television celebrity in the 1950s, received a full-blown condemnation, especially for his implication that the miracle of television was equivalent to the incarnation of Christ. This "blasphemy" shocked the editors: how could the Roman Catholic hierarchy with their elaborate system of censorship let this pass into public discourse?[51] For the most part, the would-be televangelists were not taken very seriously by *The Christian Century*, while the Roman Catholic Church was considered to be a grave threat to Protestant America.

More disturbing than Roman Catholic broadcasting efforts, however, was the hierarchy's censorial approach to commercial culture. While Protestant clergy in the 1850s had blamed Catholics for "introducing permissiveness into American society," in the 1950s they blamed them for introducing repressiveness.[52] Throughout the 1940s, the Roman Catholic association with fascism brought sharp rebuke on the pages of *The Christian Century*.[53] Viewing the terms "American," "Protestant," and "Democratic" as largely interchangeable, *The Christian Century* found great fault with the Roman Catholic efforts to monitor and affect the culture at large. A conflict with the Roman Catholic Church over the film *Martin Luther* exemplifies this position.

Outraged that a local Chicago channel had canceled a movie about Martin Luther under pressure from the archbishop, *The Christian Century* commented "This is the beginning of tyranny. Sectarian censorship is based on fear of the truth and fear of the uses people will make of their democratic freedom."[54] Yet in the same article the writer evokes the privilege and rights of the Protestant majority: "While Protestantism is the faith of the majority of people in the Chicago area, it has never previously spoken with one voice. So the illusion has easily been kept alive that the largest Catholic archdiocese in the country must be granted everything it asks, whether or not what it asks is consistent with American principles."[55] The author implicitly assumes that mainline Protestantism, in its very nature, exemplified American principles, while the Roman Catholic Church with its hierarchical structures was in direct contradiction with them. In another article entitled "Censorship: A Case History," Robert A. E. Lee seriously questioned the Roman Catholic Church's right to influence the public agenda at all: "Is one religious group really attempting to dictate what the public can see and hear through mass consumption media? Is the Roman Catholic church becoming more aggressive in extending its censorship program beyond its own sphere?"[56]

Censorship, however, was not the real issue at hand. After all, the mainliners themselves had pressed the networks for "self-restraint" in broadcasting liquor ads and quiz shows. What was disturbing about the Martin

Luther case, was not that a particular group had lobbied the TV station and won, but the fact that a Protestant television show had been censored by the Roman Catholic Church. The mainliners' attempts to ban particular uses of television were justified because they represented the "right kind . . . of religion," which reflected the popular sentiment of most Americans. In other words, the Roman Catholic Church's actions violated the implicit rules of acceptable censorship. Censorship was acceptable when enacted on behalf of the (perceived) Protestant majority. Censorship that appeared to be motivated by the Roman Catholic Church's hierarchy was not. Censorship that protected little children from viewing too much violence was acceptable. Censorship of the great Protestant reformer was not. Thus, *The Christian Century* could suggest that the FCC regulate quiz shows because they violated the work ethic and were therefore essentially anti-American. In hindsight these positions seem clearly to reflect Protestant theology, but in the 1950s the mainliners found it difficult to distinguish American from Protestant.

The Secular Threat

After Catholicism the next enemy was secularism. The commercialization of the sacred holidays was a disturbing phenomenon to *The Christian Century*, and the editors were quick to blame the TV for its part in this process. Programming on Easter of 1952, for example, was condemned by *The Christian Century* as deceiving and nonrepresentative:

> Last year as our readers will recall, they prostituted this day supposedly sacred to the most important triumphant festival of the Christian year to commercial and theatrical exploitation so crass that it revolted every decent viewer. They employed their technological resources to make the world believe that this country, though it may pretend to keep the Christian feast, is a pagan wilderness.[57]

While the commercialization of Easter had been a long process (Leigh E. Schmidt dates its beginnings to the period of 1860 to 1890), the 1952 televised version of the New York Easter Parade brought special protest, with the television held partly responsible for the new heights of holiday commercialism.[58] The national image of Protestantism had been irredeemably tarnished and the TV was to blame.

And if Easter on Fifth Avenue was not bad enough, the great success of the weekly quiz shows, such as *The $64,000 Question*, seemed to indicate that a great percentage of the American public did not object to gambling at all and were foolish enough to believe "that at last the magic has been found that will lead them to a pot of gold at the rainbow's foot."[59] Long before the Quiz Show Scandal of 1958/1959, the editors questioned the ethical integrity of such shows: "Any device which encourages gambling and leads people to put their faith in 'getting something for nothing' mars the integrity of the individual personality for which the churches have a particular concern."[60] The Protestant work ethic was being publicly chipped away. Worse than promoting cheating, the quiz show "offered opium to broad-bottomed viewers, it dragged those who might have been ambitious. It dangled the illusion of easy money before people who work for a living but spite the necessity."[61] The scandal gave the editors momentary hope that America would finally reject the "get-rich-quick pabulum" once and for all and give "the moral leadership of the country its chance."[62] Even as the younger generation of *Century* writers such as Martin E. Marty was beginning to plea for Protestants to come to terms with their new minority status, they still held hope that in a moment of crisis, like that of the Quiz Show Scandal, Americans would turn back, embrace their religious roots, and recognize their true moral leaders.[63]

While quiz shows offered ethically problematic entertainment, Westerns were violent and sadistic: "It cannot even be said of the sadist [TV] 'on the seventh day he rested.' Sunday proposes Maverick, Alfred Hitchcock, Colt 45, The Lawman and Northwest passage for its offering."[64] Variety shows were not much better, offering vulgar and base entertainment: "Since the popularity of the Paar show presumably reflects the mental climate and entertainment tastes of a considerable share of the American public, it provides occasion for serious concern."[65]

"Turn It Off"[66]

In the end, TV was worthy only of protest. If TV could not be redeemed as an educator, or as a political tool for democratization, then the editors could see little reason to spend time viewing the television. Abstention was the only answer: "Neither the Western or the shocker can outlive a yawn, or a flip of the knob. Turn it off."[67] The TV, like any other vice (including the alcohol and cigarettes it advertised), provided an opportunity to exhibit self-control.[68] Indeed, *The Christian Century* editors really seemed to believe that Americans would just get tired of the base forms of entertainment offered: "The fact is that TV is now censoring itself. As the novelty of television sets wears off, the lure of the sexy and the macabre wears thin.

In regions where TV has been in operation for a year or more there are already hundreds, probably thousands, of sets which are hardly turned on from one week to the next."[69]

For the most part, television was viewed as a moral problem rather than a new form of entertainment. The television was a vice that needed to be personally regulated by each individual viewer. Strict government regulation was not an option for these great believers in the free, self-regulating market system. The editors could only advocate self-restraint. In their eyes, American Protestantism's self-definition rested upon its advocacy of cultural and political democracy. As a 1945 editorial "Protestantism and Tolerance" stated:

> Protestantism, by virtue of its history and its own principles, is under a mandate to preserve this cultural democracy. It does not preserve it by suppressing its own convictions in sentimental deference to others. Protestantism is the spiritual guarantor of cultural and religious freedom. In contrast with Catholicism, it guarantees—to the limit of its power—the very freedom Catholicism enjoys in this nation. It asks no favor of the state, nor any privileged position in relation to the state. Nor does it ask that any political disfavor be shown toward other religious faiths. It did not do so when it was in the clear ascendancy in numbers and influence in American life, and it does not do so now that its ascendancy—not yet in numbers but in power—is open to challenge.[70]

State intervention could only be advocated when it was clearly to protect the public interest, an interest that was implicitly defined as synonymous with the liberal Protestant leadership's interest. Even moderate forms of censorship (e.g., concerning violence on children's shows) were considered to be dangerous in the long-run, and too Roman Catholic in the short-run.[71] For *The Christian Century* editors turning off the TV was the only form of resistance to mass culture they felt comfortable advocating. While there were occasional editorials urging the church to be involved in FCC policymaking, for the most part television was just ignored. The editors, like many others in the secular elite, could not see beyond their own print culture.

Conclusions

Ann Swidler has suggested that in times of social transformation "ideologies—explicit, articulated, highly organized meaning systems (both political and religious)—*establish* new styles or strategies of action."[72] In the post–World War II period, mainline Protestant hegemony was challenged like never before. Within a very short period of time, the once dominant leaders had to quickly come to terms with an existent (if previously ignored) pluralist America. Part of this shift from hegemony to pluralism required a different approach to culture. The strategy of Christianization (that is, the efforts to reform and shape cultural life according to mainline Protestant norms) no longer worked in such a context. Torn between coming to terms with this new pluralist reality and maintaining the old ways, liberal Protestant leaders approached the new medium of television with great ambivalence. In *The Christian Century* this ambivalence was largely translated into a strategy of disregard. For the liberal Protestant editors the television was often dismissed as a passing phase, a discountable threat. But despite this rhetoric, the television also served as a focal point for expressing fears of cultural change. Older and more familiar theological and cultural assumptions about play and leisure rhetorically justified these fears. *The Christian Century* writing about television reveals Protestant anxieties about the strengths of post–World War II Catholicism, the threats of secularism and pluralism, and the weakness of mainline Protestantism. This discourse coexisted alongside articles and essays that promoted tolerance and suggested that Protestants come to terms with the end of their cultural reign. Through the rejection of television, the editors channeled their fear of these changes in familiar terms. Television, the most prominent sign of the new leisure society, was categorized as a vice and Protestant America was called upon to operate with self-restraint. Censorship was avoided, for although it may have aided short-term goals, it clashed with the editors understanding of the Protestant ethos.

As liberal Protestant leaders slowly came to recognize their decline of influence in the public sphere, they only reluctantly admitted its erosion in the private sphere.[73] In the case of *The Christian Century* editors, part of their reluctance to address television must be attributed to a general lack of interest in the domestic sphere or domestic piety; the magazine's main concern was American public life.[74] That public too was, in the 1950s, conceived in masculine terms.[75] Occasionally one reads a letter from a woman reader or an article by a woman guest writer, but the overall impression is of a magazine written by men to a largely male readership. It is perhaps not surprising, given the feminine hue of mass culture in general and television in particular, that *The Christian Century* showed little interest in this new medium.[76]

By 1960, the presuppositions underlying the Elvis editorial were becoming less and less tenable, and in the next decade this kind of cultural criticism and its founding principles were largely abandoned by *The Christian Century*, as other issues, most prominently the civil rights movement, came to occupy the foreground.[77] The television set had replaced the organ in most American living rooms, and with that transition, (as Lynn Spigel argues) the Victorian domestic sphere, which had been shaped so fundamentally by ascetic Protestantism, had been transformed.[78] The younger generation at *The Christian Century* no longer hoped to keep America Protestant. The new model was the church as sanctuary or respite from the culture. By 1969, the editors self-consciously announced that they had changed the font style of the title head in order to reflect that "transition from a triumphalist model of Christendom to the witness of a servant church, given to serving humanity in its time."[79] The editors reconceived the mainline Protestant church as an escape from the homogenized, mechanized world that was increasingly the norm in the age of TV culture. In this redefined landscape, the television would remain problematic, but for different reasons. Conceived as less of a potential personal vice and more of an important shaper of social values, the television would remain suspect for promoting violence (particularly on children's programs) and social inequality, and generally for offering a worldview that was in direct conflict and competition with mainline Protestantism.

Chapter 3

Mainline Religious Broadcasting: A Failure?

New practices do not so much flow directly from technologies that inspire them as they are improvised out of old practices that no longer work in these new settings.[1]

As a new medium, the television demanded new practices, on the part of its individual users, and at the level of community. The Mainline Protestant leadership greeted the television with an experienced radio-hand. Attitudes and practices that had been shaped during the radio era played an important role in forming approaches to the nascent television.[2] Still, in a relatively short time, mainline leaders rejected television as an appropriate site for the production of liberal Protestant culture and instead focused upon cultural critique. Heretofore, historians have attributed this choice largely to a series of Federal Communications Commission (FCC) decisions that essentially eliminated the sustained-time religious broadcasting system that had been constructed during the radio-era. While the FCC decisions eliminated the networks' motivation for donating time to the so-called mainline religious groups, these changes in regulations do not explain why mainline broadcasters would not seek alternative funding opportunities or alternative avenues for producing media. While mainline Protestants were willing and able to raise large sums of money for other purposes, they declined to buy airtime and largely forfeited their future participation in the growing media culture.

To examine this change in policy and practice, this chapter focuses upon the creation of the Broadcast and Film Commission (BFC) of the

National Council of Churches (NCC) and the role of its parent organization the National Council of Churches of Christ in the larger society. As Protestant cultural dominance became less and less of a given in the post–World War II America, ecumenical organizations such as the NCC and the National Association of Evangelicals (NAE) worked hard to reverse that process. The BFC's agenda was thus partially defined by the aim of its parent organization—to preserve "This Nation Under God."

Religious broadcasting in the public interest (and therefore free of charge) was viewed as integral part of the larger battle to maintain "This Nation Under God." Under the rhetorical guise of evangelism, mainline Protestant programming was largely focused upon building a national religious consensus. Conversion of individuals to Christianity was not really the point of early BFC programming, even if it might have been legitimated using those terms. BFC television programming aimed more to "educate" the audience in the Protestant worldview, with the hope that such an education would "prepare the ground" for conversion.[3] Gradually, however, even this modest aim was forsaken as the efficacy of TV, namely its persuasiveness, was increasingly called into question.

Academic research thus played a central role in determining BFC policy. Since the 1920s, modernist liberal Protestants had argued that social scientific studies could aid the churches in planning and decision making. The BFC leadership clearly operated under this assumption. Studies of efficacy would turn out to be far more determinative factors in the development of mainline religious broadcasting than any theological, doctrinal, or creedal imperatives.[4] Although the neo-orthodox/Christian realist camp was increasingly critical of the liberal/modernist camp that presumed a natural alliance between science and Christianity, the bureaucrats within the NCC as a whole and the BFC in particular still had to make everyday policy decisions, and social scientific research offered a powerful resource.[5] Like the mass media, however, this resource would turn out to be less neutral than it originally appeared, perhaps even contributing, as Laurence Moore has suggested, to the destruction of "Protestant claims to be the dominant cultural authority."[6]

As BFC policy shifted away from media production, it refocused interest upon media criticism, and the possible use of the media in the civil rights movement.[7] This case study of the BFC offers an important example of the way in which a religious organization addressed the challenge of a new communications medium. While it should not be considered as the sole representative of mainline or liberal Protestantism, the BFC of these early years certainly reflected a significant section of the liberal Protestant leadership. As a national ecumenical institution, the BFC's approaches may have certainly been different than a particular denomination's (such as Methodist's

Television, Radio, and Film Commission (TRAFCO) of the Methodist Church), but precisely because it operated in such a national capacity and worked with the national television networks, the BFC's approach would be disproportionately influential upon mainline Protestantism.

"This Nation under God": The Creation of the BFC

The BFC was founded in 1950 as a central department of the newly formed NCC. As the replacement for the Protestant Film Commission (1947) and the Protestant Radio Commission (1949), the BFC theoretically represented the twenty-nine member denominations of the NCC and its respective 31 million lay members in the realm of broadcasting.[8] Conceived largely in the missionary terms that dominated the rhetoric of the NCC's founding convention, the BFC's "most important function [was] to help make religion a vital force in American life through broadcasting."[9] Protestant broadcasting was one brick in what Henry K. Sherill, the first NCC president, called "the building of a Christian America in a Christian world."[10]

Such lofty and establishmentarian rhetoric hid the fragile and fractured state of mainline Protestantism.[11] From the 1930s onward, "Christian ecumenism" or "Protestant cooperation" had been increasingly trumpeted by segments of the mainline leadership as a means of preserving the privileged role of Protestantism in the nation.[12] Temporarily buoyed by the postwar religious revival, the founding of the NCC represented one of the last efforts by mainline Protestant leaders to maintain a rather tenuous cultural hegemony.[13]

Until World War II, in the religious, and more importantly, the public religious realm, Protestant dominance in America had been (and many would argue that it continues to be) a relatively steady social assumption. At the turn of the century, millions of Catholic and Jewish immigrants (particularly in urban centers such as New York) challenged this assumption. The immigration laws of 1910, 1921, and 1924 were clearly formulated as a response to this numerical threat by limiting the percentage of immigrants from non-Protestant countries.[14] Despite these legal attempts to preserve their majority, Protestant leaders would soon find their assumption of cultural (if not numerical) dominance called into question. In other words, the days of "spontaneous consent" (to use Gramsci's terms) were fading; consent to the Protestant agenda would increasingly have to be manufactured. Consolidation of the Protestant leadership, however, was a prerequisite to creating that consent. In a sense, a new historical bloc, self-conscious of its "Protestant" rather than its denominational identity, was in the making.[15]

Protestant unity, apart from being theologically sound, was considered necessary in the fight against (what was perceived as) the decaying influences of secularism, Roman Catholicism, and communism.[16] Under the banner of the council, doctrinal and worship differences were put aside for a greater good—namely, the preservation of Protestant influence in America. This new rhetorical and organizational perspective was signaled by the change in the Federal Council to the NCC. The old Federal Council had lost its credibility amongst lay Protestants—it was seen as modernizing and radical and too far removed from the concerns of everyday Christians. The National Council was to be far more embracing, if far more limiting in its potential scope. The main aim was to forge a consensus amongst the divided Protestant ranks.

A brief look at the commemorative volume of the constituting convention of the National Council shows the centrality of this agenda. On the cover of the book is a picture of the assembly—delegates sitting at tables in the shape of a cross looking toward a stage, where the theme—"This Nation Under God"—hangs from above: On stage and around the room, clusters of flags—the American, the church, and the UN—are found at regular intervals. Opening the book we find speeches and addresses devoted to the convention theme.[17] The speakers remind their audience that "the laws, the institutions, the ideals of America stem from the soil of belief in a sovereign God."[18] Religious education and missionary work were therefore promoted as services to the nation. In their eyes, democracy would flourish and survive the attacks of "communism from without and secularism within" only if Protestantism remained vital.[19] While the legal separation of church and state was considered necessary for the health of both, the church was thought to play an important, if not indispensable, civic function. As the NCC president Henry Knox Sherill declared:

> There cannot be a nation under God without there being first churches under God with all that implies in intellectual and spiritual strength and discipline. There can be no artificial division between the sacred and the secular. . . . For if worship is real, then action must follow—for all of life belongs to God.[20]

The National Council agenda thus was rhetorically defined in terms of the promotion and preservation of America's semiestablished religion, a religion that was unsurprisingly largely indistinguishable from what Gramsci might have called the "spontaneous philosophy" of mainline Protestantism. In other words, the religion of the nation reflected the language, common sense, and folk religion common to mainline Protestantism, while eliminating the specifically Protestant or denominational references that could prevent potential assent (consent) by other historical blocs such as Catholics or Jews. This philosophy would undergo substantial revision in the 1950s as the support of certain kinds of Catholics and Jews (particularly of the modernist and reformed variety) would be sought and readily incorporated. Will Herberg, in his oft-cited classic *Protestant, Catholic, Jew*, offered a description and critique of this process, calling for a return to religious specificity.[21]

The logic of this "Nation Under God" rhetoric dictated that all areas of culture fell under the jurisdiction of the council. For the sake of God, the NCC leaders undertook the responsibility of guarding the nation from its own potential pitfalls. In other words, the nation's problems and interests were perceived to be identical to that of the NCC. In this larger scheme, the BFC was appointed the difficult task of monitoring the growing field of mass communications, guiding the nation toward the proper use of these new media, and promoting Protestant broadcasting. Practically translated, this meant that the BFC was responsible for formulating media policy, providing in-house education about the media (e.g., providing training workshops for ministers interested in using media in their local churches), as well as representing ecumenical Protestantism to the networks and before the FCC.

Unity, even for the lofty and abstract goal of a Christian America, however, was not easily realized. While theoretically united, mainline Protestant leaders remained largely divided over many substantive issues, one of which was the proper approach to mass media and culture. The BFC's organizational predecessor, the Department of National Religious Radio (under the Federal Council) left behind a mixed legacy to follow.[22] Since the founding of the National Broadcasting Corporation (NBC) in 1926, the Federal Council's Radio Commission had been a national provider of public service Protestant programming. As the general secretary of the Federal Council of Churches, Charles S. Macfarland participated in NBC's Advisory Council, a council devised by the Radio Corporation of America (RCA) board chairman and made up of seventeen citizen members, whose duty was to guard NBC's virtue.[23] In that capacity, Macfarland was chairman of the religious affairs subcommittee and had an important hand in formulating the guidelines for NBC's religious programming.[24] In 1928, together with two other members of the Advisory Council, Morgan J. O'Brian (the representative Roman Catholic) and Julius Rosenwald (the representative Jew), Macfarland wrote five policies that would serve as NBC's guide to religious broadcasting.[25]

1. The National Broadcasting Company will serve only the Central or national agencies of great religious faiths, as, for example, the Roman Catholics, the Protestants, and the Jews, as distinguished from

individual churches or small group movements where the national membership is comparatively small.

2. The religious message broadcast should be nonsectarian and nondenominational in appeal.

3. The religious message broadcast should be of the widest appeal, presenting the broad claims of religion, which not only aid in building up the personal and social life of the individual but also aid in popularizing religion and the church.

4. The religious message broadcast should interpret religion at its highest and best so that as an educational factor it will bring the individual listener to realize his responsibility to the organized church and to society.

5. The national religious messages should only be broadcast by the recognized outstanding leaders of the several faiths as determined by the best counsel and advise available.[26]

These policies would remain the heart and soul of the Federal Council's religious radio policy and would continue to shape the vision of the National Council's BFC through the 1950s, until research and a changing reality in the early 1960s prompted necessary changes. The shape of early religious television would be largely determined by these policies. Although strictly speaking, each of the recognized religious bodies (Protestant, Catholic, Jew) had an opportunity to air its ideas, the NBC guide basically stripped any specificity from the programming. While rabbis might quote from the Bible, and ministers from the New Testament, the messages were broad, nondenominational, and nonsectarian. In other words, the purpose of religious broadcasting was defined as the promotion of America's semi-established religion. This common goal suited all parties concerned. In promoting America's religion, liberal Protestant leaders preserved their cultural prominence through the assent of their main competitors.[27]

Jewish and Catholic agreement to these policies, however, was probably not motivated by or conceived as consent to mainline Protestantism, but rather by the desire to explain and legitimate their traditions to the larger American public. In the tripartite melting pot of the 1950s, Catholic and Jewish leaders were thankful for being recognized as two alternatives to the historically and culturally dominant faith. Religious broadcasting, however limited in time, offered proof of this newfound status as well as an opportunity to counter charges of anti-Catholicism and anti-Semitism to a larger, and perhaps heretofore unreachable, audience. Although the religious broadcasting policies ultimately served to bolster the Protestant agenda, Catholic and Jewish interests were also served. Take, for example, the implicit agreement to the religious status quo. If messages were to be nonsectarian and nondenominational, and to promote religion in general, then their respective constituencies were not to be targets of specific evangelical campaigns.[28] This tripartite cooperation also further isolated the conservative wing of Protestantism, which had been given a solid cultural blow in the Scopes Trial only a few years earlier. While excluding conservative Protestantism from the sustained-time programming may have been advantageous in the short run, it would turn out to be the Achilles' heel of the BFC media policy.

Adhering to the 1928 guidelines, the Federal Council built a repertoire of staid, establishment-like classics such as Harry Emerson Fosdick's National Vespers program and Ralph Sockman's National Pulpit. Receiving free airtime as a public service from the network, the Federal Council chose famous and/or influential New York preachers who would also attract financial support to sponsor these programs.[29] This policy, Ralph Jennings has argued, suited the network as well as the council: "NBC found in the Federal Council a benign and beneficent radio sponsor, providing the kind of positive religious programs that would serve the network's public image."[30] Others under the liberal Protestant umbrella, however, were less satisfied with this cozy relationship.

Believing that this relationship with NBC had prevented the council from taking a critical stand vis-à-vis the industry, the Congregational-Christian Church's Board of Home Missions formed a radio department headed by Everett Parker that would eventually be sponsored by Methodists, Presbyterians (of the United States) and the United Church of Canada, and the Reformed and Evangelical Churches (the same denominations supposedly represented by the Federal Council). The Joint Religious Radio Committee, as it came to be named, steered clear from direct confrontation with the Federal Council and concentrated instead on local broadcasts, media education, and media policymaking, areas that were deemed to be neglected by the council.[31] Coming to the task with a background in broadcasting, research, and seminary training, Parker emphasized the need for more accurate research that would help evaluate the efficacy of programming and assess the different components of the audience.[32] Perceiving the traditional, sermon format of the Federal Council's programming as limiting, the committee focused on developing drama, children's programming, and music programs. In these areas, the committee was successful in carving a separate niche and approach to broadcasting. Most importantly, in the eyes of Parker (and Jennings who tells the story to us), the committee preserved its independence from the networks, and was therefore able to support liberal initiatives sponsored by the FCC, such as the 1946 "Blue Book" (or Public Service Responsibility of Broadcast Licensees).[33]

Only a few years later (1947), however, the movement toward unification would bring the Joint Religious Radio Committee and the Department of Religious Radio at the Federal Council into negotiations to form the Protestant Radio Commission, an organization that was from its inception considered a temporary body until the founding of the NCC.[34] The differences in the organizations' approaches would become clear during these negotiations. The Joint Religious Radio Committee, represented by Everett Parker, felt strongly that the commission should be headed by someone with broadcasting as well as church experience (as Parker had from his internship at NBC after seminary). He likewise felt that the commission's future policy should be determined by informed research rather than random audience mail. The Federal Council leaders, however, entered the negotiations with the desire to preserve the status quo, including the leadership of the Radio Department by Frank Goodman, an ex-bookie converted to Christianity by Billy Sunday.[35] In the end, the commission began work in 1949, with Everett Parker as director of program and production. Notably, the commission's formation did not resolve the conflict that had originally provoked the founding of the Joint Religious Radio Committee. Parker and his cadre remained dissatisfied with the Federal Council's approach to radio, and within the new commission the division in approach and labor remained separate as before.

The BFC, founded a year later (1950), inherited these divisions and tensions. Everett Parker, however, declined to work in the new BFC. The Joint Religious Radio Committee experiment had failed (at least in Parker's eyes), and the BFC seemed to be simply a newer version of the Federal Council's Radio Commission. Certainly, as we will see below, the early policies of the BFC seem to bear out this general observation. Parker, however, would continue to be indirectly influential, particularly with the publication and reception of *The Television-Radio Audience and Religion*.[36]

Producing a Protestant Culture: Sustained-Time Religious Programming

In the areas of television and radio, the BFC's main efforts revolved around sustained-time religious programming. In accordance with the 1934 Act of Communications, license renewal for radio/TV stations was contingent upon proof that the station had contributed to public service. The airwaves were considered public property, temporarily on loan to the station, and thus, the station was required to donate time to fulfill their public mandate. Nowhere does the 1934 act explicitly require religious programming for license renewal, but the renewal application had a space for listing different kinds of programming, religious programming being one of those listed. As the self-designated representative of the majority faith, the BFC (just like its earlier counterparts such as the Protestant Radio Commission) benefited directly from this requirement. By coordinating programming with the BFC, the networks met one of the conditions for license renewal, while the BFC gained a free platform for presenting their agenda to the people.[37] This sustained-time arrangement between the networks and the BFC would remain operative throughout the 1950s, ending only with a 1960 FCC ruling that allowed networks to count paid-time toward the fulfillment of the public obligation.[38]

The BFC's early approach to television was determined to a great extent by historical precedents set in the medium of radio, as well as earlier forms of commercial leisure.[39] The general tactic was to embrace TV, thereby creating a Christian presence in this new medium while at the same time pressing for the moral wholesomeness of the secular programming. Few questioned whether this tactic of cultural "Christianization" was still viable in post–World War II America. Rather all energies were devoted to penetrating the industry and to developing programming for the sustained-time slots. The pressing question of the day was whether or not the BFC "will come with 'too little, too late' as was true in the beginning of radio history."[40] The task at hand seemed immense and all-important:

> With whole continents still to be won for Christ, it is staggering to contemplate the size of the job to be done. But it is the simple truth that the instruments of mass communication have been placed not in pagan hands but Christian hands. I tremble to think of the day when we Christians of America may have to yield up these instruments unused with the words of the little, fearful man who cried to his Lord, "I was afraid, and went and hid thy talent in the earth: lo, here thou hast that is thine."[41]

The BFC, as the representative of mainline Protestantism, was obligated to harness TV for Christ. If Christians, that is, the BFC, did not move quickly, television would soon become yet another secular outpost: "In the face of organized and militant secularism, we cannot evade the charge to use the newest and most powerful weapons for spreading the Gospel to all people in concerted action."[42] Such triumphalistic rhetoric hid the leadership's fear of this new medium.

Part of this early urgency resulted from an overestimation of the TV's power to shape people's opinions. If television had the power to form people's opinions, it threatened to undermine the status and authority of the established order. As long as television's power could be used to preserve and reinforce that order, the mainline leadership could enthusiastically endorse its potential. In this sense, it is natural that television, like other new communications media before it, was first perceived as a tool for evangelism. Writing in 1949, Carothers formulated this position succinctly: "the Church can have television if it understands that through this medium we have the great evangelistic opportunity of the present era . . . It is a missionary task and we have to treat it as such."[43] Television, if properly used, offered a miraculous opportunity for bearing witness to the Word. Its invasive nature meant that it could open doors that would have been slammed in conventional missionaries' faces:

> We cannot be content to present our great personalities, our dynamic leaders, our dramatic heart-warming stories to audiences of a hundred and a thousand when we have the means at hand to reach millions. From the days when Jesus spoke to Philip and Philip to Nathaniel, personal evangelism has been central in Christian movement (sic). It is important for churchmen-strategists to perceive that broadcasting is a mass medium only in the sum of its effects; to each who hears and sees it comes individual to individual. A new and magnificent *personal evangelism*.[44]

TV was personified as the missionary par excellence, whose message would be individually received (i.e., accepted) by each viewer. Unlike the impersonal mass evangelists of the past such as D. Moody or Billy Sunday, television touched each listener and did so in the privacy of the home.[45]

Television, like other new communications media before it, prompted a renewed hope for mass evangelism.[46] Viewed as a gift from God, the television's main appeal for the BFC leadership lay in its ability to reach more people than ever before in a personal manner. As Ronald Bridges, the first director of the BFC put it: "It is important for churchmen-strategists to perceive that broadcasting is a mass medium only in the sum of its effects; to each who hears and sees it comes individual to individual. A new and magnificent personal evangelism."[47] Bypassing doors closed to conventional missionaries, the TV brought its messages directly to viewers in the privacy of their own living rooms. Unlike the impersonal mass evangelists of the recent past, such as Billy Sunday, the television touched every individual. (The effects of revival without the mess of revival.)

This personal touch was considered to be irresistible to the viewer, who was willing and waiting to be filled with any message whatsoever. For Albert Crews, the BFC television director, religious TV was not by definition any different than advertising. If goods could be sold by the commercial sponsors, so could Christ be sold: "American business believes TV can sell goods. We believe TV can serve the Christian Church equally well."[48] Of course, if advertisers and the church could use the TV so effectively to manipulate the viewer then others, less ethical than the BFC, could use this medium in a far more nefarious manner. Subsequently, BFC presence on the airwaves seemed to have far-reaching public significance. Fear of the content and affects of the competing messages on the airwaves, as much or perhaps more than the potential conversion of souls, motivated the BFC to produce religious broadcasts. As Albert Crews put it: "I think we have to be in television simply because there is television."[49] The BFC had a responsibility to the public to utilize TV, lest one more cultural outpost fall to the enemy: "In the face of organized and militant secularism, we cannot evade the charge to use the newest and most powerful weapons for spreading the Gospel to all people in concerted action."[50]

BFC programming, although seemingly directed to the conversion of the individual, was more often actually an effort to maintain "This Nation Under God." In retrospect, the 1951 descriptions of the programs and films produced by the BFC indicate the increasingly defensive posture of mainline Protestant leaders. For example, the aim of *Morning Chapel* (a Du Mont network show, 10:45 to 11:00 on Thursday mornings) was to show how spiritual values could be applied to practical everyday living.[51] *What's Your Trouble* was a program in design whose purpose was described as showing "people not actively connected with the church that there is an answer in religion to many of the problems with which people are currently plagued."[52] *To Thee We Sing* and *The Meeting House* were likewise conceived to "reach people who are not particularly interested in church affairs," but who while watching the TV for entertainment might begin to realize that "religion is not a deadly serious business but one which involves joy."[53] The recurring theme in these program descriptions is of Protestantism's contemporary relevance. One cannot help but wonder whether the opposite, the fear of obsolescence, may have driven these efforts as much as their stated goal of demonstrating pertinence.

Data derived from commercial advertising was often used to legitimate the value and effectiveness of missionary television:

> The churches don't deal in sales figures or other easily measurable commodities, but the same thousand viewers that Westinghouse reaches for $4.80 are also available to religious programs for a similar or even lesser figure. Spend say, $40 for the four Bible puppet films for your TV station . . . and you will reach more children than will be reached by all the Daily Vacation Bible Schools in your community this summer.[54]

Not only would religious television reach the same audience as advertisements, it would also affect viewers similarly. If advertisers could persuade people to consume, then religious programmers could likewise persuade people to believe in Christianity. The church, then, could learn from the advertising industry's insights: "Television missionaries must profit by the discovery of the beer manufacturers; namely that a regularly appearing personality is the best way to hold a regular listening audience."[55] TV was an expensive investment but was considered to be good value: "Compared to radio, TV is said to be four times as expensive, four times as difficult and four times as effective. In the commercial world, TV is considered a salesman with his foot practically in the door."[56] The model may have been profane, but the purpose was lofty: to build God's kingdom on earth.

Early BFC programming efforts were subsequently shaped by these missionary assumptions. While the ongoing programs listed in the 1951 general report of the BFC were intended to reach a churched audience, eight of the nine programs in work were directed to nonbelievers. *What's Your Trouble*, for example, was designed "to show people not actively connected with the church that there is an answer in religion to many of the problems with which people are currently plagued."[57] Following the advertising industry's example, they chose to frame the show around two regular hosts, Dr. and Mrs. Vincent Peale, who answered viewers' letters on the air. *Within these Portals* was designed with similar purpose in mind: "To show how Christianity and the Church can help in some of the basic problems that face large numbers of us today." Each show was intended to focus on a particular problem through a short dramatic piece. Some of the topics to be examined included "alcoholism, problems of old age, adultery, divorce, draft, marriage, counseling family problems, grief, terminal diseases, parent/child relations, and how to handle a budget."[58] Two additional shows were designed to attract unchurched TV viewers in search of relaxation and entertainment, with the intent of showing that "religion is not a deadly serious business, but one which involves joy." The assumption here was that "if we satisfy their desire for these things [relaxation and entertainment], we can utilize the opportunity of introducing more serious elements." "The Meeting House" was to be based on a real church's social hall and the activities that took place there.[59] *To Thee We Sing* was devoted to church music.[60] These early programming efforts illustrate that the BFC was intent on attracting a wide audience.[61] If they could somehow lure a nonbeliever into watching their shows by making it seem as if they were providing secular entertainment, the TV would do the rest of the job. At this early stage, no one perceived the lack of human contact with the viewer as problematic; the TV was assumed to be personal and persuasive enough on its own.

In the end, however, this rather optimistic model of the television would be short-lived. At the end of his term in 1953, Bridges, the first BFC director, remained unclear as to the true effects of religious television: "How much good do we do? Are we building the Kingdom of God or are we filling in idle hours for idle people? . . . A Yankee judgment of these three years of BFC labors would be—'well we haven't done no great damage'. . ."[62]

"What then Should We Be Communicating? To Whom? To What End?"[63] The Academic Study of Religious TV

By 1955, however, the mainliners' confidence in religious television was already waning. Dr. Liston Pope, both in an address to the BFC and in an article in *Christianity and Crisis*, questioned, "what was being broadcast by others, and by the National Council itself, in the name of religion."[64] Religious TV, he argued, was often less effective in transmitting the Gospel than secular programs such as *Father Knows Best*. He criticized the religious broadcasters for following the received wisdom of the advertising industry, noting that "perhaps the principal fault of religious broadcasting has been a tendency to focus on the audience rather than on the Gospel. Ironically, it is now becoming apparent that there is not a mass audience for religious broadcasts."[65] Pope called upon the BFC and the churches to reevaluate their approach to religious broadcasting:

> The churches have something to say, and it is their responsibility to learn how to say it. A warfare is waging for the minds and souls of men around the earth, and there are no bystanders, in the cloisters of the Church or in the soundproofed studios or in the offices where executive decisions are made with regard to the use of the new marvels for girdling the world with sound.[66]

The Television-Radio Audience and Religion

"The Television-Radio Audience and Religion," a book-length study commissioned by the BFC in 1955, also questioned earlier assumptions.[67] In this 464-page research tome, Everett Parker, David Barry, and Dallas Smythe showed just how complex and difficult it was to measure the media's effects—for good or bad—on the American audience. In over 20 chapters, 100 tables, 30 figures and 6 appendices, Parker et al. analyzed data collected from the community of New Haven, Connecticut, using several distinct research methods: statistics, content analysis, audience analysis, in-depth interviews. In their breadth of methodology and particularly in their emphasis on the audience as meaning-makers, the authors would prove to be forward-looking.[68] Although the introduction states the Protestant nature and bias of the study, analysis of Catholic and Jewish programs and audiences was included as well, providing important comparative data.[69]

Interestingly, the study offered empirical data to support Everett Parker's critique of the National Council's use of media and its lack of knowledge about the media. Most striking was how opposite the conclusions were from the assumptions used to legitimate religious broadcasting and to plan specific programs. One of the most important observations concerned the composition and nature of audience. While most of the programs were designed to reach "everyone" or the "unchurched," Parker et al. demonstrated that "insofar as the term 'mass' connotes, therefore a sameness or homogeneity as one characteristic of modern communication, it must be applied to the medium rather than to the audience reached by the content. . . . [T]he people themselves are far from uniform units of personality or taste or position."[70] People chose what they wanted to listen or view and in the case of religious programs, the New Haven audience proved that the TV was not a miraculous new tool for evangelism. The viewers and listeners of religious broadcasts were not likely to be unaffiliated, rather they tended to be those who were already churchgoers.

Only Dr. Vincent Peale's programs could claim success in converting some of his viewers, but the mainline clergy (and one guesses the authors of the book) was extremely derisive about his "technique" that included sitting and asking forgiveness, forgiving everyone you are mad at, and reading the Bible three times a day (fifteen minutes each time) for two weeks.[71] Depicted mainly as a therapeutic answer for highly anxious people, the authors did not see much in Peale's programs for the mainline broadcasters to imitate.[72]

Still even Peale's charisma could not call upon much of an audience compared to that of Fulton Sheen. In an average week in New Haven, Sheen captured a massive 23 percent of the sample viewing audience, compared to the meager 7.5 percent of the *Greatest Story Ever Told*, and the 1.5 percent captured by the Peales's *What's Your Trouble*.[73] Even more disturbing—many of Sheen's viewers were not Catholic. Still, Parker et al. warned the mainline leaders away from looking for a Protestant equivalent for Sheen.[74] Part of this hesitancy was grounded in a fear of authoritarianism. The experiences of World War II as well as a historical fear of the Roman Catholic hierarchy, both reinforced this attitude: "Indeed, it is probably not of the nature of Protestantism to voice its message through a single authority figure."[75]

Sheen's strengths, they suggested, could perhaps be duplicated in a series of programs aimed at specific audiences.

This same fear of authority guided the "Depth Studies of Individuals." Fifty-nine families, both viewers and nonviewers (about half-and-half) of religious programs, were interviewed (mostly by the authors) about their attitudes towards media. At the end, the families were asked to fill out two questionnaires, one of which focused on the family's use of leisure time. The second questionnaire was based on the controversial F-scale measure developed in the Institute of Social Research to study the authoritarian personality. Authored by Theodor Adorno with Else Frenkel-Brunswik, Daniel J. Levinson, and R. Nevitt Sanford, *The Authoritarian Personality* was part of the institute's Studies of Prejudice series, sponsored by the American Jewish Committee in 1942.[76] The F-scale was designed to empirically measure "authoritarian potential on the latent psychological scale."[77] Nine personality variables—conventionalism, authoritarian submission, authoritarian aggression, anti-intraception, superstition and stereotypy, power and toughness, destructiveness and cynicism, projectivity, sex—were tested with that aim in mind.[78] The objective of the original study was to determine when and why people, given the choice, would be likely to choose an authoritarian system. Why then would Parker and his coauthors be interested in such a study's results or in using the F-scale in their own work on religious broadcasting?

Partially, the authors found it necessary to respond to what they viewed as a weakness in the original study: "The Adorno staff exhibited what may most charitably be called naiveté in their analysis of how an individual acts in relation to his loyalty to God, as distinct from his attitudes toward human authority figures."[79] Still, even though the original study had not sufficiently differentiated these different kinds of religious attitudes, religion did not come out as a determining factor in the creation of the authoritarian personality—it was just not determinative in either direction. In other words, neither the existence of prejudice or tolerance could not be connected to one's religious affiliation.[80] Empirically, the study proved that being a Roman Catholic, for example, did *not* put one in a higher risk group for being vulnerable to authoritarianism. This seemed problematic because as the authors noted: "Roman Catholics are generally distinguished from Protestants by the type and extent of authority they attribute to the church and its priesthood and by the relatively lesser importance they reserve for the internalization of authority by the individual."[81] In other words, the research seemed to contradict a basic Protestant assumption.

Still, this legitimation for the use of the F-scale seems rather flimsy because in the sample used by Parker there would be no Catholic families. Instead, the F-scale would be used to determine the relation, if any, between viewing religious programming and the proclivity toward authoritarianism.

One could see this partly as an empirical evaluation of Adorno's critique of mass culture as authoritarian and manipulative and partly as an effort to make sure that at least liberal Protestant programming would be free of this charge (which of course would mean that it would be largely ineffective as a missionary instrument). To that end Parker and his coauthors added five statements to the original F-scale questionnaire to help evaluate the role of religion in the development of authoritarianism.[82] The results show that Fulton Sheen's and Billy Graham's viewers tended to have higher average F-scales than those who viewed National Council programs (although notably Peale's audience tended to be similar to the others).[83]

How, then, were these results interpreted? Were particular types more likely to watch certain programs to begin with or were particular types more vulnerable to the effects of the media? What were the determinative factors—class, religious affiliation, education? The authors placed great emphasis on the power of the audience to choose and make its own meanings from the programs:

> Words, which have a high degree of ambiguity, carry meanings of different kinds because of syntax, pace and intonation. It is as if the content were a conveyor belt that carries many different meanings to the audience. The audience members bring to the communication as wide a variety of tastes and needs as human experience in life. What these audience members take from the conveyor belt, what uses they make of what materials they take, how they reshape the materials they take—these processes also are as diverse as the dynamics of the individuals' personalities and life situations.[84]

Fulton Sheen's program suited the most diverse group of individuals: "It is no accident that his audience is a legion of types. For he has built a program full of ambiguity, full of cues and symbols on many levels of meaning, carefully put together in relationships and with timing that invite a maximum of disparate interpretations."[85] Notably, the National Council Radio program was precisely the opposite in that it had a loyal, older, rather homogeneous audience who liked the "respectable, literate, rational religion of the type familiar in the middle-class and upper middle-class Protestant churches of British-American background."[86]

The data collected throughout the study shed serious doubt on the efficacy of TV as an evangelist: "Radio and television do not broadcast magic messages. The amazing feature of these media is simply that they permit so many individuals to see and hear the messages simultaneously."[87] While most religious broadcasts were directed to the nonaffiliated, in reality the majority of viewers were already religiously committed. Religious broadcasters, it recommended, should recognize that their audience was small and specific and far less vulnerable to persuasion than previously thought.[88] Clergy should make an effort to gear their ministry toward a constituency that spent more and more leisure time listening to the radio and watching television:

> Television is one more threat to the influence of the church because it is one more secular voice speaking to the public, tempting and wheedling and persuading and informing and arguing and amusing people in accord with whatever interests move the sponsors and managers of the program. It cannot be ignored by the churches; it might, however be used.[89]

The overall impact of TV on society was reason enough for the church to stay involved. The authors urged clergymen to see the TV as part of a "fundamental revolution in communications technology,"[90] a revolution that directly challenged the authority of the clergy, as well as the church's role in society:

> It was not too long ago in America that a church member's general life orientation was developed in his face-to-face conversation with neighbors and friends, in his perusal of the local newspaper, in his reading of books—especially the Bible—and in his participation, weekly or more often, in large congregate assemblies in church presided over by a clergyman whose chief purpose was to give him fundamental moral orientation.[91]

And it was precisely this threat to the cultural status quo that motivated the BFC to remain on the airwaves and prompted the authors of the study report, despite all of their warnings concerning the limitations and dangers of television, to end with policy suggestions for the more effective use of TV by the BFC and other like organizations. Parker et al. emphasized the importance of educating the clergy, particularly as to the use of the media by the laity and the importance of promoting existent religious programs. Religious broadcasters should design new programs with a true awareness of their audience (the already churched), and the multiplicity of audience needs in mind. Research (not audience mail or educated guessing) should be the guiding force of these producers.[92] And above all, religious broadcasters must devise an overall policy:

> What is religious broadcasting intended to do? Win converts? Its effectiveness here could be readily measured, if this were a serious purpose. Prick the conscience of the lagging churchgoer? Present the religious life in attractive terms? Encourage a general attitude of acceptance of religion on the part of the public . . . ? Bring the church to the shut-in? Do adult religious education? Bring the "best" in American religion to the average home?[93]

While questioning whether TV was an appropriate medium of the mainline churches at all, the study seemed to imply that at this point, some religious television, however ineffective it might be, was better than none.[94]

Studies and Pronouncements: The Development of Protestant Media Criticism

Study Commission on the Role of Radio Television and Films in Religion

The New Haven study not only overturned the BFC's earlier presuppositions concerning TV but also questioned whether TV was an appropriate medium for the mainline churches at all. If TV viewers were not simply convinced by its messages, then what was the function of religious TV and, more particularly, the BFC? Franklin S. Mack, the second BFC director (1954–1963), took the results of the research seriously and asked the board for direction on this question: "What then should we be communicating? To Whom? To What End? And in what relation to the program of the church for evangelism, for education, for work, for worship? . . . The central question is not how, but what?"[95] Such basic questions, however, would take the BFC and the NCC time to answer.

The Advisory Policy Statement: The Battle against Paid Time

While the BFC questioned its basic mission, television was rapidly developing. As the industry expanded, it had less time available for sustained-time religious programs. From its earliest days, the BFC had deliberated whether or not to allow commercial sponsors for their broadcasts. It was generally "agreed that television [was] going to call for new and rather heavy financing."[96] Either the denominations would have to contribute more money to the BFC (a rather unlikely scenario as the local programming was still controlled by the denominations and depended on denominational income for success) or the BFC would need noncommercial sponsors (such as foundations) in order to finance their programs. The success of Fulton Sheen's program, which was aired in prime time because it was commercially sponsored, seemed to offer a powerful argument in favor of such a strategy.

In 1953, the BFC deliberated whether or not to allow the Peale's TV program *What's Your Trouble* to be commercially sponsored. Overwhelmingly (13 yeas, 1 nay, 3 abstentions) the board voted to approve a twenty-six-week pilot project, despite fears that such an effort might "be somewhat harmful to the Commission." Dr. Cavert, for example, in a foresighted manner "questioned whether we could be as sure of long term benefits. For instance, would the stations gradually adopt the attitude that all religious programs should be paid for and would commercial sponsors by subtle degrees come to influence or control program content."[97] In an internally circulated memo in 1953 listing fourteen arguments for and against commercial sponsorship, the weight was clearly on the "against" column. The author (perhaps Ronald Bridges) noted that even the arguments in favor of commercially sponsored religious broadcasts (such as providing needed revenue) could be easily countered with the negative effects (e.g., current revenue generated by listeners could be jeopardized) of such efforts. The "arguments for" column optimistically viewed commercial sponsorship as a neutral means for providing better access to the new medium (i.e., the commercial aspect would have no effect on the content). Such optimism was clearly negated in the arguments "against" column, which claimed that such an effort might reduce the church to the status of "the money changers in the temple," while jeopardizing the status of sustaining time programs.[98] In the end, both the Peales' program and the experiment in commercial broadcasting would turn out to be short-lived.[99] Future BFC documents seemed not even to remember (let alone refer to) this one-time experiment.

Indeed, although the BFC would increasingly express ambivalence about the affects of TV, this ambivalence did not translate into a lack of support for the system of sustained-time programming. Quite the contrary, as the BFC became less and less certain of its programming efforts and their efficacy, maintaining the privilege of sustained-time programming came to have an important symbolic value.

The Advisory Policy Statement on religious broadcasting (issued in 1956), for example, was almost completely devoted to the preservation of religious sustained-time programming. The statement repeated the favorite NCC refrain "religion is essential to the strong and healthy continuance of our life as a nation." The BFC would provide programming "free as a public service," and expected the networks "to recognize it as their responsibility to make a substantial provision of facilities and desirable broadcast time free as a public service for such programs." As a public service this airtime should be scheduled at reasonable hours and divvied up according to "the strength and representative character of the councils of churches, local and national."[100] Moreover, if the network were to resort to selling time to religious broadcasters, this kind of programming should not be considered to fulfill any public service requirements. Paid-time religious TV was contrary to the BFC's own mission, because religious TV was considered to be a *public* service, aiding America as a whole. To permit paid-time religious TV would be tantamount to denying the public significance of religion in America, and perhaps admitting to the symbolic defeat of the mainline Protestant establishment.

It seems, however, that the policy statement provoked sharp retorts by all those to whom it was directed: The National Association of Radio and Television Broadcasters (NARTB), the National Religious Broadcasters Association (NRB), and the station managers. The NARTB as well as individual station managers disliked the fact that the policy seemed to advocate government regulation of the airwaves. The NRB accused the BFC "of launching a campaign to 'throw all evangelical broadcasters off the air' and of being determined to dominate religious broadcasting."[101]

Denying that the Advisory Policy had been explicitly designed to exclude evangelicals from the air, the BFC admitted only to "sounding an alarm against what we saw as a strong, accelerating trend in broadcasting away from the public responsibility concept toward complete commercialization."[102] From the BFC's perspective, the station managers had a "moral obligation" to provide the "right *kind* and *amount* of religion in the broadcast schedule" in order to preserve "our American heritage."[103] So while the BFC recognized the right of evangelicals to airtime as part of their "policy of inclusiveness," sustained-time should be granted only to the "right kind" of religious groups—those that best represented the American public, the mainline. The NRB response was not even deemed worthy of a reply. The evangelical criticism was discounted simply as a tactic to "revive and strengthen support for the tremendous vested interest [defined by the BFC as 'the fiction of an unbridgeable gulf between Christians affiliated with the National Council and Christians who are not'] which the NRB was organized, ten years ago, to protect."[104] Operating from a self-proclaimed high ground, the BFC "refused to be drawn into open controversy" with the NRB.[105] From its perspective the NRB failed to cooperate by agreeing to "some degree of mutual self-limitation of the right of access to broadcast media."[106] Instead the NRB relentlessly claimed the right to purchase time and to broadcast whenever they chose. In other words, the NRB chose not to play the game by the BFC rules. Even the NRB's claim to represent the 21 million Protestants not represented in the National Council was derided and called into question by the BFC.[107]

The BFC clearly saw itself as America's sole moral guardian, whose task they defined as protecting the public from both the evils of commercial TV and the extremes of the NRB preachers.[108] This statement and the reactions it provoked represent a turning point for the BFC. On the one hand, the

Advisory Policy Statement demonstrates the BFC's (and thus implicitly the mainliners') supreme confidence in their role as cultural and moral director. On the other hand, the statement appears as rather a desperate attempt to hold on to that role as it was increasingly sidelined.

The actual impact of the Advisory Policy Statement seems to have been minimal. Only a year later the then TV director of the BFC Albert S. Crews bemoaned that "Station acceptance lists of filmed TV programs have shrunk during 1957. Part of this is due to a lack of new products, part to growing competition, part to a settling-down process in the industry and part to a lack of promotion and sales ability."[109] Gradually, the BFC began to recognize its limitations: "The more we learn about the mass media and the harder we try to make our use of them effective, the more we feel ourselves to be falling short in our achievement. It is painful to see our reach so far exceed our grasp."[110]

Indeed, there were also fears that the media might be secularizing the church: "Our thought and action patters are molded by the media and by the very climate in which the media are dominant 'taste-makers.' As Christians we are being evangelized continuously by the mass media more than we have ever thought of evangelizing society for Jesus Christ."[111] Television itself might be a neutral medium, but the commercial television industry was not. The Television-Radio Audience Study concluded that

> The most critical and sensitive spot in the ethics of mass communications, we believe is in the use of these media for the manipulation of people. . . . Here is the danger area for religious groups using the mass media. They are working in an environment where the secular world has elaborately rationalized and even cynically advocated the manipulation of people for the purposes of the sponsor. . . . Protestant religious groups, amateurs at best in this field, may all too easily compromise their own fundamental principles when they believe themselves to be only adapting professional communication techniques to serve the Gospel.[112]

The Study Commission on the Role of Radio, Television, and Films in Religion and the Mass Media Pronouncement

Gradually, the BFC's emphasis shifted from the protection of sustained-time programming to the development of media criticism. The battle to win TV for Christ was over, and the BFC had lost. Unable to preserve the privilege of sustained-time programming, unable to raise large sums for future programming, unclear as to the message that should be aired, the BFC was left to issue pronouncements and statements.[113]

In 1957, the BFC recommended to the General Board of the NCC that a study commission on the role of radio, television and films in religion be established to evaluate the effects of these media on society and the church and to provide the BFC with a guideline for operating. Of course, even after approval, the study commission began its work only after special funding was secured.[114] At the same time, Everett Parker was asked by the BFC to chair a committee to study mass media standards and report to the study commission.[115] By November 1959, the study commission (under influence from the mass media standards committee) had produced a preliminary draft of a report that would eventually be distributed to the General Board of the NCC.

For the first time, the BFC report dealt with the general effect of media on society. The media was deemed to have a greater impact as more and more Americans owned radios and televisions and spent more and more time listening and watching. Although the media were considered to be neutral, their effect was seen to be conditional on their use. Still contemporary programming gave reason to believe that "the media on the whole [were] lowering the cultural level."[116] Creativity, literacy, and mental discipline were potentially being threatened as the print culture was transformed into an electronic culture.[117] This electronic culture challenged the church in that its philosophy was based around the pursuit of commercial entertainment. Recognizing that, the authors claimed the church should "stand in judgment" of the media, just as it "stands in judgment on all human institutions."[118] More importantly, however, was the commission's insight that it was not just religious broadcasting that was at stake, but also the church's influence on the "the total broadcasting enterprise."[119] In other words, the commission suggested "Christian infiltration," as a solution to the increased broadcasting segregation.[120]

The end aim was notably still the Christianization of American culture. In that task, both secular and religious programming had a role to play. Secular programming, it suggested, could still provide "sensitive treatment[s] of religious themes," and the purposes of religious programming could be expanded to include "climate creation" (or the "preliminary preparation of listener-viewers to be receptive to the more direct appeal of the Gospel and the churches"), worship and inspiration, instruction and evangelism (although this latter purpose was largely disregarded as implausible).[121] Like the New Haven study, the report—considering the number of Ph.D.s on the commission and committee—unsurprisingly suggested a social scientific model for understanding the "modern personal, family and community life." Only with such a complex model could the church adequately "see the potential audience in all the complexity of human dynamics in our anxiety-driven, class-conditioned, striving and mobile age."[122]

Notably, the church's traditional models of home, family, and community were being displaced by a social scientific model that was perceived as a necessary aid if the church were to successfully enter the electronic age.[123]

In June 1960 the study commission on the role of radio television and films in religion released its pronouncement on The Church and the Mass Media. The first nine pages of the report focused on the role of the NCC as media watchdog. While avoiding censorship (that reeked too much of Catholicism), the church had a responsibility to publicly pressure the media toward self-regulation: "The task of the churches is not limited to the expression of concern over specific mass media programs that are harmful. It is certainly not to attempt over-all censorship. It is rather to take positive steps to help like-minded persons and groups to be wise stewards for the public good of these instruments which God has made available."[124] On television and radio specifically, the churches were urged to encourage the FCC to fulfill its mandate and actually hold stations responsible to broadcasting in the public interest.[125] The limitations of religious broadcasting were clearly stated: "the media are no substitute for the saving and healing work which Christ does through the living community of believers in His Body, the Church."[126]

The church and television broadcasting was issued as a practical policy follow-up to the church and mass media. With the issue of sustained-time programming, no longer relevant due to a 1960 FCC ruling, the statement was largely devoted to the development of a critical stand vis-à-vis the media in general. Recognizing that "religious organizations and individual religious broadcasters have been guilty of not using television and radio solely for the public good," the General Board of the NCC called for a broader approach to the media.[127] This approach basically entailed applying pressure on the networks, stations, and the FCC to broadcast in the public interest. The church had a role to play in insisting that concerns such as "world peace, racial and economic justice, social welfare, and progress in the arts and religion" be reflected in broadcasting.[128] The last section of the statement, which deals specifically with the churches' use of television and radio, steers clear of the whole notion of missionary TV or radio. Instead religious presentations are to "deal candidly with contemporary and controversial issues and concerns, bringing to bear on them the illumination, judgment, and healing of the gospel."[129]

In June 1962, the BFC passed the statement to the General Board, but at that point it was stalled in the NCC bureaucracy because other divisions of the council, who felt they were affected by the pronouncement, had not had an opportunity to examine it.[130] Each division (Christian Life and Work, Home Missions, Christian Education, and United Church Women) offered suggestions, and it was redrafted and finally approved on March 29, 1963.

Finally on June 4, 1963, Everett Parker (the chairman of the drafting committee) met with National Association of Broadcasters (NAB) to discuss the pronouncement (to what end is unclear?).[131]

Conclusions

In the lives and contents of these documents, one notes the major shift of concerns from producing religious programs and maintaining their airtime, to providing a church-based critique of the media. Less and less interested in producing Christian culture, the BFC increasingly came to see its role as a critic and an educator.[132] In the years to come, lobbying the FCC would come to occupy a larger part of the BFC's activities, particularly in two areas: educational television, and the protection of civil rights (see Parker's suit). While no explicit mention is made of the changes—the new policies reflect the movement toward the recognition of pluralism. This prophetic voice blended well with the new shift toward the outside.

In a remarkably short period, TV had been reconceived; no longer was it a powerful tool for evangelism, nor a means of shoring up the mainliners' cultural authority. Only six years after Ronald Bridges proclaimed that the media has been placed in Christian hands, a young historian was already claiming an end to the era of Protestant cultural domination: "Anglo-American and Puritan-Protestant culture, if it is not being displaced, is at least merely coexisting as shaper of national customs."[133] Martin E. Marty called upon Protestants to recognize their new minority status and to appreciate it:

> Nostalgia here is not productive. Yearning for the golden age of evangelical triumph in America overlooks the effects of immigration, secularization, urbanization. Participants in the dialogue should not have to be nudged repeatedly to be awakened out of a dream world. In this new quadri-conspiratorial constellation Protestantism, in the interests of truth and strategy, should begin to learn to enjoy the luxury of its minority status in a pluralistic post-Protestant society.[134]

As the mainliners (and religion in general) lost cultural currency, television was becoming (as the BFC predicted) more and more commercially oriented. In 1960, the FCC ruled that paid-time television served the public interest, leaving the door open for the networks essentially to eliminate sustained-time religious television. What the BFC had fought so hard to prevent had become a reality. Sustained-time television did not disappear overnight, but the new ruling eventually forced the BFC to reconsider its position concerning paid-time religious programming. By that point, however, the mainline enthusiasm for religious television was so diminished, that the BFC itself basically began to admit defeat. By 1960, the BFC not only questioned the role of religious television, but also began to perceive that the nation was in the midst of a cultural shift, a shift that was only partially attributable to the emergence of mass media:

> The conviction grew that there is something radically wrong with the ethical and moral climate of America. While the finger of blame was pointed at those who, in one way or another, control the use of the media of mass communications, there was abundant evidence both of governmental negligence and of public apathy. It has become increasingly clear that our use of the powerful media of mass communication has far outstripped our understanding of their immediate and cumulative effect upon the life of the nation.[135]

Early BFC reception of TV was shaped by the mainline presupposition of establishment status. Use of the TV to evangelize was justified as serving the greater cause of preserving "This Nation under God." While the idea of television as the next greatest missionary was quickly abandoned following the TV-Radio Audience study, the BFC nonetheless continued to fight for the preservation of the sustained-time system (the status quo on the airwaves). The battle to remain on the air specifically as a public service had a highly symbolic value. With the small audience and strategically minor time slots, mainline religious broadcasting was already a minor affair. The issue was important to the BFC (and the NCC) because it represented the public role of religion in an increasingly commercialized America.

With sustained-time a lost battle, the BFC's emphasis shifted to media criticism, an occupation that required far less money and resources. The position of critic rather than producer suited the changing status of mainline Protestantism. As their cultural clout declined, the mainline Protestant leadership gradually embraced genres of high culture, such as modern art, to the exclusion of other more commercial forms of culture.[136] Religious television programming would never really be considered highbrow enough to be embraced wholeheartedly, despite talk shows featuring guests such as Reinhold Niebuhr. Instead, a new emphasis would be placed on secular media, particularly noncommercial forms, such as PBS, whose messages were compatible enough with the mainline position to be grudgingly endorsed as an acceptable form of middlebrow culture.

Chapter 4

"Preserving Our American Heritage": Television and the Construction of Evangelical Identity[1]

While the mainline protestant leaders at the Broadcast and Film Commission (BFC) fought to maintain its privilege, neoevangelical leaders struggled for self-definition and public recognition, hoping to rehabilitate that part of Protestantism that had been humiliated by the Scopes Trial. The fight for the airwaves, first on radio and then on television, was part of that struggle. The National Religious Broadcasters Association (NRB)—which was founded to provide an interface between evangelicals, the television networks, and the Federal Communications Commission—was formed in direct response and as a counterpart to the BFC, just as the National Association of Evangelicals (NAE, founded 1941) was formed as a direct response to the National Council of Churches.[2]

NRB policy regarding television, for the most part, was not medium specific. That is to say, the NRB formulated guidelines concerning religious broadcasting in general and made little distinction between radio and television.[3] For the NRB, the fight for religious broadcasting was part of the larger fight to challenge the mainline or liberal Protestant hegemony and to remake the image of conservative Protestantism in the public sphere. Freedom to broadcast was construed as freedom to be an evangelical Protestant in the public sphere and tantamount to being culturally respectable.

The construction of evangelical identity, as both Tona J. Hangen and Joel Carpenter have suggested, was closely related to evangelical negotiations with broadcast media—radio and then television.[4] The entrepreneurial spirit of radio/T.V. religious broadcasters, their defiant opposition to the notion of public broadcasting, and their early recognition that both the radio and television could be effectively targeted to a specific market segment rather than the American public as a whole—these approaches would turn out to be forward-looking. In other words, while evangelical culture would be marked by its contact with television, the medium itself would be affected by evangelicalism.

The evangelical negotiation with broadcasting was part of the larger struggle to define a new conservative Protestant identity—evangelicalism. The fight for religious broadcasting was an extension of a broader cultural strategy to make conservative Protestantism respectable. The radio and then the television provided new platforms for evangelicals to wage their symbolic battle for the future of Protestantism in America. The NRB approach to religious broadcasting was an important element in the larger evangelical battle to "preserve our American heritage."

To contextualize the NRB's response to television, we must first understand something about fundamentalism and its progeny evangelicalism.

Evangelicalism and Fundamentalism: Terms and their Meanings

Although both the NRB and the NAE became umbrella organizations that would encompass a variety of traditions (including previously marginalized churches, denominations, and missions from the Holiness and Pentecostal traditions), the early visible leadership as Joel Carpenter and George Marsden have documented largely identified itself as fundamentalist in origin.[5] While the cross-cultural usage of fundamentalism remains, to some extent, fairly contested, scholars have more or less come to agreement over the contours of American Protestant fundamentalism in the 1910s, 1920s, and 1930s. In this period, fundamentalism refers not only to a particular theological or religious perspective, but also to a mobilization of a social movement. In his book, *Pious Passion: The Emergence of Modern Fundamentalism in the United States and Iran*, Martin Riesebrodt describes fundamentalism as a "radical-traditional reaction to rapid social change."[6] In the eyes of fundamentalist leaders, American institutions such as the family, the church, and the public schools were threatened by the changes wrought by Darwinism, higher Biblical criticism, and increasing religious and ethnic pluralism. The family altar and the Bible-reading, prayer-directing father were perceived as rarer and rarer in American homes.[7] The decline of family piety and the subsequent changes in attitudes toward personal morals, leisure habits, consumption and accumulation were perceived by fundamentalists as proof of the severity of the social crisis.[8]

Most worrisome, in fundamentalist eyes, were the changes in the churches, denominations, and seminaries that reflected the liberal or modernist Protestant agenda. Leaders perceived the decay in the churches as the source and cause of the general social decay. Society could only be salvaged if the churches were saved from the liberal Protestant blight. Ultimately the salvation of the churches would only be achieved through the salvation of individual souls—evangelism. In ignoring this task (or interpreting it in a different light), the Social Gospel not only misdirected energies but also caused damage to the church and by extension the society at large. Fundamentalists thus fought the liberals for control of church institutions, from denominations and mission boards to seminaries and colleges. In such a context, schisms were inevitable. Churches, denominations, and seminaries were forced to choose sides and by the 1930s and 1940s the lines between fundamentalist and liberal camps had been clearly drawn.

The liberals claimed the victor's mantle, while the defeated fundamentalists retreated from the public eye. From the liberal point of view, the rationalists had triumphed over the irrational fundamentalists. From a sociological perspective, however, it may be more helpful to follow Martin Riesebrodt in viewing the transition and resulting schism as an adaptation to competing audiences (or constituencies). The liberal clergy adapted itself to the changing middle-class suburban culture, while fundamentalist leaders looked toward a more traditional audience shaped by different sets of values than their suburban peers.[9] As more and more church institutions came to be dominated by liberal leaders, fundamentalists began with earnest to found their own competing institutions to meet the particular needs of their constituency.[10] Eventually there would be conservative churches, seminaries, publishers, and ecumenical organizations parallel in function to their liberal counterparts. American Protestantism had developed into what Martin E. Marty has called a "two-party system."[11]

Under further scrutiny, however, this two-party system (liberals versus conservatives, modernists versus fundamentalists, etc.) was even more fragmented. The liberal party was divided between the neo-orthodox and the classic modernists; the fundamentalists, from the 1940s forward, were divided between the neoevangelicals (later just called evangelicals) and the separatist fundamentalists. If we understand the liberal/fundamentalist split to be partly an adjustment to the social and economic changes in the early twentieth century and the different ways in which these religious constituencies were affected by these changes, the split of the fundamentalist camp into neoevangelicals and fundamentalists can be explained as a later development of a similar dynamic. In other words, Riesebrodt's insight into the social causes of the fundamentalist/modernist split can be expanded to explain the dynamics within the fundamentalist camp that led to the creation of an evangelical tradition, particularly in the post–World War II period.[12]

In the late 1940s and early 1950s, neoevangelicalism emerged as a distinctive and separate movement from fundamentalism. For the most part, the neoevangelical leaders did not have major theological points of disagreement with their fundamentalist brethren, but they did disagree with their approach to culture at large.[13] In their eyes, gross and generalized hostility was simply not utile any more. Evangelicals, like the rest of Americans in post–World War II, were becoming more and more educated, and more middle-class.[14] They did not want to leave their traditional mores behind but rather hoped that in adopting a moderate, less antagonistic agenda they could attract that portion of middle America that had become increasingly alienated from traditional or conservative religion. In other words, evangelicals adapted themselves to a particular subset of the traditional constituency, a subset that in outward (or sociological) terms was becoming more and more similar to its liberal, suburban counterparts.[15] Evangelicalism emerged as the "old-time religion" for the new middle classes of the traditional milieu in the 1950s, 1960s, and 1970s. (Henceforth in this chapter, to prevent confusion, the terms neoevangelical and evangelical will refer to those conservative Protestants who wished to distinguish themselves from their fundamentalist brethren. The descriptions conservative Protestantism or "old-time religion" will be used as umbrella terms to encompass both of these traditions).

Through a close examination of the newsletters of the NAE, as well as the existing but scanty archival material from the early years of the NRB, this chapter looks at the general rhetorical climate during the early years of the evangelical movement and suggests how that climate may have shaped or contributed to the evangelical approach to mass media in general, and the television in particular. How did evangelicals define themselves as distinct from liberals and fundamentalists? How did this self-definition translate into organizational, rhetorical, and strategical differences? How was the mass media constructed and employed in the evangelical effort "to win America?"

The focus is on this group of evangelical leaders whose experiences or responses to television were not necessarily representative of the larger evangelical mosaic.[16] In the interests of comparison this chapter focuses on a group that defined itself as the challenger to the Federal and then National Council of Churches and the counterpart to the BFC. From the beginning, the NRB membership was constituted from a much wider spread of the evangelical tradition than its early leadership, which was part of the same group of ex-fundamentalists who founded the NAE. Both the NAE and NRB were meaningful (and arguably important) organizations because in their founding and presence (if not in their actual acts), the founders provided umbrella organizations for a wide variety of conservative Christian traditions that felt marginalized by the mainline Protestant establishment. In so doing, they created an evangelical identity that unified previously splintered and nonassociated conservative Protestants of many different stripes.[17] The founding of the NAE and the NRB thus constructed and at the same time reflected the new cultural boundaries between the evangelical and the fundamentalist, and the evangelical and the liberal. Evangelical responses to the television were formulated in this context.

The use of mass media, particularly the use of the most modern and technologically sophisticated media—the radio and the television, would be an important symbolic touchstone in the early evangelical movement. Evangelical and fundamentalist leaders legitimated their use of radio and television in terms of their efficacy, presuming that these media could persuade individuals to accept Christ as their savior. In their adoption of a heavy-effects model of the media, that is, a belief in the unmediated efficacy and all-persuasiveness of the media, conservative Protestant leaders differed little from their mainline Protestant counterparts.[18] This model, according to Elihu Katz, assumed "that the media would operate totally (on every eye and ear), directly (without interference), and immediately (evoking collective reaction, as if from one man)."[19] Evangelical leaders interpreted these effects in positive terms. In other words, they worried less about the effects of competing messages and focused more upon the absolute effects of the Gospel on the viewer. Religious broadcasting was deemed important, precisely because the effects were so total and direct. Although NAE resolutions from conventions occasionally mentioned the problematic programs on television and radio, the evangelical leadership was far less interested in the societal effect of these mass media per se, and far more interested in using whatever media possible to further spread the word. Contact and conversion were considered equivalent. If one could just reach people with the Gospel, conversion would follow. The television and radio were instruments for reaching a larger audience. Evangelicals made little or no distinction between traditional forms of revivalism and newer mass-mediated versions.

How the antimodernist evangelicals came to embrace and legitimate this paradoxical position, and how early evangelical responses to television, in so far as they are reflected in the leadership's discourse in this era, were embedded in contemporary cultural, political, and theological debates are discussed below. Evangelical access to the airwaves came to be considered as access to the broader society and denial of that access seemed only to point to the lost status of Protestantism in general and traditional Protestantism in particular. Although evangelical leaders seemed unaware of media theories or social scientific theories concerning the effects of mass media on the listeners and viewers (in particular those theories that contradicted their assumptions), they demonstrated a remarkable amount of media savvy. By placing emphasis on numbers (i.e., how many souls could be reached by the media), evangelical leaders bypassed the issues of efficacy that so plagued mainline Protestant leaders involved in media. The goal of evangelism largely mitigated all other worries concerning the negative effects of the television. In adopting such an approach, evangelical leaders walked a thin line between modernity and fundamentalism, reflecting, as Martin E. Marty has pointed out, that despite the initial appearance of complete negation, there is perhaps a much greater symbiosis between these two traditions than it would seem at first glance.[20] As Quentin J. Schultze has suggested, the importance of evangelical radio and television does not lay in the number of converts, but in its role in the creation of an evangelical subculture. While evangelicals legitimated the use of these media by depending upon missionary metaphors, they unintentionally reinforced and recreated a newer conservative Protestant identity that was increasingly middle-class, better educated, and more technologically sophisticated.[21] Through their practical responses to television, evangelical leaders (often unwittingly) recreated the evangelical identity and the conservative Protestant presence in the public sphere.

"Cooperation without Compromise": The NAE (1941)[22]

The NAE was founded in 1942 as the answer to the liberal-leaning Federal Council of Churches. Perceiving religious liberalism to be "The Great Apostasy of the 20th Century," the early leaders of the NAE believed that only through a unified front could the old-time Gospel religion face "The Battle of the Century." Throughout the 1930s, these neoevangelicals had watched the fundamentalist faith become socially and culturally marginal, as liberals increasingly overtook religious seminaries ("strategic chairs of religion in universities") and served as the supplier of religious broadcasts for the major national radio networks.[23] Severe separatism, such as that advocated by the American Council of Christian Churches (1941), was not a viable option for these men, who wished not only to refute the heresies of liberal Protestantism, but also to "express and implement the[ir] constructive ideals."[24] While Carl McIntire (and his organization, the American

Council of Christian Churches) advocated the complete separation of Bible-believing Christians from the apostate modernist denominations and accepted only those churches that had separated from their erring mother denominations, the newly formed NAE welcomed all churches, even if their denominations were affiliated with the Federal and then National Council of Churches. For the founders of the NAE, who aimed to preserve "old-time religion" and to win America back to that religion, separatism of such a severe nature was considered to be unnecessary and self-defeating. In the foreword to the Report of the Organization of the NAE for United Action, this position is stated forthrightly. Liberal Protestants (alluded to as the "leaders of one school of thought") are chided for their inability to unify on the basis of doctrine: "they have been unwilling or afraid to provide a doctrinal foundation which would be an anchor against the tendency to drift into the sandbars of heterodoxy."[25] In like manner, separatist and combative fundamentalists are reproached for insisting

> upon the inclusion of doctrines which are not essential to the salvation or Christian fellowship, thus giving the cold shoulder to some Bible-believing and Christ-loving groups which are needed to assist in a common cause.
>
> There is also an unfortunate tendency in certain groups to adopt a martyr complex. Some have appeared to go out of their way to seek opposition in order that when the opposition is aroused they may burn gloriously at the stake in the view of a great national gallery.[26]

By distinguishing themselves from the militant, combative tactics of self-defined fundamentalists such as McIntire, the neoevangelicals hoped to represent a different side of conservative Protestantism to the American public. This was in some ways an image campaign: how should the old-time Gospel be presented in the public sphere? In this arena, the neoevangelicals tried hard to distinguish themselves from the fundamentalists in tone and manner, and the liberals in theology and doctrine. An explanatory brochure published by the NAE after the Constitutional Convention in Chicago, May 1943, made this point clear in a question and answer format.

> What is its attitude toward the Federal Council of the Churches of Christ in America?
>
> The Federal Council, because of its lack of a positive stand on the essential doctrines of the Christian faith, its inclusion of leaders who have repudiated these doctrines, and its active support of programs and institutions which are nonevangelical or apostate, does not represent the evangelicals of America.
>
> What is its attitude toward the American Council of Christian Churches?
>
> Doctrinally there is no disagreement between the American Council and the NAE. The leadership and policy of the American Council are not satisfactory to

the great body of evangelicals. There is no prospect of its ever attaining sufficient strength to become an important factor in the solution of our major problems because its policy of indiscriminate destructive criticism contributes to the defeat of its own purpose.[27]

Rhetorical Strategies

Rhetorically, evangelicals tried to steer a middle course between fundamentalists and liberals, with the aim of winning middle America to their cause. Rhetorical difference thus became a marker of evangelical identity. In 1956, in his history of the NAE, *Cooperation without Compromise*, James DeForest Murch recounted the interactions between Carl McIntire, the president and founder of the American Council of Christian Churches (ACCC), and the committee that preceded the founding of the NAE. In his opinion there were three irreconcilable differences between the two sets of leaders. The American Council advocated complete separatism from apostate denominations and churches, while the nascent NAE accepted individuals and individual churches as long as they subscribed to the statement of faith. The American Council believed in the concept of a "council" of churches rather than just a fellowship of evangelicals. Evangelical leaders counseled the necessity of "a constructive program as against one with a polemical and negative approach."[28] (The implication being that the American Council was both polemical and negative.) Evangelical leaders, from early on, thus took pains to be less aggressive and combative than their fundamentalist counterparts. Stephen Paine, president of Houghton College, in his speech at the first NAE convention, prefaced his comments thus: "Let me say that in every one of the causes I shall cite, I could give you chapter and verse if that were necessary. However, I'm not going to do this. I am not going to call any names, because I am not talking against anyone."[29] In retrospect, this new rhetorical strategy was also a cultural strategy for making evangelicalism "respectable" and less associated with the discredited tactics and approaches of the fundamentalist movement in the public sphere.

In particular, evangelical leaders made efforts not to attack other conservative Christians (particularly on issues of separatism and doctrine), hoping to create the widest consensus possible. Attacks against mainline Protestantism, while more vehement, were not directed at the laity (which the NAE leadership viewed as potential members) but at the leadership (which was perceived to be largely disconnected with the views of the people in the pews). The harshest polemics were usually reserved for analyses of the structure and purposes of the Federal Council of Churches, its successor the

National Council of Churches and the liberal theology that supported the organizations' policies.[30] Nonetheless, the early evangelical leaders were still quite strident in expressing their views, particularly concerning the problematic aspects of liberal Protestantism.

In the keynote address to the convening convention of the NAE, entitled "The Unvoiced Multitudes," Dr. Harold J. Ockenga stated the situation bluntly: "Evangelical Christianity has suffered nothing but a series of defeats for decades. . . . The enemy has won his victories in overwhelming fashion in Russia, in Germany and Japan, and now he is knocking at our very door."[31] In Ockenga's eyes, evangelicalism faced three competing enemies: Roman Catholicism, "that terrible octopus of liberalism," and secularism.[32] James DeForest Murch in two series of articles in *United Evangelical Action* in 1946 and 1951, and again in his 1956 account of the history of the NAE, described liberalism as "The Great Apostasy" that spread like a "virus" managing to penetrate all aspects of the church, particularly theology and education.[33] The Federal Council, while purporting to be fearful of the Roman Catholic Church, was itself on its way to becoming "a sort of neo-Catholic church."[34] Even more problematic was the planning of an even larger, more comprehensive council—The National Council of Churches. Murch claimed that thousands of evangelicals feared this development: a "super-church" that would be led by the same "liberal clique" that would propagate a liberal evangelism with social and educational programs "based on a humanistic religion, a pragmatic philosophy and a naturalistic ethics; and a left-wing political program not far removed from communism."[35] Such an organization would be too weak to fight the true enemies of Protestantism, enemies such as "atheism, liberalism, paganism, communism, statism, and Roman Catholicism." At the same time, the "super-church" with its "tentacles of liberal regimentation" would impede noncouncil old-time Gospel preachers from adequately filling that role.[36] Murch's articles often describe liberalism as parasitic and "man-centered," and the NCC as a "Super-Church" or "leviathan." Equally problematic, in evangelical eyes was the perceived relationship between the liberal Federal Council and "pink" or "red" doctrines. Again, the problem lay with the leadership, not the laity:

> There is no question in our mind that a small number of "liberal" clergymen are deliberately using the apparatus of the Council to play upon the minds and humane sympathies of good men and women in the Protestant churches, luring them along a step at a time in Socialism. They never call it that. They camouflage it under such labels as "The Good Society," "The Kingdom of God," "Industrial Democracy," and "The Planned Society." But it is definitely not the American way of life.[37]

Often the language used by the neoevangelicals to describe liberal Protestantism recalled language used in polemical treatises against Catholics (and Jews) in the 1920s and 1930s.[38] Indeed, one of the striking things is that the evangelicals regularly accused the liberal leadership of being Catholic-like, both in their aspiration for power and in the actual structuring of their organizations. Although evangelicals were not committed to a particular well-thought-out, conspiratorial theory, they did use conspiratorial terms such as monopoly, manipulation, domination, and communist infiltration. Take, for example, William Ward Ayer's description of modernism in his speech to the National Conference for United Action Among Evangelicals in 1942:

> Modernism destroys foundations and provides a culture for the growth of the germs of all forms of evil. It destroys faith in the Bible, in Christ, in righteousness, in revivalism, and has given us the God-forgetting paganistic civilization which is so disastrous to every good thing in our land. Today, this same modernism would silence every voice raised in behalf of Christian patriotism, for many modernists have a greater interest in the outworking of some form of Marxism than in the salvation that comes through our Lord and Savior, Jesus Christ. The inroads of wild socialistic theories through the power of organized minorities in government are creating a cancerous condition in America. Not only is there a surreptitious entrenching of radicals in high places in our governmental life, but a tendency is manifest even on the part of high officials to smear any who call attention to these cancerous adhesions to our body politic.[39]

The image of the octopus, which could place its tentacles everywhere, taint everything, and eventually squeeze the life out of its prey, as well as the image of the virus that penetrates even more obscure corners, and the parasite that lives off the life blood of others were well-used metaphors in right-wing writing.[40] Such extreme metaphors were usually reserved by evangelical leaders for their descriptions of liberal institutions and leaders, although Catholics, seculars, and communists too were favorite targets.

As the evangelical movement developed in the 1950s, even these polemics, at least in the public sphere, would become less and less frequent. Take, for example, the decennial report of the board of administration to the annual convention of the NAE prepared by Dr. Rutherford L. Decker, entitled "The Holy Spirit Works Through the NAE," in which he recounts the founding of the NAE. The emphasis in his article is on the role of the Holy Spirit, and the inclusiveness of the NAE, including Pentecostals. The polemics against modernism and separatism, which had dominated the convening convention, are nonexistent.[41] Even the anti-Catholicism has been toned down. In the NAE Presidential Address in 1952, Frederick Curtis

Fowler recounts the problematic position of the Roman Catholic Church vis-à-vis the state. The position is the same: the Roman Catholic Church violates separation of church and state, which is both antibiblical and anti-American, but the style of rhetoric is different. Here Fowler quotes canon law and scripture to make his point and constructs an argument based on these sources.[42] The style is far more "rational" and far less polemical.

In part, this shift can be explained by the increasingly moderate tone and direction of the dominating group of evangelical leaders. Although fundamentalists such as Bob Jones were part of the early organization, they began to "separate" out again from the NAE after the first decade. Marsden claims that the real breaking point was the Billy Graham Crusade in New York. Graham first received an invitation in 1955 by a fundamentalist organization, but he turned it down in favor of an invitation from the Protestant Council of New York in 1957. Accepting the invitation from the Protestant Council meant that converts summoned from the crusade would be sent to local churches, even liberal churches. Fundamentalists could not accept this compromise.[43] For Graham and his backers, however, this kind of cooperation, particularly in such a public context, was an essential step in transforming the public image of conservative Protestantism. *Christianity Today*, for example, was founded in 1956 with similar aims in mind. Subsequently, Billy Graham and his father-in-law, L. Nelson Bell, initially hesitated about proposing the editorship to Carl F. H. Henry because he might be too closely associated with fundamentalism.[44] Once hired, Henry wrote to potential contributors: "It is our purpose to win over those of liberal learning and training. Therefore an attempt should be made not to antagonize."[45] Indeed, the tone of *Christianity Today* would be less vehement than the more "in-house" *United Evangelical Action*. Evangelical rhetoric was still conservative rhetoric, but it was becoming more and more distinctive from fundamentalist rhetoric, and at the same time, evangelicalism was becoming more of a challenge to mainline Protestantism and its hold on the religious status quo.

Organizational Strategies

Another dimension of this cultural strategy to reinvent conservative Protestantism was expressed in organizational terms. Although suspicious of the ecumenical liberal bureaucracies such as the NCC, evangelical leaders could certainly see the positive reasons for uniting as many like-minded Protestants together, regardless of denominational affiliations. "Unless we can have a true revival of evangelical Christianity, able to change the character of men and build up a new moral fiber, we believe Christianity, capitalism and democracy, likewise to be imperiled," concluded Ockenga.[46] Under such threats, true Christians had to unite around "the cross of Jesus Christ."[47] Doctrinal issues and historical differences as expressed in denominational distinctiveness needed to be set aside in favor of unity, at least for organizing purposes. Anticipating Robert Wuthnow's thesis concerning the declining significance of denominations in American religious life, Ockenga concluded that

> The division is no longer between denominations; the division is between those who believe in Christ and the Bible, and those who reject Christ—the Christ of the cross and the Bible. Now is the time to forget all these differences and join together as one with the Crucified One.[48]

To be effective (and distinguishable from the liberal efforts), joint action would have to be premised upon an agreement of basic truths. In this step, the NAE positioned itself as diametrically opposed to the strategy of the Federal Council, which had based cooperation upon service rather than any shared doctrine.[49] The motto was "Cooperation without Compromise," and the doctrinal statement certainly allowed little room for theological dissent, at least not for liberal dissent.

Statement of Faith Unanimously Adopted in Chicago Constitutional Convention in 1943 (May 3–6).

It shall be required that those holding membership shall subscribe to the following doctrines:

1. That we believe the Bible to be the inspired the only infallible, authoritative word of God.
2. That we believe that there is one God, externally existent in three persons; Father, Son and Holy Spirit.
3. That we believe in the deity of Christ, in his virgin birth, in His sinless life, in His miracles, in His vicarious and atoning death, in His bodily resurrection, in His ascension to the right hand of the Father and in His personal return in power and glory.
4. We believe that for the salvation of lost and sinful man regeneration by the Holy Spirit is absolutely essential.
5. We believe in the present ministry of the Holy Spirit by whose indwelling the Christian is enabled to live a godly life.
6. We believe in the resurrection of both the saved and the lost; they that are saved unto the resurrection of life and they that are lost unto the resurrection of damnation.
7. We believe in the spiritual unity of believers in Christ.[50]

Cooperation in the evangelical context did not refer to a federation of churches, a concept that Murch and others deemed to be a step on the road to a "super-church." The autonomy of individual churches and denominations would remain intact; the model was rather a "functional type of cooperation" similar to the Interdenominational Sunday School Association (ISSA) founded in 1875.[51] Until the rise of liberalism the ISSA had been a model of successful twentieth-century Christian cooperation, setting the standards for Sunday School curriculum across the country. The neoevangelical leaders envisioned that the NAE would be the umbrella for a number of similar parachurch efforts, in areas such as relations with government, broadcasting, public relations, evangelism, missions, Christian education, and other such areas.[52] Cooperation in this context was premised upon doctrinal unity and the pragmatic desire to create a kind of conservative consensus and culture. If they cooperated, evangelicals could publish magazines with a 2 million circulation (instead of the 40 to 50 thousand circulation of the existing magazines), organize their colleges and Bible schools, coordinate missionary efforts overseas, and provide more effective protection for religious broadcasting.[53] By cooperating (here the word "united" was rarely used as it reeked too much of liberal versions of ecumenism), evangelicals could challenge the pretension of the Federal Council of the Churches of Christ in America (FCCA) to be the official representative of American Protestantism. In the eyes of the evangelical leaders, the majority of lay people in the twenty-two national churches claimed by the FCCA did not feel represented by the organization's policies. In addition, another 40 percent or so of Protestants were completely outside of the FCCA jurisdiction and lacking representation on the national level. All of these underrepresented and misrepresented Protestants formed the potential constituency for the NAE.

"The Rescue of Evangelical Broadcasting": The NRB (1944)

The liberal near-monopoly of the religious radio airwaves from 1927 forward provided an opportunity for the constructive action of a united neoevangelicalism. Early on, the "Rescue of Evangelical Broadcasting" was listed as one of the top priorities of the new organization.[54] In 1939, the National Association of Broadcasters (NAB) passed a Standards of Practice Code, which required religious programs to be nonsectarian and generally banned the sale of time for controversial issues.[55] The networks generally abided by this code, preferring to get rid of preachers such as Father Coughlin, and to provide the mainline Federal Council of Churches with sustenance (or free time) to air their programs.[56] Independent religious broadcasters found it increasingly difficult to buy airtime, and in 1943 when the Mutual network's policy changed, independent broadcasters found it difficult not to blame the liberal Federal Council policy for these bad fortunes.[57] By 1944, James DeForest Murch, Walter Maier and his business manager Eugene Bertermann had suggested that the NAE sponsor a specific organization for all evangelical broadcasts. The new umbrella organization, the NRB, would include any independent religious broadcasters willing to agree to its code of ethics and statement of faith, including individuals whose denominations were not affiliated with the NAE. In April 1944 at the annual NAE meeting, the NRB was founded to actively represent the interests of independent broadcasters (e.g., nonaffiliated with the Federal Council of Churches) to the networks and to the federal government.[58] In September 1944, they held the first meeting of the NRB and adopted a constitution and a code of ethics.[59] Members agreed to sign a statement of faith identical to that of the NAE and to adopt the NRB code of ethics.

The NRB was separately incorporated from the NAE, but the majority of the NRB executive committee were expected to be NAE members. In addition, the NAE Commission on Radio was considered to be synonymous with the NRB—their agenda differing slightly.[60] The main aims of the organizations were to fight for the "right" to purchase airtime, to fight for their fair share of sustained-time Protestant programming, and to protect the "right" to preach doctrinal sermons on the air (instead of broad truths). As a first step toward these goals, the NRB compiled a code of ethics, with which they hoped to change the image of independent religious broadcasters. Channels feared airing such programs because of problems with extreme broadcasters in the past. The code promised that associated broadcasters would (1) represent nonprofit organizations devoted to the propagation of the Gospel; (2) present their messages in a "positive, concise, and constructive" manner; (3) produce programs "consistent with the program standards of the station" and in accordance with federal and state law and FCC regulation; (4) cooperate with the station or network management; and perhaps most importantly; (5) request audience donations only for "legitimate religious purposes and . . . in a dignified Christian manner," with receipts issued to donors and the right of the NRB board of directors to request an accounting.[61]

Although the NRB was a kind of lobby group (its office was strategically placed in Washington DC from early on), it did not advocate particular legislation but believed that owners and broadcasters could be convinced that it was in their interest to broadcast their members' shows. In contrast to its mainline counterparts (The Protestant Radio Commission and then the

BFC), the NRB was not engaged in creating educational media and curricula, producing religious programs, or sponsoring research about the media per se. With such focused goals, the NRB could afford to be far less bureaucratic and to act on a need only basis. On a practical level, this meant that the NRB required far less funding than the BFC, membership dues being used mainly for office expenses alone.

The earliest efforts by the NRB concerned the sale of radio time to Gospel broadcasters, who were finding it increasingly difficult to purchase airtime. The "broad truths" policy devised by the networks and the NAB in conjunction with the mainline Protestant churches, likewise threatened to end doctrinal sermons on the air, even on paid-time.[62]

In 1948, T. Elsner, president of the NRB, reported that he had been trying to establish goodwill with the radio industry, and to avoid "increased radio legislation." He noted that changes have been made in the NAB code so as not to conflict with NRB.[63] By 1949, the NRB could claim some limited success in gaining access to sustained time on radio as well. By 1952, the fight to purchase time on TV was well underway. By this time, the NAE and the NRB were more organized. The NAE convention in 1952, from the very outset, recognized that they would have to fight for the right to purchase airtime on TV. The resolutions passed at the convention note the National Association of Radio and Television Broadcasters (NARTB) code of ethics, which recommended that no charge should be made for TV time for religious broadcasts. The NAE interpreted this as "a violation of our fundamental constitutional religious rights." They believed that station owners were using these recommendations as a means of preventing sale to Gospel broadcasters.[64] The NRB viewed the NARTB code as a "means to hinder every evangelical church, religious body and broadcaster from purchasing television time."[65] The NRB president Dr. Elsner responded by noting that if beer or cigarette companies have the right to buy advertising time, surely the churches should as well: "It will be a sad day for America when the television industry refuses to sell time to churches and religious bodies for the presentation of that which embraces the preservation of our Nation and the salvation of our Eternal Souls."[66] Children would be exposed to clowns, cowboys, and crime through the television, but not the Gospel. He ended his plea to NARTB by concluding that he was for free enterprise and the right of the station owners to ultimately decide.

The fight to buy time to broadcast the Gospel was described as an issue of freedom of religion. In the words of DeMurch:

> The government has no right to meddle with such matters or to force or compel allegiance to any particular form of religion, but does have the obligation

to guarantee the full and complete right of individuals and establishments of religion to exercise their freedom without let or hindrance.[67]

In his analysis, the closing of "channels" to "intelligent religious discussion and the dissemination of facts about religion" was a clear infringement upon freedom of religion. One should have the right to explain one's faith in the press, the radio, and TV and do so without being "smeared as a bigot, a mossback, a fanatic or a religious queer."[68] The networks' commitment to the "broad truths" policy, which had brought about general campaigns to go to church, or Sunday school, covered the controversial aspects of religion, particularly those aspects that are connected to theology and beliefs. In Murch's evaluation, "religious freedom involve[d] a guarantee of the right of controversy."[69] Ecumenism and the wish for harmony and goodwill were simply ways to avoid the controversy and in the end to limit true religious freedom.

Of course, the evangelical desire for "true religious freedom" and the right to a controversial kind of Christian message did not necessarily mean that they viewed Roman Catholics, communists, and secularists as having the same rights. Indeed, since they viewed Catholics, communists, and secularists as ultimately undermining freedom of religion, they allowed them little if any of the same theoretical right to controversy.[70] Still, the most frequent suggestions for dealing with these ideological threats were prayer and evangelism.[71] While their rhetoric continued to be anti-Catholic, anticommunist, and antisecular, evangelicals were likewise engaged in pragmatic steps to ensure their voice in the public sphere. The preservation of paid-time religious broadcasting was an issue of "religious freedom" for evangelicals, partly because it was an issue of agreement between diverse parties and partly because it had concrete practical goals. Unlike some of the other projects that evangelicals pursued in this era—such as the founding of Fuller Seminary or *Christianity Today*—religious broadcasting was a very public issue.

Same Rhetoric, Different War: The Advisory Policy Statement of 1957[72]

Both the BFC and the NRB were founded out of the conviction that the preaching of the Gospel on the airwaves to the nation was a public service that needed to be protected. This conviction, however, was interpreted from completely different perspectives. First, what did preaching of the Gospel mean? The NRB knew exactly, and anything that differed from its seven-point statement of faith was to be considered apostasy.[73] The BFC, however, like its parent organization, had no creed but ecumenism, leaving the second director of the BFC to ask, "What then should we be communicating? To Whom? To What End?"[74]

Public service was an equally contentious concept. While the BFC claimed to be the rightful historical heir of American Protestantism, the NRB quickly denounced this pretension and claimed to represent the true undefiled remnant. Who would wear the crown? Who could speak on behalf of America's religious majority? On the economic side, was this public service to be subsidized by the stations or the networks? Did the Federal Communications Commission have the right to legislate that networks provide free airtime for religion?[75]

All of these questions came to a rhetorical head when the BFC issued its Advisory Policy Statement on Religious Broadcasting in June 1956. While playing lip service to the existence of religious diversity, the statement clearly restated the BFC's nonnegotiable position regarding sustaining time.[76] Recognizing that "religion is essential to the strong and healthy continuance of our life as a nation," the BFC provided Protestant programming as a public service. In return, the stations were expected to donate free broadcast time to fulfill their public mandate. This airtime was to be allotted according to "the strength and representative character of the councils of churches, local and national."[77] Subsequently the BFC advised against paid-time religious programming, which in any case should not be considered to fulfill any public service obligation. To permit paid-time religious TV would be tantamount to denying the public significance of religion in America, and perhaps to admitting to the symbolic defeat of the mainline Protestant establishment.

Perceived (rightly so, although the NCCC did not admit as much) as a direct attack against independent religious broadcasters, the advisory policy statement galvanized the NRB's forces. Many in the industry, including Harold Fellows, president of the National Radio and Television Broadcasters, sided with the NRB, seeing the BFC's policy as "misguided" and as unjustified "propaganda."[78] This testimony encouraged the NRB "we feel that our cause is greatly strengthened with the industry at both the national and local level." Nonetheless immediate and swift action was necessary if paid religious broadcasting was to survive. The *Radio-Tele-Gram* newsletter reported of "scores of evangelical broadcasters [having] [been] taken off the air in local communities all across the land." Without a powerful response from independent religious broadcasters, "the Council [would] [be] increasingly determined to exercise the prerogatives of a 'super church' in the control of Protestant broadcasting in America."[79] Steering away from the paranoid tone used by other Federal Council critics (such as Carl McIntire), the NRB nonetheless portrayed the BFC as an opponent to religious freedom and liberty. As Eugene Bertermann, the president of the NRB put it, "Freedom of speech and freedom of religion, guaranteed to us by the Constitution of the United States, involve the right to proclaim one's faith through the avenue of communication normally available. Respected groups such as the churches should not be barred from the unhampered utilization of an important medium of mass communication."[80]

In a counterattack, the NRB defended the right to purchase time for religious programming and promoted the dissolution of the BFC monopoly over Protestantism's share of sustained-time programming. Claiming to represent nearly half of the 21 million Protestants not represented by the National Council and BFC, the NRB lobbied the networks to redistribute sustained-time accordingly, and to force local stations to let their preachers buy adequate time for their programming.[81]

In the eyes of the BFC, the intent of the Advisory Policy Statement was to sound "an alarm" against the increasing commercialization of broadcasting.[82] Harold Fellows's criticism was dismissed as proof that the NARTB was "allergic to anything that sounds like criticism of the industry, especially anything that seems to suggest government regulation or review."[83] The NRB's response was dismissed as self-serving. Criticism of the policy statement was being used to "revive and strengthen support for the tremendous vested interest which the NRB was organized, ten years ago, to protect."[84] Nonetheless, this defensive posturing hid an increasing realization of the problematic nature of the Advisory Policy statement. S. Franklin Mack suggested that the BFC "clarify" its position vis-à-vis paid-religious broadcasting. The BFC had not intended to imply that it was "morally wrong or unethical to purchase or sell time for religious broadcasting," but had "simply advised against it."[85] Moreover, the BFC had "no desire to control all religious broadcasting," or to "get anybody off the air."[86] These last minute efforts to transform the policy's image had little effect.

In the end, the BFC had not been misunderstood, either by the NARTB or the NRB, but rather the leadership had fundamentally miscalculated the contemporary scene. In the process, the theologically conservative independent broadcasters came to identify themselves as defenders of free speech and religion against an increasingly defensive BFC leadership, whose raison d'être was being called into question on almost every level. The working assumptions underlying the Advisory Policy Statement were no longer operative. The ecumenical movement as a whole was experiencing a denominational decline in participation, and the BFC was no exception.[87] In addition, the mainline assumption of establishment status was gradually being chipped away. Even within the ranks, there were those who challenged the mainline to come to terms with living in a "post-Protestant America."[88] The neoevangelicals and fundamentalists, contrary to the popular theory of secularization, had not just disappeared, but in fact were gaining momentum as they invested in institutions and organizations such as the NRB. Occupied by the everyday operation of the organization and constrained by the nearsightedness endemic to such an endeavor, the BFC leadership was unable to see the changes on the horizon of the religious landscape.

Three years after the Advisory Policy Statement was published the Federal Communications Commission declared that paid-time programming could serve to fulfill a station's public obligation, leaving the door open for the networks to severely curtail sustained-time programming efforts. The symbolic fight for religious airwaves was basically over, and the NRB had essentially won. Largely unwilling and uninterested in raising the money necessary to purchase airtime, the BFC would turn from production and programming to the role of media critic and public advocate. Meanwhile, under the directorship of Eugene Bertermann and, later, Ben Armstrong, the NRB's power and prestige would continue to increase throughout the 1960s and 1970s, laying some of the foundation for the rise of the Christian right as well as the televangelist empires.[89]

Conclusions

Like their mainline counterparts, evangelical and fundamentalist leaders perceived that the Protestant influence in America was on the decline. In their eyes, whatever Protestant influence remained was largely of dubious religious value. The fundamentalist/modernist schism had left the evangelical and fundamentalist community with a sense of marginality and an increasing sense that their faith presuppositions had lost relevance in the modern era. While mainline Protestant leaders feared and fought their loss of hegemony, evangelical leaders fought for a new presence in the public sphere. Evangelical responses to television should be viewed as part of this larger strategy for gaining lost respectability.

In the 1950s, evangelical leaders consciously constructed a different style of discourse, a discourse that was neither as antagonistic and militant as the fundamentalist discourse, nor as accommodating or rationalist as the mainline discourse. The distinctiveness of the evangelical discourse lay both in its style and its content. The new evangelical was more civil in his approach to fellow believers and in the public sphere than the fundamentalist, and more committed to the "fundamental truths" than the liberal (or at least that was how the ideal evangelical was presented in their discourse). While the liberal provided the evangelical with a model of what not to say, the fundamentalist provided the evangelical with a model of how not to say it.

Robert Wuthnow has suggested that it is not enough to look at the content of a particular discourse, and to extrapolate the worldview of either its writers or readers. Instead, one must also look at the different ways in which discourse is constructed and structured. The style of discourse, he argues, may be as important as the actual content.[90] He suggests that differences in discourse might also explain the "cultural chasm currently separating religious liberals and religious conservatives."[91] Here it could be suggested that in the aftermath of the fundamentalist/modernist controversy, the contours of Protestant discourses were being renegotiated. On the mainline side, Reinhold Niebuhr and the neo-orthodox challenged the modernist, progressive optimism that had heretofore characterized liberal or mainline Protestant discourse. On the conservative side, the neoevangelical leadership counseled a more moderate and positive approach to the culture at large than that of separatist fundamentalism. The emergence of evangelicalism played an important role in these redefinitions. Relative to the sharp distinctions that characterized the two-party Protestant landscape in the 1920s and 1930s, the 1950s seemed to be a moment of consensus.[92] Thus, accounts of religion in America in the 1950s by Martin E. Marty, Mark Silk, and Thomas Berg stress the points of "convergence" and potential for cooperation between evangelicals and mainline Protestants, but mostly on so-called defensive or negative issues.[93]

Mainline and evangelical leaders alike feared religious pluralism and the erosion of Protestant hegemony in America. Roman Catholicism and secularism were similarly shared enemies, as were the solutions proffered: cooperation and evangelism. To fight the growing numerical influence of Catholicism, American Protestants needed to cooperate across denominational and church lines. Evangelism was likewise conceived as an important tool for "preserving our American heritage." Not only did Protestants have to fight the increasing numbers of Catholics, they also needed to provide a counterbalance to the propaganda and missionary work of the Roman Catholic Church. Signs of the Roman Catholic Church's powers were palpable, the most evident being the growth of its membership by a million members a year.[94] Particularly disturbing was the appointment of an American ambassador to the Vatican, as part of a larger cold war strategy against communism.[95] Both liberal and evangelical Protestants viewed the appointment as a strike against the separation of church and state and a sign of the increasing power of the Roman Catholic Church in America.

Notwithstanding these common areas, evangelical and mainline discourses differed in their particular contents and styles. Cooperation might have seemed momentarily realistic only because, as Mark Silk has suggested, the end goals of both groups were similar—the preservation of Protestant hegemony.[96] Despite similar terms and issues, mainline and evangelical discourses remained worlds apart. Evangelism, for example, might have been the stated goal of both mainline and evangelical Protestants of the 1950s, but the content of that evangelism, both in its aims and method, varied. As a trope, "evangelism" operated differently within each discursive community. For the evangelicals, evangelism largely meant revivalism, particularly in its urban version and as represented by the golden boy of evangelicalism in the 1950s—Billy Graham. While there were mainline leaders who were more pro-revival, there were also mainline leaders who found revivalism, and the so-called religious revival of the 1950s, distasteful and regressive. Although Reinhold Niebuhr, for example, recognized that Graham represented a new generation of conservative Protestants, he nonetheless remained critical of the kind of Christianity Graham represented: "For what it may be worth, we can be assured that his approach is free of the vulgarities which characterized the messages of Billy Sunday, who intrigued the nation about a quarter century ago. We are grateful for this much 'progress.'"[97] Niebuhr might have perceived that there was a revival of interest in religion in the 1950s, but in his eyes it was not an interest in old-time religion, but a deeper desire for answers in wake of World War II, the rise of the atomic bomb, and the cold war.[98]

Evangelicals, despite the moderated tone of their discourse and relative intellectual openness, still believed in the fundamental truths of the Gospel, and all attempts at cultural accommodation began with that premise. In contrast, mainline Protestant discourse, both in content and style, was far more influenced by secular sources, secular issues, and academic research. Even when the discourses seemed to agree, from a closer perspective, their contents and styles differed enormously. In the realm of media, this would likewise be the case.

Evangelical leaders in the 1950s (unlike their separatist brethren) were hopeful that America could be Christianized, and that the culture could be turned toward godly ends. The fight for the airlanes, or the right to doctrine-specific religious broadcasting, was part of this larger battle to "preserve the American heritage." In this general aim, evangelical leaders differed little from their liberal counterparts. In contrast, however, evangelical leaders viewed religious broadcasting simply as an extension of an older revivalist tradition that placed great emphasis on reaching the masses. The NRB fought for the right to buy airtime and to preach doctrine, while the BFC attempted to protect sustained-time religious broadcasting and to maintain a broad-truths policy. Unlike their fundamentalist counterparts, evangelical leaders self-consciously guided their policies with their public image in mind.

In order to effect policy change at the networks and at the federal level, a new kind of conservative Protestant discourse that emphasized civility and moderation would be essential. New boundaries were being drawn within the conservative Protestant camp, and fighting for the airwaves became an integral part of the newly shaping evangelical identity. In their battle with the BFC, NRB leaders actively defined what it meant to be evangelical and created an evangelical consensus. In the process, they challenged the mainline's monopoly on the definition of Protestantism in the public sphere.

For the majority of evangelical leaders, new media including the TV were perceived as missionary tools rather than leisure creators. In this sense, evangelicals ignored the dominant use of the media. (There is notably far less media criticism in *Christianity Today*, than in *The Christian Century*.) They legitimated the use of the media as a neutral tool. Unlike the mainline, they did not employ social scientific studies to measure their efficacy or to determine the so-called neutrality of the media. Instead, they relied upon their observation of the "facts." What were the philosophical foundations that informed the evangelical approach to media? How did evangelicals legitimate their use of new technological innovations? What did it mean for old-time Gospel religion to come to terms with the space age?

Chapter 5

"The Age of Space Requires Space Age Teaching Tools": Technology on Evangelical Terms

Although evangelicals rejected new developments in science and scientific method, they remained friendly to new technologies, including communications technologies. In this sense, evangelicals, like their fundamentalist and liberal counterparts, strove to find a balance between tradition and modernity.[1] Ultimately evangelicals accepted the technological fruits of science in so far as they could be Christianized or at least in so far so they failed to threaten the foundations of evangelical Christianity. In rejecting science but ambiguously embracing technology, evangelical leaders pursued a paradoxical and often contradictory position that required legitimation and justification. Their understanding and use of television as new medium was part of this broader evangelical discourse concerning the role of science and technology in society. Through an examination of articles published in *United Evangelical Action* and *Christianity Today*, this chapter examines how evangelical leaders responded to the increasing prestige of science in post–World War II America, the rise of new technologies in general (and in the household) and the new medium of television in particular. These strategies of accommodation were not "natural" or "inevitable" but rather chosen and pursued. Why did evangelical leaders choose to accommodate to technology rather than reject it wholeheartedly along with the scientific philosophy that produced it? Why were evangelicals scientifically phobic yet technologically friendly? How did they accommodate this position intellectually? What did the terms "technology" and "science" mean to evangelical leaders in the 1950s and 1960s?[2] Why did they perceive technology in neutral or even positive terms? How did this discourse shape evangelical responses to television? For evangelical leaders, the realms of science and technology offered yet another opportunity for self-definition. Here as well, evangelicals searched for an intellectual position that could be labeled as neither fundamentalist nor liberal.

While the editors at *The Christian Century* discussed television in terms of its cultural effects (usually its undesirable effects), in *Christianity Today* the radio and television usually appeared in different contexts—the missionary and technological realms. For each community, the appearance of the television prompted a different set of concerns and a different set of responses. The medium of television makes few appearances in *Christianity Today* or even in other NRB or NAE publications. When television does appear, it is most often grouped together with radio or in connection to religious broadcasting in general. These few references, together with the relatively meager archival materials available for those early years of the NRB, provide an important contrast to the materials presented in the early chapters on liberal Protestant responses. By highlighting the ways in which the evangelical response was dissimilar from the liberal response, the specifically evangelical response to television is clearer. And despite the relative paucity of sources, the evangelical viewpoint that emerges is distinctive.

In the evangelical context, discourses on science and technology intersected with discourses concerning mass media and broadcasting. New media technologies were viewed and construed in that context. Understanding the evangelical approach to television, therefore, requires a general understanding of fundamentalist and evangelical approaches to science.

Fundamentalist Science: Baconianism in the Twentieth Century

From the 1920s, and particularly from the Scopes Trial in 1925, a central component of fundamentalist and evangelical identity has been the rejection of the theory of evolution.[3] Subsequently, fundamentalists and their evangelical kin have been often identified by outside commentators as antiscientific or antimodern, while the debate at the Scopes Trial is popularly remembered and portrayed as one of science versus religion.[4] While liberal and modernist Protestants searched for ways to adjust theology and doctrine in relation to new scientific discoveries or promoted the strict separation of religious and scientific spheres, fundamentalists rejected the concept of accommodation and accepted only that which did not contradict with their received religious, biblical and scientific ideas.[5] Throughout the nineteenth century, conservative or Old School Presbyterianism as represented at Princeton Theological seminary wed its intellectual destiny with the inductive science of Baconianism as interpreted by Scottish commonsense philosophy.[6] Baconianism began with the assumption that knowledge was obtained through the senses. Through observation one gathered facts, and from these facts one induced the true nature of the physical world. Science, from this perspective, was defined solely as description and classification and not as the formulation of theories of explanation.[7] Indeed, nineteenth century Baconianism could be described as antihypothesis; explanations were garnered from direct observation of the natural world rather than critical thought or speculation. In this context, "discovery" referred to the results of observation alone. As Ian G. Barbour has suggested: "The Baconian account leaves out the whole theoretical side of science, and above all it omits the role of creative imagination in the formation of new concepts."[8] Such a populist understanding of science suited Jacksonian America in general and blended well with the trends in American Protestantism. Just as ministers did not need any special training beyond a calling from God, scientists, in this paradigm, needed little more than common sense.[9]

From this theoretical understanding of science, fundamentalists built their notion of biblical literacy, a hermeneutic that claimed the possibility of literal readings based on the observable "facts" of scripture. Fundamentalist claims to the contrary, this method and perhaps more importantly the legitimation of its use was an innovation even within the Protestant tradition that emphasized unmediated and plain readings.[10] Baconianism therefore played a central role in defining the intellectual, theological, and social character of fundamentalism. Consequently the theory of evolution challenged far more than the biblical story of creation. In a broad sense, Darwinism, as Paul J. Croce has suggested, disrupted "expectations of certainty in either science or religion."[11] In the fundamentalist world, this disruption was unwelcome. The rise of Darwinism represented a wide variety of social and intellectual changes, the majority of which were understood by fundamentalists in negative terms. For example, the fiery fundamentalist spokesman William Riley described Darwin as the "father of skepticism, agnosticism, modernism, higher criticism, unitarianism, and Hitlerism." In Riley's words, "evolution was antibiblical, antisocial, antimoral, antinational, and antiglobal."[12] Fundamentalists viewed the scientific undermining of Baconianism to be largely equivalent to the undermining of the conservative Protestantism worldview.

Employing Thomas Kuhn's work *The Structure of Scientific Revolutions*, historian George Marsden has suggested that the American fight over evolution is best understood as a debate between two alternative scientific paradigms—Baconianism versus Darwinism.[13] He observes that fundamentalists often defended the Bible as scientific and as based on facts, while they depicted evolution as unscientific and based merely on hypothesis.[14] Although he claims it is unnecessary to "subscribe to Kuhn's extreme view of the subjective character of knowledge" in order to adopt the paradigm theory, Marsden seems to do just that by implying that there was some kind of intellectual parity between Baconianism and Darwinism.[15] One does not have to be a supporter of either Science with a capital S or the Enlightenment with a capital E (i.e., in its French guise rather than its Scottish) in order to argue that although Baconianism was an important American tradition amongst American religious intellectuals in the antebellum period, it was at heart, as Theodore Bozeman has shown, a doxological science, formulated with the intent of harmonizing religion and science, and ultimately, as the definition would imply, of praising God above all. The underlying principle of such a science was to show how it "could be held true to religion."[16] To suggest, as Marsden and more recently Mark Noll have, that there is some kind of parity between Baconianism and Darwinism on a scientific (not cultural) basis is to adopt the very kind of epistemological relativism that evangelicalism (and one would assume a Calvinist or Christian historian) rejects and abhors when applied to ethics, morals, or generally to the principles of religion.[17] Fundamentalists remained loyal Baconians because Darwinism posed substantial threats to their worldview from an intellectual and social perspective.

Nonetheless, Marsden and Noll's efforts (in tandem with Bozeman) provide the present chapter with important insights concerning the evangelical attitude toward science and technology in the 1940s and 1950s. Most importantly Marsden and Noll have demonstrated how important it was for fundamentalists and then evangelicals to legitimate their beliefs in terms that could be seen and presented as "scientific."[18] In other words, even though contemporary science had ceased to be epistemologically compatible with conservative Protestantism, fundamentalist and evangelical leaders still remained committed to a rhetoric that employed scientific terminology to describe religion.[19] The general social status of scientific discourse was (and is) clearly a motivating factor in its use.[20] If nineteenth-century Protestants felt compelled to address the implications of contemporary scientific discoveries and theories and were successful in creating some kind of philosophical synthesis (Baconianism), twentieth-century science would prove to be far more out of reach—both in terms of its content matter (which was far more complex) and in terms of its societal status, which was growing steadily with each technological accomplishment. Science was increasingly becoming an area of knowledge limited to specialists, and subsequently scientists were becoming more and more of an elite. While evangelical leaders built Fuller Seminary, the National Association of Evangelicals, the National Religious Broadcasters, *Christianity Today*, scientists built the nuclear bomb, launched the man to the moon, invented the computer, the television, and various other household gadgets. In such a time of technological change, even the proponents of "old-time religion" found it hard to ignore these achievements.

Evangelicals, Science and Technology in the Space Age

How then did conservative Protestants cope with the increasing prestige of science and its application in the form of technological innovation? While fundamentalists tried their utmost to combat the increasing acceptance of evolution and its consequences in the public sphere (particularly in public schools), they simultaneously celebrated America's technological innovations, often adopting the latest invention with great enthusiasm. In positing a sharp distinction between science and technology, fundamentalists (and later evangelicals) remained critical of ideas that directly competed with or challenged conservative Protestantism, without resorting to complete cultural separation or withdrawal.[21] George Marsden has suggested that fundamentalist thought was actually highly compatible with technology and technological thought:

> Fundamentalist thought is in fact highly suited to one strand of contemporary culture—the technological strand. Unlike theoretical science or social science, where questions of the supernatural raise basic issues about the presuppositions of the enterprise, technological thinking does not wrestle with such theoretical principles. Truth is a matter of true and precise propositions that, when properly classified and organized, will work. Fundamentalism fits this mentality because it is a form of Christianity with no loose ends, ambiguities, or historical developments. Everything fits neatly into a system.[22]

In separating science (or at least normative science) from technology, fundamentalists were, according to Marsden's evaluation, able to embrace technology wholeheartedly. Fundamentalists thus conceived technology as a "neutral" tool, and "technological thinking" as practical, atheoretical, and therefore unthreatening to the underlying theological assumptions of the movement. To arrive at this conclusion, fundamentalists relied upon the Baconian model of science, which, as described above, promoted an understanding of "discovery" that was solely mechanical and completely detached from theoretical science. In this sense, new mechanical inventions were simply the products of observation, seemingly unconnected to any larger theoretical science that might contradict aspects of fundamentalist theology. In other words, by working from the "scientific" perspective that they had defined and accepted, fundamentalists could legitimate "technology." Technology came to be associated with the acceptable form of science (i.e., the form of science that did not threaten biblical literalism) and unassociated with any theories that may have actually engendered it (or made it possible). Neutrality became for fundamentalists an essential property of technology itself. From this perspective, the value of any particular technology depended upon the morals of those who used the technology. Communists, for example, were understood by fundamentalists to be misusing technology, for they were not god-fearing individuals, but mass manipulators. In contrast, Americans, as protectors of democracy and Christianity, used technology as God intended—to spread democracy and Christianity.[23]

While fundamentalists largely remained committed to Baconian science and its corresponding understanding of technology, evangelical leaders adopted a more moderate and more ambiguous position. Here they differentiated themselves from contemporary fundamentalists, whom they believed to be almost irredeemably inflexible, and the modernists, whom they viewed as far too limber and accommodating. Carl F. H. Henry, the first editor of *Christianity Today*, noted that the contributors to *The Fundamentals*, although opposed to evolution, were "neither suspicious nor distrustful of science. They [were] open to the facts, but unconvinced that all the facts [had] been introduced."[24] While criticizing fundamentalists as being ahistorical and lacking in theological perspective, Henry managed to identify with their basic critique of Darwin without engaging in antiscientific rhetoric: "Contributors to *The Fundamentals* doubtless agreed on the inadequacy of any explanation of the universe and man in merely evolutionary terms."[25] A year later a *Christianity Today* editorial (probably authored by Henry), noted how orthodox religion had declined in prestige as the respect for science had risen post-Darwin. According to the author's analysis, orthodox Protestantism had remained mistakenly committed to the scientific, mechanistic worldview that was popular prior to Darwin: "By an irony of history, and while deriding liberal thinkers for their deference to scientism (of a later generation), fundamentalists canonized the scientism of an earlier generation."[26] The solution to the problem (or threat) posed by Darwin and science in general was to refrain from wedding theology with any particular science or scientific theory:

Deriving the essential content of a theology of revelation from the fashionable scientific views of the day—of *today* no less than *yesterday*—is a perilous pursuit. Unless science a century after Darwin has suddenly mounted a stage whereon its convictions are no longer subject to revision and reversal—so that scientific progress has now become a thing of the past—we had best ready ourselves for novelty and surprise in the science of today and tomorrow. It remains risky for Christian theology to absolutize and finalize the present verdicts of empirical science, and foolhardy to baptize them with the authority of revelation. This is as true of the current indeterministic views of nature as of the older mechanical view. In fact, it is well to greet the whole range of scientific pronouncements with full respect for the revisionary ideal that science itself champions.[27]

While more strident fundamentalists might continue to condemn Darwinism and science outright (and in doing so, perhaps continue to endorse an older scientific view), Henry and other evangelical leaders advised against any such future close alliance between science and theology—until scientific discoveries and science itself stabilized (a requirement that in essence contradicts the modern notion of science). Yet, despite the change in tone and the slight shift in emphasis, the underlying argument—that one should not rely on theoretical science, which by definition would continue to change in the future—remained embedded in a Baconian worldview that rejected theories or hypotheses in favor of the facts. For these evangelicals, God's revealed word remained an unchanging constant. This emphasis on the unchanging, traditional biblical "truth" was in stark contrast to the model of evolving, changing, progressing, Christianity of modernist Protestantism. In this sense, evangelicals remained firmly opposed to evolution, as item number four on *Christianity Today*'s statement of principles declared: "We believe man created in God's image is moral, intelligent and free, of unique dignity and potentiality for good or evil, versus all views of man as a product of materialistic evolution."[28] At the same time God and his word were timeless truths, regardless of whatever progress had been made in other spheres:

> That is not to deny the magnificent contribution of science to our knowledge of the intricate behavior of the universe. Whoever closes his eyes to that contribution does so, of course, by the denial of his own modernity. But the fact remains that the great truths of the biblical creation narrative retain their validity for our scientific era, and that the twentieth century is in dire moral and spiritual straits for having neglected them.[29]

For evangelical leaders, science and its accomplishments were often understood as "moral" distractions that contributed to the general spiritual decline, a decline directly linked to the rise in popularity of the philosophy of naturalism.[30] While naturalism "gave new impetus to the study of the natural sciences with many salutary benefits to humanity," it also had led to "a tragic contempt of spiritual things."[31] In the eyes of James DeForest Murch, the liberal attempt "to accommodate Christianity to scientific naturalism" was a perfect example of this contempt as was the "obnoxiously anti-cultural, anti-scientific" approach of the fundamentalist.[32] In contrast, evangelical leaders most often viewed science and technology (on the one hand), and religion and morality (one the other), as belonging to separate spheres. The problem was not with scientific accomplishments per se, but with the cultural privileging of the scientific over the religious and moral domain:

> Scholars must indeed distinguish scientific and religious truth. But these men do so in an objectionable manner damaging to the Judeo-Christian revelation. They imply the superiority of scientific truth to religio-moral truth. With seeming humility, they properly acknowledge that scientific knowledge is relative; with underlying dogmatism, they consign religious knowledge to a wholly different order, to the realm of faith as contrasted with knowledge. In so doing they conceal the indebtedness of all truth to faith; they obscure the Hebrew-Christian emphasis that revealed religion rests on superior knowledge; and they say things about the spiritual-moral world that prepare the way for the naturalistic assault upon faith in God and the supernatural.[33]

Evangelical leaders viewed technology and technological accomplishments in a similar manner. The problem was not with technology per se, but rather with the misuse and misinterpretation of technology. From the evangelical perspective, technology was a god-given gift that provided proof of America's greatness and testified to God's sovereignty. The main problem was that far too many Americans failed to acknowledge God's primacy and importance in the technological era. Technology was slowly usurping religion:

> Without any doubt the dominant feature of our age is the spectacular triumph of applied science. In no other field of human endeavor have such astounding advances been made, and every one of us lives in the glow of technological achievement. It is natural that the man of science who dives into the mysteries of the physical world and comes back to us with automobiles, radios, television and nuclear devices, seems to speak with much more authority than those who speak of the mysteries of God.[34]

When properly used and understood, technology reflected the glory of God. When misused and misunderstood, technology threatened the status and credibility of old-time religion (even in its newer evangelical version). A correct interpretation required simply that technology be assigned its proper place in the hierarchy of creation (God above all). Proper use was defined by intent and by the moral standing of the user. Thus, in the eyes of evangelical leaders, the value of technology was partially determined by the meanings imparted by the user, and partially determined by the character of the user. This approach to technology was likewise reflected in evangelical understandings of broadcast media.

In the technological age, many Americans viewed science rather than God as the ultimate cultural arbiter. To combat such a misnomer, evangelical leaders adopted a tactical position. On the one hand, they acknowledged the social importance and impact of new technologies without acknowledging the theories that supported them.[35] On the other hand, they remained committed to a theology that gave priority and authority to the religious and moral realms. In suggesting that technology and science belonged to separate realms, evangelicals followed their fundamentalist ancestors. In suggesting that science and religion inhabited separate spheres, evangelicals moved away from their orthodox ancestors and adopted an intellectual strategy similar to that of German liberals such as Albrecht Ritschl and Rudolph Otto.[36] In following such a path, evangelical leaders balanced their desire to remain true to orthodoxy while differentiating themselves from the liberals they so despised.

The Atomic Bomb, the Space Race and the Cold War

While evangelical attitudes toward science and technology pre-dated the cold war, many of the articles on the topic in *Christianity Today* and other sources reflect this larger cultural discourse. Anticommunist rhetoric abounds throughout evangelical writings of this era, resounding with themes common to its secular counterparts. Indeed, there were explicit political alliances between evangelical leaders and some of the more notorious cold-war warriors. J. Edgar Hoover, for example, wrote for *Christianity Today* and spoke at National Religious Broadcasters Association meetings in the 1950s. Hoover believed that clergymen had a fundamental role in the fight against communist subversion.[37] Evangelical leaders abhorred communism for its blunt atheism, and restriction of freedom of religion in communist states.[38] Subsequently their attitudes toward the atomic bomb and the space race were shaped as much by political as by theological considerations. They were in awe of and proud of American achievements in the technological domain and were convinced that such accomplishments were a necessary part of preserving the American way of life, as long as moral and spiritual priorities remained in the foreground. Only by preserving such a cultural hierarchy could America fight the evils of communism.

The Russian launching of Sputnik in 1957, which called America's technological and scientific prowess into question, was for evangelicals a sign that Americans had lost their trust in God:

> We take great pride in our technological prowess, our scientific acumen, our economic strength, our atomic weapons—the kind of pride that has made us lose our sense of dependence on God. We have been arrogant, and have displeased our Creator. We have forgotten we are not a self-made people. Nor have we any business worshipping ourselves.[39]

If science was not the enemy per se, it certainly had become for evangelicals far too central in most Americans' minds. These writers, however, did not refute scientific accuracy or theory but, like the rest of Americans, remained in awe of its impact. The evangelical approach to these new technological feats was to call Americans back to their creator, and to thank Him for these advances instead of mocking Him through immorality:

> Do we thank God who has so blessed us? No! Rather we consume more liquor than any nation in history; we have a higher divorce rate than any country of modern time; we spend more money on pleasure than any people before us—sin, clamor and licentiousness try hard to drown out the small voice of thanksgiving which those few who are devout seek to make heard. Sputnik has uncovered our condition.[40]

In the end, man's essential condition and predicament was, in the eyes of evangelicals, undetermined by the changes wrought by technological and scientific inventions. Despite new discoveries, particularly the discovery of space (or the heavens), man remained, in evangelical theology, a sinner in need of God's reconciliation: "The 'beep' of Sputnik may bring valuable scientific data. Only the grace and truth that came with the angels' song can redeem mankind."[41] Ultimately, these discoveries, were, like all of creation, illustrations of God's sovereignty. Soviet announcements that claimed that the space age had discredited Christian dogma (i.e., that the cosmonauts did not see angels or meet God on the way to the heavens) were met with a direct response in a *Christianity Today* editorial.[42] In the view of the editor, the ability of man, "a finite" mind, to achieve such accomplishments only enlarged the possibility that an infinite power, such as God, created the world. Scientific discovery ultimately reinforced the biblical worldview and the evangelical way of life. One should fear communism not for its scientific accomplishments but for its rejection of God and the commandments.

Ultimately the cold war battle was a moral and spiritual battle, and not a scientific one.[43] On the home front, evangelicals believed that they had an important role to play in this battle. As Mrs. Herman E. Eberhardt, wife of the director of the Central Union Mission in Washington DC and "Mother of the Year," answered in a *Christianity Today* survey of prominent Christian mothers: "A space age mother needs to keep her feet on the ground and her heart in the heavenlies. The man in the moon will never replace the man in the home with a dedicated mother working with him to raise a Christian family."[44]

The possibility of atomic warfare, for example, only reinforced the evangelical belief that the destiny of the world was in God's hands.[45] Although adherence to dispensationalism was not a litmus test for membership in evangelical organizations (such as the NAE or the NRB), many evangelical leaders remained committed to a premillennialist eschatology that resonated well with the "prophecies of doom" so associated with the cold war.[46] In the eyes of the premillennialists, global holocaust could well be a sign of Armageddon and the end of the world as prophesied in the Bible, especially in the book of Revelations. Remarkably, however, on this point (the destruction of the world), secular scientists and evangelical leaders were grudgingly in agreement. An editorial in *Christianity Today* ushering in the New Year of 1960 began with precisely this articulation:

> But the so-called "prophets of doom" are not confined to the pulpit. Eminent physicist Edward Teller predicts Russian unquestioned world leadership in science ten years from now and sees the world modeled after Russian ideas rather than Western by the end of the century. Men are asking, "For earth, what time is it? Are these still her evolutionary birth pangs, or are we hearing the final cadence of God's countdown for her history?"[47]After evaluating the year's achievements, the editorial ended with a reference to the atomic clock: "Whatever the hour on God's clock, the ultimate triumph is secure. But the countdown is not yet ended . . . and there is yet work."[48]

Ironically, prophecy might be fulfilled through a technological means—atomic warfare—indicating that, at least in the evangelical mind, the scientific/technological and the biblical worlds were perhaps not that different. Evangelicals conceived of atomic anxiety, particularly the feeling that the world was coming to an end, as a parallel, secular version of premillennialism. One *Christianity Today* writer believed that atomic anxiety could perhaps compel unbelievers to understand how the destiny of the universe was ultimately in God's hands, not man's.[49] If the end of the world was near, evangelicals still had an important task to perform—to preach the word, and to reach out to as many people as possible with the word. In this context, the new advances in communications technology such as radio and television proved to be essential tools.

"The Age of Space Requires Space Age Teaching Tools."[50]

For the most part, evangelicals viewed new forms of mass media simply as an extension of God's other gifts of communication—such as the common world language under the Roman Empire and the printing press during the Reformation.[51] The *Christianity Today* editors, for example, commented that

> The world of today differs greatly from the world of St. Paul . . . With rockets and missiles now exploring outer space, Paul at one time was having difficulty sailing in a wooden ship safely to Rome.

Man-power and horsepower have given way to the power of atoms and nuclear fission. With modern equipment, one can do the work done by thousands in Paul's day. Epistles, laboriously written on parchment and delivered weeks later by personal messengers, have been superseded by communications media delivering messages across continents in seconds.

> All these advancements do *not* mean that man himself has improved and become morally better. He is still the same sinner, in need of the same Savior of whom Paul preached.[52]

The challenge of the space era was to understand which tools God provided and to use them to promote this timeless message. Radio and television were perceived as "special teaching tools for an age that is *complicated, confused* and *complacent*."[53] But how did evangelicals know which tools were God's and which tools were Satan's? What kind of guidelines could the Bible give?

> Our world today seems far removed from the world of the Bible. What have we, with our nuclear weapons, space satellites, television, and mechanized way of life, in common with a an age of chariots and horsemen, and herdsmen, nomads and primitive tillers of the soil? Has not modern man reduced the Bible to a religious curiosity, virtually prehistoric and definitely prescientific and therefore outmoded and irrelevant?[54]

The challenge was to convince modern man that despite these seemingly large disparities between the space age and the biblical world—the biblical message remained essential. Dr. Ockenga, for example, conceded that the new cosmology of the space age provided a clearer understanding of angels, redemption, and heaven than the old cosmology. At the same time, however, he emphasized that "the eternal principles enunciated in the Word have permanent application to the problems and perplexities of societal man in his human relationships." Subsequently, "an intelligent Christian ought to be more adapted and equipped to makes this transition [to the space age] than a non-Christian who is a materialist or naturalist."[55] Edward J. Carnell made the same observation in even clearer terms:

> From one end of the land to the other millions of people are deluded into believing that man's hope is science. Nothing could be more removed from the full truth. Man is spirit as well as body. The bread of science will never bring happiness to the spiritual side of man.[56]

As regards the broadcast media, Ockenga's prediction turned out to be farsighted. Evangelicals would be far "more adapted and equipped" to meet the requirements of radio and television than their liberal brethren. Through modern communication tools, evangelicals could hypothetically reach more people than ever before, and in a manner that demonstrated the contemporary relevance of the old-time Gospel.[57] Evangelicals thus perceived the new communications tools as neutral tools provided by God to distribute his messages across the globe. At the same time, the powers of these new technologies deceived people into believing that they no longer needed the Bible or biblical faith. Evangelicals believed they had a responsibility to use these communications tools in the way God intended for them to be used (that is to disburse the word of God) and simultaneously to convince people that technology could not influence the spiritual state of man.

Underlying these assumptions, was an understanding of the broadcasting media as somewhat neutral tools. The content of the message and the purpose of its use determined the value of the medium. One could and should use the broadcasting media in order to further God's will (namely, to spread his message), but at the same time there was a fear that the medium itself (namely its prestige and stature in society) was undermining the status of religion, particularly old-time Gospel religion. In other words, evangelical leaders feared that the social and cultural prominence of new technologies was distorting man's perception of the world. Little, if any, consideration was given to the potentially distorting influence of the media upon the content and reception of God's word. In general, evangelical critiques of the media were concerned with the moral dimension.

Edward John Carnell's *Television:*
Servant or Master?

Edward J. Carnell, systematic theologian at Fuller Theological Seminary, was one of the first evangelical leaders to appraise the new medium of television from a biblical perspective. Published in 1950, *Television: Servant or Master* evaluated the potential impact of the new medium on society as a whole and on the evangelical community in particular.[58] While Carnell's observations cannot be generalized to the evangelical leadership as a whole, the book does touch upon a number of issues that are represented in other later writings in *Christianity Today* and *United Evangelical Action*.[59] In so far as it was the only 1950s book-length treatise on the subject of television published by an evangelical theologian, *Television: Servant or Master* deserves closer analysis.

Trained at the Harvard Divinity School, where he wrote a dissertation on the notion of dialectic in Reinhold Niebuhr's thought, Carnell approached the subject of the television with the same kind of rigor.[60] Although television was a mass medium, Carnell believed that its potential social and cultural effects warranted a careful theological analysis. Adopting Augustine's metaphor of two cities, Carnell divided the world into the children of the dark and children of the light, with society defined as a mixture of both elements. Social products, such as technology, were therefore also mixed— reflecting the nature of society and of men's hearts: "Technological efficiency is a neutral powder keg: It can move the world for God or it can blow civilization apart. These termini define the outside limits of TV's promises and threats."[61] To limit television's threats and to highlight its promises, the children of the light (evangelicals) needed to reflect upon the new medium, to evaluate their usage of it and its potential effects upon society. Carnell offered his book as the first step in this process. Carnell's invocation of Augustine provided a classical theological legitimation for the fundamentalist understanding of technology as neutral.

Unlike his liberal Protestant counterparts, Carnell recognized and understood the therapeutic and entertainment value of the television. Beginning with the presumption that man both needs and craves laughter, Carnell believed that the television would entertain and distract, both important tasks in the modern world. Even more importantly, television had an important emotional value for the viewer—promoting relaxation and well-being:

> TV therapy is a welcomed anesthesia in this now proverbial "aspirin age." In this mid-twentieth century upheaval, where on every hand hearts are failing

for fear, men must either retain the fine custom of relaxation or reckon with the threats of a destroyed equilibrium in body and soul. Well-being is not an automatic blessing. It must be cultivated with the same skill and artistry as growing a delicate rose. Television will painlessly assist in the mechanics of its cultivation.[62]

Television provided a means of escaping the routinization of everyday life. In that capacity, Carnell believed that television could provide an important escape valve. Although he provides few examples (one wonders whether he might be drawing upon personal experience), Carnell thought television could help people relax and subsequently be more capable of successful social interaction (thus increasing what he called "personality quotient"). Carnell's insights into the therapeutic function of television foreshadowed the therapeutic talk shows of the 1980s and 1990s.[63] While the escapist quality of the television provided relaxation and therapy, it likewise exposed the viewer to new landscapes, operating like a "travel bureau in the home" and forcing viewers to move beyond their received narrow frames of reference and to broaden their cultural views.[64] In such a capacity, television encouraged men to cultivate their deeper virtues.

Religious education, therefore, could potentially be very effective on television. For Carnell, the fact that the television was a family medium, broadcast in the home away from the crowds, allowed man to lower his pride and find God:

> Television arrests man in near solitude. Thus TV, while it may threaten to convert every home into a theater, can also turn every parlor into a church. The home is a neutral area now. Whether it will become a theater or a church depends once again on both the skill and the morality of those controlling the medium. Religious telecasters therefore must be courageous, remembering that by overtaking man in his solitude TV enjoys an access into hearts which the organized church does not. Many, whose self-pride might otherwise prevent them from entering a church, may eventually find God through television.[65]

The television enjoyed a unique kind of access to the masses. On the one hand, television reached greater numbers than any revivalist preacher could imagine. On the other hand, the television could potentially reach individuals alone in their homes, far from the influence of the crowd (at the movies or at the revival tent). Here, Carnell provides a positive interpretation of TV solitude—a characteristic of the medium that would often come under attack by future critics. Interestingly, he does not view the solitary nature of TV viewing as problematic or erosive of church community.

To reach these solitary viewers and convert them to Christianity, religious telecasters had to remember that television was primarily a medium of entertainment. Carnell suggested that effective religious television required a minister with a natural, folksy, and informal demeanor, one who avoided long speeches.[66] The minister would have to be genuine, for TV would "put an end to any sham a religious broadcaster might outwardly display."[67] Unlike the radio listener, the TV viewer was able to view the preacher and was thus better equipped to evaluate the preacher's manner and sincerity, and due to the high cost and competitive nature of the television schedule, only the truly talented and honest would survive.[68] In contrast to Roman Catholics, whom Carnell predicted would be as successful on the small screen as they had been in the movies, evangelicals would have to work hard at creating a place in the new medium. The most effective (although expensive) solution was for evangelicals to become television station owners and operators (foreshadowing Pat Robertson's technique). These efforts would be important, if not crucial, in the television age, for man's previously private world would now be invaded by all sorts of influences:

> Whereas formerly a man could close out the world when he shut the door of his home, now the world with its good and evil, marches right into the living room and boldly takes its place beside the family hearth. The furniture in the home is being rearranged to make room for the television set. The invasion of the world into both the homes and hearts of men has been incredibly accelerated in the age of television.[69]

While the location of the television in the home provided more opportunities for witnessing, it likewise threatened to secularize the home. If more and more leisure time was being spent watching the television, less and less time was being spent on alternative hobbies, or on prayer and fellowship with God.[70] As the time watching television increased, the more influence the medium would have on the Christian home: "Television will greatly step up the problems of Christian sanctification. With the world in the front room of the home, it will require new skill to be *in* but not *of* the world."[71] In Carnell's mind the greatest problem posed by the existence of television was rooted not in the content of the programs but in the fact that the presence of the medium itself might promote the "delusion" that "man's hope is science." Carnell quickly discounted such a belief, noting that "the bread of science will never bring happiness to the spiritual side of man."[72]

While Carnell's book did not garner much attention either in the evangelical or mainstream Protestant press, his arguments foreshadowed the positions that would be articulated over the next decade or so within the evangelical community. Carnell's beginning premise—that technology was neutral and therefore television, like the radio before it, could be redeemed as a religious educator or witness—remained the starting point for televangelists in the decades to come. His practical suggestions for broadcasting successful evangelical programs were likewise perceptive. Numerous contemporary commentators (notably liberal Protestants among them) have suggested that the success of televangelism partially resides in its entertainment value. Remarkably, Carnell was able to foresee the ambiguous and mixed impact of the television on the American home in general, and on the evangelical home in particular. Unlike the majority of early mainline Protestant commentators who feared the impact of television far more than they valued its potential, Carnell pragmatically recognized that the television would be an influential social and cultural force in the years to come. Since entertainment would be the TV's primary social function, evangelical broadcasters would also need to entertain while they preached. Evangelical parents would need to moderate and control their children's access to the medium, which as a product of this world, by definition, contained both good and evil. Carnell suggested that parents install the television and recite the following blessing:

> To Thee, everlasting Father, we dedicate this television set. Be pleased to protect it, and all who use it, from evil; and may its presence in the home increase our comfort and happiness. If ever we forget this covenant with Thee, remove us from this treasured set and in its stead place sorrow.[73]

By consecrating the television to God, Carnell hoped to instill within children the necessity of being "Christ-conscious" while viewing.[74] To booster such consciousness, parents would need to monitor programs and discuss their contents. Carnell's reluctance to suggest a complete ban on television stood in contrast to both the fundamentalist position (which viewed TV as too worldly) and the mainline position (which encouraged people to just "turn it off!"), both of which were far more condemnatory of the new medium.

Sex, Smut, and Censorship

Although evangelical leaders, such as Carnell, recognized the potential contribution of TV to missionary and outreach work, they remained concerned about the potential affects of the new medium on their community and on the American people as a whole. While *The Christian Century* editors were far more concerned about violence and gambling on television, *Christianity Today* devoted more column space to "moral laxity" and "sex and smut" in the communications media in general. Smoking and drinking fell under these moral categories as well.[75] Evangelical leaders viewed the increasing appearance of "sex" in public life as a sign of secularization (or "the godless concept of life that is destroying America").[76] L. Nelson Bell, for example, claimed that

> Sex obsession is a moral and spiritual cancer which has fixed itself on America and which is designed to destroy us as surely as untreated cancer destroys human life. This diagnosis is open to all who can see. Our literature, stage, screen and accepted standards of life literally reek with an obsession about sex which has now reached unbelievable proportions.[77]

And Bell was not alone in this analysis. A *Christianity Today* criticism of Cecile B. DeMille's movie *The Ten Commandments* focused upon two main points—gratuitous sex scenes and the omission of the Gospel. Guest columnist J. Edgar Hoover likewise described an America where

> on every hand, deliberate pandering to the lower instincts is apparent. Innuendo permeates once wholesome publications. Movie ads and paper-backs flaunt violence and sexuality. Sexual brutality and sadism are too often emphasized unduly on both television and movie screens. Moral degenerates spew forth a surreptitious torrent of outright obscenity in the form of films, playing cards, comic books, paperbooks, and pictures.[78]

For Carnell, one of the more problematic aspects of the new medium of television was the advertisers' use of sex as "a drawing force."[79] He compared the advertisers' tactics to that of the Kremlin who employed female sex "slaves" to engage in espionage![80] If "the children of light" were not careful, American television would quickly slip into the moral decadence of French television, where "show girls, wearing no brassieres and having midriffs free, are beamed out for the French to lust upon."[81] From an evangelical perspective, the moral character of cultural products was determinative. Unfortunately far too many Americans were indifferent to such cultural criticism. The editor of *Christianity Today* chided the church for not speaking out enough against immorality, noting that in the contemporary context such a task was often not easy: "Any reference to Puritanism will bring either a sneer or the raised eyebrows of a people sated by twentieth-century sophistication."[82]

In contrast to the liberal NCC and BFC officials who found boycott and censorship to be "reprehensible to traditional Protestant thinking," evangelicals were ambivalent about both.[83] This difference in attitude can be partly attributed to a genuine evangelical desire to promote "common standards of decency." Evangelical leaders (like their liberal counterparts) felt that they could not leave the moral realm to Catholic leaders alone. As the mainline leadership focused less and less on traditional moral issues, evangelicals took up the torch. For evangelical leaders, pornography could not be simply dismissed as the cost of living in a society that valued freedom of speech. Pornography was problematic not just because it was amoral but because it was "openly and avowedly anti-Christian."[84] Indeed, any aspect of contemporary entertainment that was indecent was considered to be only a degree away from pornography. Even the billboards advertising movies were suspect.[85] As regards television, Carnell hoped that the industry would write a code of decency, perhaps one similar to that undertaken by the film industry. To reinforce positive moral messages on televisions, evangelicals were encouraged to write letters in support of shows that *did* adhere to acceptable standards. Still, if these positive efforts to encourage the industry to conform to moral standards should fail, Carnell saw no other choice than to protest: "All public mediums ought to match standards of public conscience. If they will do not it voluntarily, they must be coerced."[86] Despite such strong language, Carnell offered no programmatic plan toward that end, and other evangelical leaders likewise found it difficult to advocate straightforward censorship. Joseph Martin Dawson, for example, in a *Christianity Today* column on censorship, cited Milton and Thomas Jefferson as examples of figures who opposed such measures as antidemocratic.[87] Still, it was difficult to count upon the audience to self-censor their viewing. A *Christianity Today* editorial published in the wake of the Quiz Show Scandal questioned whether viewers could even be expected to participate in a boycott:

> Perhaps only public indignation can force a revision of television morality. But are the viewers really indignant? Are they inclined to bypass a shady program, or to snub a shady product? Or do they too welcome comfortable delusion above the hard truth? Has the true and the good grown too demanding for us—something our age expects only when it becomes "public necessity"? Have humanistic pressures deteriorated our reverence for human life to dramatic farce, devoid of dignity and duty, and openly disdainful of high and holy things?[88]

Another *Christianity Today* editorial questioned the policy maintained by some evangelicals, of boycotting the movies while viewing television at home. The editorial questioned whether even "selective forays into the medium" could affect one's spiritual life. Unwilling to completely give up on the industry, the editorial called upon readers to write more letters to networks, advertisers, and producers.[89] In the end, evangelical leaders were unable to offer a viable alternative to old-fashioned censorship.

"The Minister in the Mirror"

In addition to sex and smut, evangelicals found other aspects of television content problematic. Like their liberal counterparts, *Christianity Today* editors bewailed the representation of Protestantism on the air. Comparing the Protestant minister to the ever more filmable Catholic priest, both liberals and conservatives worried that the Protestant minister was being portrayed in a problematic light, and that this portrayal signaled something more about the status of the minister in American society. In the evangelical mind the decline in status of the minister was actually connected to the liberal tendency toward rationalization: "The bureaucratization of the denominations is one of the chief causes of the clergy's declining prestige, since it tends to brand him as one of the herd rather than as God's spokesman."[90] A proposal for a television play involving an adulterous Protestant minister evoked a *Christianity Today* editorial that noted, "The minister is presented to the American people as a hypocrite, as a cad, as a heel, as a deadbeat, as a charlatan, as an extortionist, as an incompetent."[91] Conservative Protestant ministers were subject to even worse depictions than their liberal counterparts. Only a year earlier, NBC's Sunday afternoon series (Kaleidoscope) had aired a program entitled *The Third Commandment* that portrayed a fraudulent evangelist and faith healer. The editorial surmised that both Billy Graham and Oral Roberts were the indirect targets of this play.[92] Generally, there was a sense that conservative Protestantism did not fare well on secular television.[93]

"All in Color"[94]

Generally, columns in *Christianity Today* and *United Evangelical Action* remained in the practical and programmatic realms, but occasionally writers speculated about the effects of these new technologies (and their uses) upon the church. Otto A. Piper, a German refugee and professor of New Testament at Princeton Theological Seminary, noted that

> with the result of rapid technological growth based on theories of rationalism and positivism, modern life has become dominated by the idea of technological efficiency and high returns. We see congregations and also many ministers looking to outward success, expressed in exact figures, as the goal to be pursued; and thus the belief is implied that the most elaborate organization is the best guarantee of success.[95]

In Piper's mind, the churches were modeling themselves after businesses, and expecting preachers to act like corporate managers. A few years earlier, an editorial in *Christianity Today* had specifically addressed the dangers of advertising and the advertising mentality to conservative Protestantism:

> The concept that human behavior can be manipulated by promotion and advertising poses still another peril for the churches. To neglect the supernatural elements of the Gospel, in deference to mechanical motivation enthroned by behavioral sciences, may result in the idea that a direct proportion exists between the amount of promotion and number of converts. Indeed business success stories may encourage even quite orthodox church boards to share the sentiment: "If we were promotionally alive, we'd double the (regenerate) church membership!"[96]

The editor directly repudiated the idea of using secular social scientific research to increase the efficacy of evangelism. Advertising was not to be used as a model for evangelism. One could use "promotion" as a tool to reach more people with the Gospel, but care had to be taken lest evangelism itself turn into yet another form of advertising. In his mind, secular research *promoted* advertising as an effective means to reach more potential converts. Clearly evangelicals were not reading the same studies as the mainline Protestants, who relied upon social scientific research in order to legitimate their *withdrawal* from television.

While advertising and its demonic effects were easy to discern, other effects of television were subtler. Eutychus, *Christianity Today*'s satirist, devoted a whole column to the appearance of color television and its impact upon the church:

> It is plain that we must have religion with color added. In the church visual, the more pageantry the better. We now have color bulletins and color movies, but so many affairs remain drab. Even the local Easter sunrise service has very little color except for the sun, and the new choir robes are disappointingly charcoal. Stained glass windows help, but the pictures don't move. Projected film techniques ought to be able to outstrip a craft of the Dark Ages. Since these windows are not functional in any case, a vista-vision screen might provide an interesting substitute.[97]

The medium of color television was having a direct effect on the role of color in everyday life in general, and on the church in particular: "Life is now a four-color process."[98] Carnell feared that the advent of color television would make viewers less willing "to snap off the set."[99] Would the traditionally ascetic Protestant Church be able to compete with the colorful, image-laden world represented on color television? In what ways would church life be transformed by these technological innovations?

Were these developments a sign that we were already living in a postliterary age.[100] Eutychus satirically and cynically described a future world of automation, a world in which the pastor would simply play recorded messages during his visits to ailing widows:

> His simple visitation technique is to bring a table, find an extension cord, plug in the machine, replace a fuse, splice the tape, then nap with a subtly benign expression while his best oratory thunders at the widow.[101]

No longer would the pastor's office be lined with book shelves. Eutychus prophesied that in their stead "gleaming silver-green machines will line . . . [the] study wall, and weekly sermons will be automatically recorded (in the pastor's individual voice) from a centralized office."[102] Eutychus's vision tells us several things about evangelical approaches to new communications technologies. On the one hand, Eutychus clearly bemoans the passing of the literary world and the interpersonal communication between pastor and widow. On the other hand, Eutychus anticipates the sophisticated usage of these new technologies by the church and although the tone is rather negative, it is realistic. While there is a sense of loss expressed, there is also a sense of realism—the Gospel will be increasingly mechanized in the new technological world.

Conclusions

Evangelical approaches to the television were conceived within a larger discourse concerning science and technology. While evangelical leaders refrained from adapting any particular approach to science (steering clear of both Baconianism and Darwinism), they embraced its "neutral" technological fruits. In so far as new communications technologies could be used to further the greater goal of evangelism, evangelical leaders remained committed to their use. At the same time, they remained fearful of the general impact of these technologies on society. Most of these fears were articulated as concerns about the role of conservative Protestantism in a technological age. If man could travel to the moon, why did he need old-time religion? For evangelical leaders, the answer was clear. In such a time of change, God's unchanging word anchored the present in the past and created a clear sense of priorities. In many ways the atomic age and the cold war seemed to legitimate premillennialist views.

If the end of the world was near, evangelism took on a new urgency. The new communications media provided a means to reach a mass audience in a contemporary manner. Technology was a god-given gift, with a god-given purpose. By broadcasting the Gospel evangelicals hoped to reach more people with God's word, but they also hoped to demonstrate that old-time religion was an integral part of the contemporary world. The new communications media would provide proof of the relevance of the message (the Gospel). In the process, evangelical faith would become an increasingly visible part of public culture.

Generally more open to television than their liberal counterparts, evangelical leaders did find elements of the new medium problematic. As a new form of entertainment it posed new moral challenges, particularly as public prudery declined. Still, evangelical leaders would often prove to be prophetic in their evaluation of television culture. J. Edward Carnell, in particular, wrote with an empathy for TV viewing that no liberal Protestant leader could ever imitate. In the age of television, evangelicals understood that to communicate God's Word, cultural adjustments would have to be made.

Chapter 6

Protestants and the Television: The Paradox Reassessed

Fast forward to the year 2006: television is no longer a new medium. We take for granted that we live in a media-saturated world. The Christian right is not so new anymore—the new evangelical imagined by the NAE leaders in the 1950s is no longer marginalized or scorned as a "fundamentalist" but rather is now courted as a potential voter and as an important market segment (and not just for so-called Christian goods). The decline of mainline Protestantism, both in numbers and in influence, is readily apparent to all. What then can we learn from these case studies of Protestantism and the television in the 1950s? What can these stories tell us about the adoption and domestication of new technologies today and their importance in understanding the role and kind of religion in the public sphere?

Sixty years have passed since the advent of television, but the organizations that were formed to approach this new communications medium— the BFC (now renamed the Communication Commission) and the NRB—are still around, and the NRB has become one of the more important hierarchies in Protestant America, a hierarchy that wields both economic and political pull. With the advent of the Internet, digital media, cellular phones, and other such communication tools, these organizations still have as much or more to contend with in the digital age as they did in the age of mass media.[1] The difficulty in accessing the broadcasting networks has been replaced by an overabundance of channels on radio and television, and endless possibilities for using the Internet to produce alternative media of all kinds from more static, less interactive Web pages, and podcasts (see www.godcasts.com) to virtual or online communities through list serves, and blogs.[2]

Considering all of these technological innovations, one might conclude that the issues raised in this book are no longer relevant. Yet, mainline and evangelical approaches to these new media remain significantly different: the NRB remains committed to broadcasting an evangelical message to reach nonbelievers (and not just born again Christians) and the National Council of Churches Communication Commission predominantly engages in media education and criticism. In a 2005 news release describing the rapid rise in the number of Christian radio stations (again a medium that one might have thought would become irrelevant or extinct), the NRB confirmed that its threefold vision was: to (1) "proclaim the Good News of eternal life through Jesus Christ, (2) transform the culture through the application of sound biblical teaching, and (3) preserve religious freedom by keeping the doors of electronic media open for the spread of the Gospel."[3] In other words, the NRB uses the media for evangelizing to nonbelievers (although they recognize them to be a very small percent of the audience), for creating an alternative evangelical culture, and in addition sees itself as preserving the "right" to purchase air time from the larger media producers.

In contrast, a quick glance at the Web page of the Communication Commission (the BFC's descendant) demonstrates that it remains committed to "serve as a professional development resource . . ., a channel of collaboration, . . . a moral and educational force in the communication field."[4] While the Communication Commission, under the rubric of the Interfaith Broadcasting Commission (which included the U.S. Conference of Catholic Bishops, the Broadcast Group of the Southern Baptist Convention, and the Jewish Theological Seminary of America), provided eight programs to the networks as a public service (i.e., the contemporary version of sustained-time programming), it mainly views itself as an ecumenical clearinghouse for media education and cultural critique.[5] Indeed, in the "Church and the Media: An NCC Policy Guide,"[6] several of the positions formulated in the 1950s are reiterated:

> Television, whether in the U.S. or in other nations, is creating a "mass" culture of the lowest common denominator of all of society. TV programming and images often appeal to the base instincts of humanity and exploit such instincts for private gain. Thus, both entertainment and news media are dominated by affirmations of greed, instant gratification, the use of violence rather than negotiation as a way of solving problems, titillation (sex rather than love), exploitation of the weak by the strong (particularly women, children, older persons, and ethnic minorities), satisfaction of curiosity rather than a deeper consideration of issues, and single viewpoints rather than multiple viewpoints. We do not attribute the negative effects of media to the individual creations of writers, reporters and producers as much as to the cumulative effects of a way of viewing the world brought about by the technical demands of the media themselves.[7]

Thirty-three years after the Elvis editorial was printed in *The Christian Century*, the mainline Protestant leadership still condemns the media industry for appealing to the "lowest common denominator."[8] From their perspective the mainstream media is lowbrow, and as a consequence the American public needs protection from it. The mainline Protestant establishment should therefore work to convince the networks that "since all elements of social communication are first of all God's creation, and not our creation, they must be considered as being held in trust for the community by those who control them. Therefore stewardship is a necessary corollary of creation."[9] The commission's responsibility is to ensure that the media are therefore held in stewardship for the public good, which is predictably defined as airtime for public broadcasting, restraint from broadcasting overly violent programming, and other such stipulations. What is striking about both the NRB and NCC documents is how little the organizations' positions have changed over time.

If television was once the medium under attack and under discussion, today it is the Internet.[10] While churches have recognized the ability of the Internet to bolster communication—particularly to use Carey's terms again, in a ritual capacity—they also look to the Internet for E-vangelism. And with the blurring of genres—the Internet is also now the site of a variety of Christian activity (for podcasts or Godcasts, see www.godcast.org; for radio stations, see www.christianradio.com; for television stations, see www.christian.tv). More than ever, producing media is a relatively easy proposition, although finding a relevant audience has become increasingly difficult.

Still, a quick comparison of Web sites is instructive(http://www.ncccusa.org/; http://www.nae.net/; http://www.nrb.org/; http://www.christianitytoday.com/; http://www.christiancentury.org/). The National Association of Evangelicals Web site is clean, well-designed (with one message from the president), and other links clearly marked. The National Council of Churches of Christ Web site is by far a better resource of texts—there are proclamations and policies, headlines and press releases, but it is almost overwhelmingly wordy. *Christianity Today* has turned into a Christian publishing empire with magazines of every genre—Christian parenting, fashion, leaders, and other popular lifestyle topics. There is a very active community board with chats, and there is also an online store where one can buy Christian music, videos, sermons, gifts, travel books, materials for home schooling. In contrast, *The Christian Century* Web site looks similar to *Harper's Magazine* (small unobtrusive ads along the side of the magazine)—making for a much more passive experience, with less opportunity for the surfer to participate.

Clearly, mainline Protestants and evangelical Protestants are negotiating the world of cyberspace in different ways and, in the process, as users and as nonusers they are shaping our understanding of the Internet and its place in our daily lives and practices. What repercussions will these negotiations have on the future landscape of American religion? On the nature of religion in cyberspace?

In chapter 1, I noted that, paradoxically, those Protestants who define themselves as "conservative" and/or "antimodernist" have historically been innovators in the area of media. In contrast those Protestants who define themselves as "modernist" or "liberal" have often been antagonistic to new media and slow to adapt to changing realities. In the example of television, this was likewise the case.

In this study, I endeavored to understand and unravel this paradox through a historical comparison of evangelical and mainline leaders' responses to television, during the period it was first assimilated into American homes (1945–1960). I suggested that the rise of televangelism—the focus of most previous scholarship on the subject—must be contextualized and compared to mainline Protestant responses to television. Previous studies have most often described the success of televangelists as almost predetermined or predestined. Some placed emphasis upon structural factors such as money or FCC decisions, while others emphasized the "televisable" nature of "old-time" religion. Notably, these kinds of explanations either view "Protestantism" as static, and the television itself as the causal factor, or view the religious transformations within American Protestantism as the causal factor and the television as a nonvariable. In contrast, this study has focused upon the *responses* of mainline and evangelical Protestant leaders to the medium of television. That is to say, the emphasis has been on understanding the ways in which mainline and evangelical leaders construed and constructed the new medium of television and its potential for harm or good to society in general and to their constituencies in particular. The model has been an *interactive* one, which assumes that media are constituted in social and cultural contexts and that religious identities are in flux. To write, therefore, of mainline and evangelical Protestant responses to television is to write about a changing set of cultural objects and a range of causal factors. To unravel the paradoxical relationship described above, subsequently, is a multistep process that relies upon a number of partial explanations that together provide a plausible framework for understanding.

Theology

As religious leaders with religious agendas, Protestant leaders' responded to television from within a theological context. In mainline Protestantism, the dominant triumphalist modernist theology was being challenged by a more chastened Christian realism. In chapters 2 and 3, I suggested that this theological transformation provided the backdrop and legitimation for the mainline leadership's shift away from media production toward media criticism. Within the conservative Protestant camp, evangelical leaders endeavored to create a specifically "evangelical" theology that was neither hostile to the world nor embracing of it. John Edward Carnell, for example, approached the television with great equanimity—neither rejecting the television as satanic nor embracing it as the messianic harbinger. Carnell's television theology was (in his eyes) an application of Augustine's observations concerning the nature of this world. Notably Carnell did not turn to eighteenth- or nineteenth-century American Protestant figures for legitimation but viewed his theological task in terms of a longer Christian history (an approach he shared with many of his neoevangelical contemporaries as they reformed fundamentalism). Theology, therefore, was a significant factor, in so far as it shaped the responses of Protestant leaders to the new medium of television, but it was not the sole determinant. In any case, it is difficult, if impossible, to distinguish between the effects of theology upon media policy and the after-the-fact theological legitimation of that policy.

The Medium of Television

In this study, I have shied away from arguments based solely upon medium theory. At the same time, medium theory has informed parts of my research approach. Following the dictum of theorist Joshua Meyrowitz, who suggests that a particular "medium environment is most visible when the medium is just beginning to be used by a significant portion of the population," I have confined this study to the early years of television.[11] At the base of this observation lies the assumption that the medium of television was historically and culturally constructed rather than created by technological fiat. The "television," as we know and understand it, was shaped by a variety of influences, a small portion of which could be termed as the audience "response" to the new medium. In so far as Protestant leaders were just one part of the TV audience, they too, helped to shape the nature of television. The medium of television may have influenced the kinds and types of religion that would be successful on air, but that is due to the way in which the medium was socially and culturally constructed, in part by its Protestant users.[12]

The Christian Century editors, for the most part, discussed the television using negative terms. At times, the contents of this dystopic discourses differed, but generally the starting point was that of disdain. In the eyes of the editors, the TV embodied or symbolized the negative aspects of post–World

War II American life. In contrast their evangelical counterparts (at *United Evangelical Action* and *Christianity Today*) approached the television in positive terms, viewing the medium as a gift from God with a divine purpose—to spread the Gospel to as large an audience as possible. From their perspective, the TV witnessed to the strength and power of divine will. These differing interpretations—the TV as Satan versus the TV as savior—tell us less about the nature of television per se, and far more about the difference between evangelical and mainline perceptions of the medium (whatever its determining traits might be). While the medium of television may (or may not) be more or less suitable for particular kinds of messages (i.e., simple and straightforward ones) with particular purposes (namely entertainment and leisure rather than education), the willingness of evangelical Protestants to adapt to those constraints (and the refusal of mainline Protestants) reflects their respective sets of cultural presuppositions. In this case the resistance of mainline leaders toward the television may have opened the public sphere to their evangelical competitors.

Cultural Boundaries

As a product of the post–World War II American society, the television connoted different sets of cultural references for evangelical and mainline leaders. For evangelical leaders, the television was associated with technology and the technological society. Through the savvy use of television, evangelicals hoped to demonstrate the continued pertinence of the Gospel. The logic was one of association. Technology was relevant (and even prestigious), therefore, competent use of television in doing Christian work demonstrated the relevance of old-time religion. In evangelical sources, the television was not berated as popular or mass culture—rather it was discussed as an esteemed tool for distributing the message of the Gospel. Evangelical leaders did occasionally find the contents of secular television programming immoral or unsuitable, but this did not imply a cultural evaluation of television as a pastime or form of entertainment.

In the early years of the medium, mainline leaders viewed the television as a deceptive and potential mass manipulator, although these fears remained largely unarticulated by their evangelical counterparts. After Everett Parker et al.'s BFC-sponsored research project concluded the opposite—that television was an ineffective persuader—mainline Protestant leaders continued to disregard the TV. Even when these fears of brainwashing were somewhat abated, mainline leaders continued to perceive the television as a debased form of entertainment. The television represented, both in its contents and in its concept, a basic challenge to the Protestant work ethic. Mainline leaders defined television viewing as a passive spectacle sport that had very little intrinsic value. Mainline Protestants leaders counseled their constituents to refrain from viewing television, stating that it was a waste of time.

Self-Definition

Why did mainline and evangelical leaders view the television so differently? Why did mainline Protestant leaders think that the television was lowbrow entertainment, while evangelical leaders remained convinced that it was a divinely inspired medium? The difference in these cultural evaluations must be partly traced to issues of self-definition. What did it mean to be Protestant in post–World War II America, an era during which Protestant hegemony was increasingly tenuous? Mainline and evangelical Protestant leaders offered different answers to this question, and their responses to television were part of this differentiation process. In chapter 4, I suggested that the NRB was an important part of the larger evangelical effort to present a positive alternative to fundamentalism. In chapters 2 and 3, I suggested that mainline Protestants were increasingly convinced that the end of Protestant hegemony was nigh. The BFC media policies reflected this changing self-definition. The de-Christianization of the public sphere was understood in positive terms as a necessary step toward a pluralistic society. Evangelical leaders viewed these same processes as problematic. In an increasingly pluralistic public sphere, evangelicals felt they must reassert the Christian heritage of the nation.

Conclusions

In attempting to maintain the cultural high ground, the mainline leadership reacted in remarkably conservative ways. While the mainline leadership was able to accept the challenges of biblical criticism, and Darwinism, TV culture was ultimately out of bounds. This rejection of television typified the mainline leadership's attitudes toward popular or mass culture. Herbert J. Gans has argued that intellectuals are far more likely to criticize popular culture when their own status and power is in question or in decline.[13] In this case, mainline Protestant leaders, whose cultural hegemony had been contested from the mid-1930s forward, became more suspicious of television (and other forms of mass culture) as they became more and more resigned to the prospect of religious and cultural pluralism. During the early years of television, which coincided with the so-called religious revival of the early 1950s, the mainliners benefited from their prominent societal position by receiving the majority of free (or sustained) airtime devoted to religious programs, and they held hope that the programs aired might actually sway Americans toward church. As television became a truly mass medium, and as it became clear that the post–World War II revival was just a temporary anomaly, the mainline leadership gradually became less involved in television production and started to moved into a new cultural role—that of educator and critic. The decision to focus more on criticism and policy advocacy notably coincided with an increasing realization that the assumption of mainline hegemony was no longer viable.[14] No longer sure of their role as the moral, cultural, and spiritual guardians in America, mainline Protestant leaders began to slowly accept the reality of pluralism. As this shift in self-perception (and reality) occurred, the mainliners became less and less interested in "Christianizing" the culture. The new model was of the church as sanctuary or respite from the increasingly commodified outside world.

In contrast, the evangelicals (who granted had a lot less cultural capital to lose) were able to be much more culturally accommodationist. While remaining critical of secular television programming, evangelicals remained optimistic about the potential of this new technology to convert the masses. During the early years of television, most of the evangelical battle concerned the right to purchase time for their programming. Through their membership in the National Religious Broadcasters Association, disparate evangelical broadcasters united in their struggle to undermine the Broadcast and Film Commission (of the NCCC) as *the* representative of Protestantism. These evangelicals were no longer willing to cede the public sphere to the mainline. Nor were they willing to accept the secularization of America as inevitable or necessary. As the mainline became more and more resigned to being on the religious and cultural sidelines, evangelicals became less and less satisfied with their role as religious and cultural outsiders. By Christianizing television as well as other forms of popular culture, evangelical producers provided Christian alternatives to secular culture. In doing so, they adapted "old-time" religion to the media age. While remaining committed to a discourse that legitimated no form of theological change, evangelical leaders proved to be far more accepting of technological change than their mainline counterparts.

Afterword

Michele Rosenthal in her last chapter wrote her own virtual "Afterword," but did not claim that it was a "Last Word," nor will my pages titled "Afterword" claim to be that. She asked what the readers might have learned from her inquiries in dusty nonelectronic archives about electronic inventions, events, and responses, and answered both succinctly and cogently. Rather than be seen as a superfluous add-on, I deduced that I was to bring a sort of insider-outsider view in another summary. Captive of existence in the confines of print-media and not adept in the fields of radio, television, or the internet, this historian of religion and commentator in journals long led me to keep an eye out for what was being projected on screen and an ear out for argument about what the images meant for the media themselves and, more fatefully, for religion. Fatefully, one says, because in the period about which the author writes, "mainline Protestantism" had been positioned to be influential in "mainline culture," or to be influenced by it to the point that it might have revised its religious message and strategy.

This account of events and opinions in the other cluster in Protestantism is fateful because, again during the period covered in this book, the agencies and influences labeled fundamentalism and later evangelicalism rose from relative obscurity in the larger culture to a situation in which these had displaced standard-brand Protestantism and even challenged the Catholic impact on culture. For Dr. Rosenthal, this shift was not only reflected in the writings of all parties involved but actually given propulsion by them, whether as positive agents or cautious and often negative commentators and critics of television when it shaped religious people or was found to be useful to some of them.

A perspective I would bring confirms the author's findings and would project them on a global scale, where the intermingling of media and religious signals and symbols was concurrently occurring. During more than a decade of intense study of militant religious fundamentalisms around the world, my colleagues and I noticed something in the chronology of the rise and metamorphoses of these movements. That "something" suggested that more than coincidence was involved in the putative "religious retreat from modernity," which secular and liberal commentators thought the new "old-time religion" movements were, and the growth of such religions thanks to the "exploitation of the instruments of modernity" by those whom the secular agents shunned, disdained, and refused to imitate.

Modern religious fundamentalisms appeared in many religious cultures in the 1920s. One could cite the American Protestant patent, the Muslim Brotherhood in Egypt after 1928, and two main strands of Hindu assertive movements in India after 1925. These were cultures in which traditional religion had been put on the defensive by technology, modernization in politics, and disruption of traditional societies. Rather than roll over and languish in comatose state, leaders appealed to audiences to rally over against whatever could be labeled or experienced as "modernity." Precisely in those years of the 1920s and 1930s radio presented itself as an instrument for rallying the discontented, labeling "the moderns" with stigmatizing and often demonizing terms, and devising strategies for counting them.

Fast-forward to the 1950s, when television appeared on the scene. While the expense of the medium for a time limited its usability by second-generation leaders of the movements, the more venturesome of them began to eye it and employ it, as fundamentalism metamorphosed into neoevangelicalism and evangelicalism in the United States, and with corollaries in other religious spheres. Again, the rhetorically gifted and those who were at home with images as broadcast over television, rallied a new generation of the discontented, spelled out what led to that discontent, and became a mass medium for organization and giving impetus to previously only latent supporters. All the while, the standard-brand or mainline Catholics, Protestants, Jews, and for all I know other-religionists were bystanders, languishers, or fumblers in the use of media.

Author Rosenthal quite properly focuses on the United States as a case study, thanks in part to its prominence in world religion and technological development. Her focus allows for careful examination and makes possible an awareness among readers of themes that by analogy "fit" other cultures as well as America with its Protestant heritage. One did not get far in reading her without finding a need to cope with *paradox* and *irony*. North Americans "mainliners," who were developing theologies to help them embrace and be embraced by forces often called "modern," paradoxically were virtual noncontenders with the media. And "evangelicals," who were developing ever more blatant and bold dismissals of modernity and some of its symbols—among them "pluralism," a sexual revolution, and new styles of international and domestic politics, ironically found themselves more at home than not in the emerging pop-cultures. Of course, their radio and television avatars selected certain areas for figurative strategic bombing, among them soft-porn television, liberal politics, legal abortion, and calls for homosexual rights, while they selected many others to embrace. A quick illustration: in the 1960s into the 1980s, rock music was seen by evangelicals to be the devil's instrument, but by the 1990s and 2000s evangelicals had produced "Christian rock," a $1-plus billion dollar a year venture. The lyrics were changed; words about "Jesus" replaced those about the embraced earthly lover, but the once-derided and attacked "beat" and what it did to stimulate pelvic movements and attract boundary-violating garb, now could be redeemed by evangelicals to promote Jesus. They could seek to win converts and to entertain the already converted.

One could study the paradoxes and ironies in many areas, among them politics—in which evangelicals, long passive and in hiding, were now masters; commerce—in which evangelicals had once asked for restraint, fearing the role of Mammon, now became capitalist venturers and advertisers; and popular entertainment, once seen as the devil's distraction but now, with often minor changes, converted to a converting agent for Jesus.

Michele Rosenthal has traced the television case study with historical finesse, and both those who favor and those who are critical of religious use, abuse, or avoidance of television will learn from it. She has implied certain theological judgments made along the way. Schooled to know the long history of religious establishment, the ancestry in Europe or in the thirteen American colonies as background to the "mainline," she is aware that descendants in that mainline "coasted" and served as chaplains to the recessive establishment which was itself changing to a point of unrecognizability. Meanwhile, the heirs of evangelical dissenters of eighteenth- and nineteenth-century America knew and demonstrated that they knew that there would be no churchly voice for their heirs if they did not convert their heirs and neighbors. Television became one of the main instruments for this.

Mainline Protestants, all the while, were developing theologies that encouraged affirmation of the modern secular order, however It was defined, were lowering the boundaries between religion and secularity to the point that there seemed fewer reasons for members to "stay in" and fewer reasons for outsiders to "sign up." The theological section is a bit underdeveloped in this book, and one hopes that Ms. Rosenthal will follow up with a volume two. She has concentrated single-mindedly on television, but along the way found that she had her hand on a cultural story of vast dimensions. Fortunately, since she enjoys discerning and pointing to paradoxes and ironies, her is not a grim study but a good read that should inspire readers to look at television and religion differently, and may move some to be more than passive in the face of television and the internet "about going along" with evangelicals or "going against" with the longer-established versions of Protestantism in America.

MARTIN E. MARTY
Fairfax M. Cone Distinguished Service Professor Emeritus
The University of Chicago

Notes

Introduction: The Triumph of Televangelism and the Decline of Mainline Religious Broadcasting

1. Razelle Frankl (*Televangelism: The Marketing of Popular Religion* [Carbondale, IL: Southern Illinois University Press, 1987], pp. 6–8) attributes the hybrid term—televangelism—to Jeffrey K. Hadden and Charles Swann, *Primetime Preachers: The Rising Power of Televangelism* (Reading, MA: Addison Wesley Pub., 1981).

2. See Mark Silk, *Unsecular Media: Making News of Religion in America* (Urbana: University of Illinois, 1995), particularly chapter 7: "Hypocrisy," pp. 80–90. See also, R. Laurence Moore, *Selling God: American Religion in the Marketplace of Culture* (New York: Oxford, 1994), especially chapter 5, "The Marketplace for Religious Controversy," pp. 118–145.

3. Ben Armstrong of the National Religious Broadcasters preferred the term "electric church" while William Fore of the Broadcast and Film Commission preferred the term "electronic church."

4. See Will Herberg, *Protestant, Catholic, Jew* (Garden City, NY: Anchor, 1955).

5. For a clear summary of classical and neoclassical sociological thought on the issue of secularization see Karl Dobbelaere, "Secularization: A Multi-Dimensional Concept," *Current Sociology* 29:2 (March 1981): 3–153. For a personal view on the decline of the secularization theory see Peter L. Berger, "The Desecularization of the World: A Global View," in *The Desecularization of the World: Resurgent Religion and World Politics*, edited by Peter L. Berger (Grand Rapids, MI: Eerdmans, 1999), pp. 3–18.

6. On the debate over the decline of the mainline denominations and the rise of conservative churches, see Dean Kelley, *Why Conservative Churches Are Growing* (New York: Harper and Row, 1972) and Roger Finke and Rodney Stark,

The Churching of America, 1776–1990: Winners and Losers in Our Religious Economy (New Jersey: Rutgers University Press, 1992).

7. Daniel Dayan, "The Peculiar Public of Television," *Media, Culture and Society* 23 (2001): 743–65.

8. Martin E. Marty and R. S. Appleby, *The Fundamentalism Project*, Vols. 1–5 (Chicago: University of Chicago Press, 1993–2004).

9. Jim Wallis, *God's Politics: Why The Right Gets It Wrong and the Left Doesn't Get It: A New Vision for Faith and Politics in America* (San Francisco: HarperSanFrancisco, 2005), p. 346.

10. This is in and of itself rather interesting given that Wallis appears regularly on talk radio, edits a magazine (*Sojourners*), and wrote a New York Times bestseller.

11. See Heather Hendershot, *Shaking the World for Jesus: Media and Conservative Evangelical Culture* (Chicago: University of Chicago Press, 2004).

12. See, for example, B. Alexander's study entitled, *Televangelism Reconsidered: Ritual in the Search for Human Community* (Atlanta, GA: Scholars Press, 1994), which discusses the ritual aspects of the televangelist audience or Janice Peck's *The Gods of Televangelism: The Crisis of Meaning and the Appeal of Religious Television* (Cresskill, NJ: Hampton Press, 1993), which focuses on the rhetoric of religious television, in both cases the medium is largely unquestioned. At the other end of the spectrum, Steve Bruce in his study *Pay TV* (London: Routledge, 1990) and Frankl in her book *Televangelism* (Carbondale, IL: Southern Illinois University Press, 1987) both make the common assumption that "Television is not a neutral medium" (p. 145) and from that point suggest that the conservative Protestant message because of its simplicity (in contrast, of course, to the "complexity" of the liberal Protestant message) is better suited to the television and the mass media in general. Frankl and Bruce rely upon a variation of medium theory or what Claude Fischer calls "impact analysis" or "soft" forms of technological determinism (*America Calling: A Social History of the Telephone to 1940* [Berkeley, CA: University of California Press, 1992], p. 12).

13. See Claude S. Fischer, *America Calling: A Social History of the Telephone to 1940* (Berkeley, CA: University of California Press, 1992); Carolyn Marvin, *When Old Technologies Were New: Thinking about Electric Communication in the Late Nineteenth Century* (New York: Oxford University Press, 1988); and Raymond Williams, *Television: Technology and Cultural Form* (Hanover: Wesleyan University Press, [1974] 1992) for examples of this dialogical approach.

14. Fischer, *America Calling*, p. 5.

15. Raymond Williams, *Towards 2000* (New York: Penguin, 1985), p. 146.

16. Lynn Spigel, *Make Room for TV: Television and the Family Ideal in Postwar America* (Chicago: University of Chicago Press, 1992).

17. See, for example, Peter G. Horsfeld's pioneering book *Religious Television: The American Experience* (New York: Longman Inc., 1984).

Chapter 1   American Protestantism and the Television: A Paradoxical Relationship

1. On contemporary evangelicals' approaches to communication see Quentin J. Schultze, "Evangelicals' Uneasy Alliance with the Media," in *Religion and Mass Media: Audiences and Adaptations*, edited by Daniel A. Stout and Judith M. Buddenbaum (Thousand Oaks, CA: Sage, 1996), pp. 63–64. Despite the fact that mainline Protestants are less "evangelistic" they also approached and conceived of new media (like the television and radio) as tools for evangelism.
2. Martin E. Marty, "Protestantism and Capitalism: Print Culture and Individualism," in *Communication and Change in American Religious History*, edited by Leonard I. Sweet (Grand Rapids, MI: Eerdmans, 1993), p. 100.
3. Daniel J. Czitrom, *Media and the American Mind: From Morse to McLuhan* (Chapel Hill, NC: University of North Carolina, 1982), p. 6.
4. Carolyn Marvin, *When Old Technologies Were New: Thinking about Electric Communication in the Late Nineteenth Century* (New York: Oxford University Press, 1988), p. 125.
5. Marvin, *When Old Technologies Were New*, p. 124.
6. James W. Carey, *Communication as Culture: Essays on Media and Society* (Boston: Unwin Hyman, 1988), p. 15.
7. Ibid.
8. See D. Dayan and E. Katz, *Media Events: The Live Broadcasting of History* (Cambridge, MA: Harvard University Press, 1992) and E. Rothenbuhler, *Ritual Communication: From Everyday Conversation to Mediated Ceremony* (Thousand Oaks, CA: Sage, 1998).
9. See B. Alexander, *Televangelism Reconsidered: Ritual in the Search for Human Community* (Atlanta, GA: Scholars Press, 1994); Stewart M. Hoover, *Mass Media Religion: The Social Sources of the Electronic Church* (Newbury Park, CA: Sage Publications, 1988); and Janice Peck, *Gods of Televangelism: The Crisis of Meaning and the Appeal of Religious Television* (Cresskill, NJ: Hampton Press, 1993).
10. E. Katz described Israeli television viewing as equivalent to the tribal campfire.
11. Elizabeth L. Eisenstein, *The Printing Press as an Agent of Change: Communications and Cultural Transformations in Early-Modern Europe, Vol. 1* (London: Cambridge University Press, 1979), p. 310.
12. See Robert W. Scribner, "Oral Culture and the Diffusion of Reformation Ideas," *History of European Ideas* 5 (1984): 237–256 for a critique of Eisenstein's thesis and also S. Ozment's *Protestants: The Birth of a Revolution* (New York: Doubleday, 1991), p. 46.
13. Ozment, *Protestants*, p. 46.

14. Ibid., p. 66.
15. Eisenstein, *Printing Press as an Agent of Change*, p. 440.
16. Ibid., p. 78.
17. Mark Edwards, *Printing, Propaganda, and Martin Luther* (Berkeley, CA: University of California Press, 1994), p. 7.
18. Marty, "Protestantism and Capitalism," p. 93.
19. Ibid., p. 102.
20. Harry S. Stout, "Religion, Communications, and the Career of George Whitefield," in *Communication and Change in American Religious History*, edited by Leonard Sweet, (MI: Eerdmans, 1993), pp. 122–124.
21. Lambert Frank, *"Pedlar in Divinity": George Whitefield and the Transatlantic Revivals, 1737–1770* (Princeton, NJ: Princeton University Press, 1994), pp. 64–94.
22. Ibid., p. 44.
23. Ibid., pp. 226–231.
24. Stout, "Religion, Communications, and the Career of George Whitefield," pp. 122–124.
25. Lambert, *Pedlar in Divinity*, p. 94.
26. Hatch, *Democratization of American Christianity*, pp. 125–127.
27. Ibid., p. 127.
28. William McLoughlin, *Revivals, Awakenings, and Reform* (Chicago: University of Chicago Press, 1978).
29. On televangelism see Bobby Chris Alexander, *Televangelism Reconsidered: A Ritual in the Search for Human Community* (Atlanta: Scholars Press, 1994); Steve Bruce, *Pray TV: Televangelism in America* (London: Routledge, 1990); Razelle Frankl, *Televangelism: The Marketing of Popular Religion* (Carbondale, IL: Southern Illinois University Press, 1987); Jeffrey Hadden and A. Shupe, *Televangelism: Power and Politics on God's Frontier* (New York: Henry Holt and Co., 1988); Hoover, *Mass Media Religion*; Peter G. Horsfield, *Religious Television: The American Experience* (New York: Longman Inc., 1984); Peck, *The Gods of Televangelism*; Quentin J. Schultze, *Televangelism and American Culture: The Business of Popular Culture* (Grand Rapids, MI: Baker Book House, 1991).
30. Horsfield, *Religious Television*, pp. 15–23.
31. For a summary of the debate over audience size see Stewart Hoover, *Mass Media Religion: The Social Sources of the Electronic Church* (Newbury Park, CA: Sage, 1988), pp. 63–72 and Stewart Hoover, "The Religious Television Audience: A Matter of Significance or Size?" *Review of Religious Research* 29 (December 1987): 135–151. While the National Religious Broadcasters estimated the audience at 100 million, critics claimed the true number was closer to 10 or 20 million viewers.
32. In the earliest research of religion and television conducted in 1952 (published in 1955), Parker et al. suggested that the television was not such a great missionary to the undifferentiated mass audience. (Parker et al., *The Television-Radio Audience and Religion* [New York: Harper Brothers, 1955], pp. 401–414).

33. For Steve Bruce this is the main effect of televangelism (*Pray TV*, pp. 237–240). See also Alexander, *Televangelism Reconsidered*, p. 162, and Hoover, *Mass Media Religion*, pp. 222–223. Estimates of the evangelical population in America vary widely from 20 to 25% of the general population.

34. See Robert Wuthnow, "Religion and Television: The Public and the Private," in *American Evangelicals and the Mass Media*, edited by Quentin J. Schultze (Grand Rapids, MI: Zondervan, 1990), pp. 199–213 and Robert Wuthnow, "The Social Significance of Religious Television," *Review of Religious Research* 29 (December 1987): 97–210.

35. Wuthnow, "Religion and Television," p. 211.

36. Stewart Hoover suggests that the cultural meaning of the electronic church has three levels: individual, community and social ("The Meaning of Religious Television: The 700 Club in the Lives of its Viewers," in *American Evangelicals and the Mass Media*, edited by Quentin J. Schultze, [Grand Rapids, MI: Zondervan, 1990], p. 245).

37. Bobby Alexander's study emphasizes how the programs perform ritual functions for their viewers. Bobby Alexander, *Televangelism Reconsidered: Ritual in Search for Human Community* (Atlanta, Georgia: Scholar Press, 1984). Janice Peck looks at the different ways in which Jimmy Swaggart and Pat Robertson's programs appeal to "viewers' collective memories of the past and their visions of the present and future." Janice Peck, *The Gods of Televangelism: The Crisis of Meaning and the Appeal of Religious Television* (Cresskill, NJ: Hampton Press, 1993), p. 23.

38. Quentin J. Schultze, "Keeping the Faith: American Evangelicals and the Media," in *American Evangelicals and the Mass Media*, edited by Quentin J. Schultze (Grand Rapids, MI: Zondervan, 1990), p. 41.

39. Peck, *Gods of Televangelism*, p. 19. Peck begins with the assumption that the faith crisis wrought by modernity has produced three different rhetorical strategies: adaptation and accommodation, rejection, and somewhere in-between. While there may be some truth to such a typology, one of its problems is that it is ahistorical. Even fundamentalist rhetoric that seems uncompromisingly to reject modernity has changed over time. Likewise to claim that liberal Protestants completely embraced modernity and adapted their beliefs completely seems more like evangelical polemic than history. Both evangelical and liberal Protestants have *selectively* adapted to the constraints of modernity. Indeed, in many ways one could argue that liberal Protestants while adapting intellectually to many of the challenges of modernity have been more successful than evangelical Protestants in resisting the effects of consumer society, the very development that Peck finds so problematic (see pp. 240–241).

40. Peck, *Gods of Televangelism*, pp. 228–231.

41. On mainline religious broadcasting see John W. Bachman, *The Church in the World of Radio-Television* (New York: National Board of Young Men's Christian Associations, 1960); J. Harold Ellens, *Models of Religious Broadcasting* (Grand Rapids, MI: William B. Eerdmans, 1974); William F. Fore, *Television and Religion: The Shaping of Faith, Values, and Culture* (Minneapolis: Augsburg, 1987); Stewart M. Hoover, *The Electronic Giant: A*

Critique of the Telecommunications Revolution from a Christian Perspective (Elgin, IL: Brethren Press, 1982); Martin E. Marty, *The Improper Opinion: Mass Media and the Christian Faith* (Philadelphia: Westminster Press, 1961); Everett C. Parker, *Religious Television* (New York: Harper and Brothers, 1961); Parker et al., *Television-Radio Audience*.

42. Ann Swidler, "Culture in Action: Symbols and Strategies," *American Sociological Review* 51 (April 1986): 280.

43. Horsfield notes two other FCC decisions that led to the rise of televangelism: the "Fairness Doctrine," and the exemption from fundraising regulations (Horsfield, *Religious Television*, pp. 13–14). See also Hoover, *Mass Media Religion*, pp. 54–55.

44. P. A. Crow, "National Council of Churches of Christ in the USA," in *The Dictionary of Christianity in America*, edited by Daniel G. Reid, Robert D. Linder, Bruce L. Shelley, and Harry S. Stout (Downers Grove, IL: InterVarsity Press, 1990), p. 799. For a comparison, the contemporary evangelical population is estimated at anywhere from 20 to 50 million. In addition, the mainline churches stood firmly in middle class America. While mainline Protestant leaders were quick to point to the lack of finances for television, the real question is why they were unwilling or unable to call upon their communities for finances.

45. See Horsfield, *Religious Television*, pp. 52–75; Fore, *Television and Religion*; and Marty, *The Improper Opinion*.

46. Fore claims the mass media offer a worldview that contradicts Christianity (*Television and Religion*, pp. 26–38).

47. Fore, *Television and Religion*; William Fore, *Mythmakers: Gospel, Culture and Media* (New York: Friendship Press, 1990); Horsfield, *Religious Television*; Marty, *The Improper Opinion*.

48. For an overview of medium theory see Joshua Meyrowitz, "Medium Theory," in *Communication Theory Today*, edited by David Crowley and David Mitchell (Stanford, CA: Stanford University Press, 1994), pp. 50–77. See also Czitrom, *Media and the American Mind*. For an example of this kind of critique, see Neil Postman, *Amusing Ourselves to Death: Public Discourse in the Age of Show Business* (New York: Penguin Books, 1985), particularly pp. 114–124. Hoover (basing his observation on a comment by George Marsden, a self-defined Calvinist historian) likewise claims this kind of relationship: "Simplicity in theology and social critique always has been a basic tenet of fundamentalism as it appeals to those who are troubled by the intellectualism of modernity. Popular communication styles and approaches have always favored such simplicity" (*Mass Media Religion*, p. 46).

49. See Horsfield, *Religious Television*, pp. 63–64. Unsurprisingly, supporters of televangelism often resort to a combination of medium theory and theology in order to legitimate their approach. They claim (somewhat tautologically) that their success is God-given and it is no mistake that the conservative form of Christianity has been so favored or that the television (as God's miracle tool/gift) would favor such success.

50. As Meyrowitz (himself a medium theorist) notes: "Medium theory has also tended to ignore vast *cultural differences* that mute and alter the development,

use and perception of various communication technologies." (Joshua Meyrowitz, "Medium Theory," in *Communication Theory Today*, edited by David Crowley and David Mitchell [Stanford, CA: Stanford University Press, 1994], p. 71, emphasis mine).

51. On the distinction between modernism and liberalism in American Protestantism, see William R. Hutchison, *The Modernist Impulse in American Protestantism* (Cambridge, MA: Harvard University Press, 1976), pp. 1–11. On cultural adaptation see also Laurence Moore, *Selling God*.

52. Hutchison, *The Modernist Impulse*, p. 90. Newman Smyth, for example, one of the new theologians, thought that hostility to the process of adaptation (to science and culture) was counterproductive.

53. Swidler, "Culture in Action," p. 277.

54. As Swidler suggests: "culture appears to shape action only in that the cultural repertoire limits the available strategies of action" ("Culture in Action," p. 284).

55. Raymond Williams, *Television: Technology and Cultural Form* (Hanover, NH: Wesleyan University Press, 1992 [orig. 1974]), p. 17.

56. Lynn Spigel, *Make Room for TV: Television and the Family Ideal in Postwar America* (Chicago: University of Chicago Press, 1992); Cecilia Tichi, *Electronic Hearth: Creating an American Television Culture* (New York: Oxford University Press, 1991).

57. Spigel, *Make Room for TV*, pp. 11–35.

58. Tichi, *Electronic Hearth*, p. 7.

59. In other words, I'm not using "reception" to describe a particular audience's reaction to a particular program, but rather in a much more general way.

60. By viewing televangelism as one possible response we steer clear of arguments that imply the inevitability of such an outcome.

61. Lawrence Levine, *Highbrow/Lowbrow: The Emergence of Cultural Hierarchy in America* (Cambridge: Harvard University Press, 1988); Paul DiMaggio, "Cultural Boundaries and Structural Change: The Extension of the High Culture Model to Theater, Opera, and the Dance, 1900–1940," in *Cultivating Differences: Symbolic Boundaries and the Making of Inequality*, edited by Michele Lamont and Marcel Fournier (Chicago: University of Chicago Press, 1992), pp. 21–57.

62. Levine, *Highbrow/Lowbrow*, p. 86; DiMaggio, "Cultural Boundaries and Structural Change," p. 34.

63. Levine, *Highbrow/Lowbrow*, pp. 85–168.

64. On the visual culture of Protestantism despite its self-proclaimed iconoclasm see David Morgan, "Introduction," and "The Visual Culture of American Protestantism," in *Icons of American Protestantism: The Art of Warner Sallman*, edited by David Morgan (New Haven, CT: Yale University Press, 1996), pp. 1–23; 26–60.

65. Levine, *Highbrow/Lowbrow*, p. 150; Moore, *Selling God*, p. 109.

66. Levine, *Highbrow/Lowbrow*, p. 155. Levine quotes a trustee of the Philadelphia Art Museum who suggested that particularly for foreign-born visitors the museum took the place of a Cathedral.

67. Moore, *Selling God*, pp. 12–39, 90–117.

68. For secondary accounts of this debate see James Hudnut-Beumler, *Looking for God in the Suburbs: The Religion of the American Dream and its Critics 1945–1965* (New Brunswick, NJ: Rutgers University Press, 1994), pp. 102–106 and Andrew Ross, *No Respect: Intellectuals and Popular Culture* (New York: Routledge, 1989), pp. 23–64.

69. Pierre Bourdieu, *Distinction: A Social Critique of the Judgment of Taste* (Cambridge: Harvard University Press, 1984). My understanding of Bourdieu and the applicability of his concepts in the American context has been shaped by Michele Lamont and Annette Lareau, "Cultural Capital: Allusions, Gaps and Glissandos in Recent Theoretical Developments," *Sociological Theory* 6 (Fall 1988): 153–168.

70. As the quiz show scandal is represented in the film *Quiz Show*, Van Doren's parents notably do not have a television to watch their son until he gives them one.

71. Parker et al., *Television-Radio Audience*, pp. 163–165.

72. On fundamentalist attitudes toward science in this era see James Gilbert, *Redeeming Culture: American Religion in an Age of Science* (Chicago: University of Chicago Press, 1997), pp. 121–169.

73. On the history of the discipline in America see Everette E. Dennis and Ellen Wartella, eds. *American Communication Research: The Remembered* History (Mahwah, NJ: Lawrence Erlbaum, 1996); and Everett M. Rogers, *A History of Communication Study: A Biographical Approach* (New York: Free Press, 1994). See pp. 11–15 on communication research in D.C. during the war years.

74. Columbia's Bureau of Applied Social Research was one of the first institutions to do empirical research on mass communications (See E. Katz, "Diffusion Research," in *American Communication Research* , pp. 61–70).

75. Rogers, *History of Communication Study*, p. 12.

76. For an important discussion on the development of the study of communications in the United States, and in particular the longevity of the hypodermic needle metaphor, see Ellen Wartella, "The History Reconsidered," in *American Communication Research: The Remembered History*, edited by Dennis and Wartella (Mahwah, NJ: Lawrence Erlbaum, 1996), pp. 169–179.

77. Wartella, "History Reconsidered," p. 177.

78. Martin E. Marty, *Modern American Religion, Vol. 1: The Irony of it All* (Chicago: University of Chicago Press, 1986), pp. 5–8; Robert Wuthnow, *Producing the Sacred: An Essay on Public Religion* (Urbana, IL: University of Illinois Press, 1994), pp. 27–29.

79. Wiebe J. Bijker, *Of Bicycles, Bakelites, and Bulbs: Toward a Theory of Sociotechnical Change* (Cambridge, MA: MIT Press, 1997).

80. R. Silverstone, E. Hirsch, and D. Morley, "Information and Communication Technologies and the Moral Economy of the Household," in *Consuming Technologies: Media and Information in Domestic Spaces*, edited by R. Silverstone and E. Hirsch (London: Routledge, 1992), pp. 15–31.

81. On nonusers see the collection edited by Nelly Oudshoorn and Trevor Pinch, *How Users Matter: The Co-Construction of Users and Technology* (Cambridge, MA: MIT Press, 2005), particularly pp. 51–102. See also, Diane Zimmerman

Umble, *Holding the Line: The Telephone in Old Order Mennonite and Amish Life* (John Hopkins University Press, 1996); and Rivka Ribak and Michele Rosenthal, "From the Field Phone to the Mobile Phone: A Cultural Biography of the Telephone in Kibbutz Y," *New Media and Society* 8(4): 553–574.

82. R. Kline, "Resisting Consumer Technology in Rural America: The Telephone and Electrification," in *How Users Matter*, edited by Oudshoorn and Pinch (Cambridge, MA: MIT Press, 2005), p. 52.

83. S. Wyatt, "Non-Users Also Matter: The Construction of Users and Non-Users of the Internet," in *How Users Matter*, edited by Oudshoorn and Pinch (Cambridge, MA: MIT Press, 2005), pp. 67–68.

84. I am grateful to Rivka Ribak for her idea of a dialogical relationship between users and technologies.

Chapter 2   "Turn It Off!": The Liberal Protestant Critique of Television

1. "What a Twisted Scale of Values!" *The Christian Century* 77 (May 25, 1960): 630.

2. The title "Turn it Off!" comes from "Yawn and Flip the TV Knob," *The Christian Century* 75 (October 22, 1958): 1198.

3. The television received far less page space (despite the fact that it was a new medium) than book reviews, and film reviews. In general cultural matters came second to church politics, and politics in general.

4. R. Laurence Moore, *Selling God: American Religion in the Marketplace of Culture* (New York: Oxford, 1994), p. 236.

5. For Moore's account of liberal Protestant responses to the moving pictures see *Selling God*, pp. 159; 222–230; on the radio see pp. 232–235, and on the television see pp. 244–254.

6. On liberal Protestant responses to mass culture in the 1950s see Sally M. Promey, "Interchangeable Art: Warner Sallman and the Critics of Mass Culture," in *Icons of American Protestantism: The Art of Warner Sallman*, edited by David Morgan (New Haven: Yale University Press, 1996), pp. 167–173.

7. Moore, *Selling God*, p. 236. Leonard Sweet has suggested that the decline of liberal Protestantism was largely due to "theological dry rot." Leonard Sweet, "The 1960s: The Crises of Liberal Christianity," in *The Shaping of Contemporary Evangelicalism*, edited by George Marsden (Grand Rapids, MI: Eerdmans, 1984), p. 32.

8. Bruce briefly (and perhaps a bit too simply) defines the theological and sociological differences between liberal and conservative Protestants, which would explain their different approaches to the media (pp. 44–48).

9. Charles Clayton Morrison, "Can Protestantism Win America," *The Christian Century* 63 (April 3, 1946): 425–427.

10. Charles H. Lippy, ed., *Religious Periodicals of the United States: Academic and Scholarly Journals* (Westport, CT: Greenwood Press, 1986), p. 112; Martin E. Marty, "Peace and Pluralism: The Century 1946–1952," *The Christian Century* 101 (October 24, 1984): 979–983; Mark G. Toulouse, "*The Christian Century* and American Public Life," in *New Dimensions in American Religious History*, edited by Jay P. Dolan and James P. Wind (Grand Rapids, MI: Eerdmans, 1993), pp. 44–82.

11. Lippy, ed., *Religious Periodicals of the United States*, p. 112; Marty, "Peace and Pluralism," pp. 979–983; Toulouse, "*The Christian Century* and American Public Life," pp. 44–82.

12. Lynn Spigel, *Make Room for TV: Television and the Family Ideal in Postwar America* (Chicago: University of Chicago Press, 1992), p. 32.

13. For an example of the debate on the revival in the 1950s see Seymour M. Lipset, "Religion in America: What Religious Revival?" in *Review of Religious Research* 1(Summer 1959): 17–24 and Will Herberg's response, "There is a Religious Revival!" *Review of Religious Research* 1(Fall 1959): 45–51. On religion in the 1950s see James Hudnut-Beumler, *Looking for God in the Suburbs: The Religion of the American Dream and Its Critics, 1945–1965* (New Brunswick, NJ: Rutgers University Press, 1994); Martin E. Marty, *Under God, Indivisible 1941–1960*, Modern American Religion, Vol. 3 (Chicago: University of Chicago Press, 1996); Robert Wuthnow, *The Restructuring of American Religion* (Princeton: Princeton University Press, 1988).

14. Harold Fey, "Can Catholicism Win America?" *The Christian Century* 61 (November 29, 1944): 1378–1380; Charles Clayton Morrison, "Can Protestantism Win America," *The Christian Century* 63 (April 3, 1946): 425–427. See Marty, *Under God*, pp. 144–149 for an account of the significance of this series.

15. Charles Clayton Morrison, "Protestantism and Commercialized Entertainment," *The Christian Century* 63 (May 1, 1946): 553.

16. Ibid.

17. Ibid., pp. 554–555.

18. Ibid., p. 554. On the development of aesthetic theory in *The Christian Century* see Linda-Marie Delloff, "'God as Artist': Aesthetic Theory," in *The Christian Century 1908–1955* (Ph.D. diss., University of Chicago, 1985).

19. Morrison, "Protestantism and Commercialized Entertainment," p. 556.

20. Moore, *Selling God*, p. 97.

21. Ibid., p. 98.

22. Ibid., p. 100.

23. Herbert J. Gans has argued that intellectuals are more likely to criticize popular culture when their own status and power is in question or in decline (*Popular Culture and High Culture: An Analysis and Evaluation of Taste* [New York: Basic Books, 1974], p. 7).

24. For an overview of secular critiques of mass culture in the 1950s see Andrew Ross, *No Respect: Intellectuals and Popular Culture* (New York: Routledge, 1989), pp. 42–64. On high art as Protestant art see, for example, Paul Tillich's essay on "Protestantism and Artistic Style," where he calls Picasso's *Guernica* "a great Protestant painting" (*Theology of Culture*, p. 68). On liberal Protestant

responses to mass culture see Promey, "Interchangeable Art," in *Icons*, pp. 167–173. Notably, Morrison did not embrace all high art as sacred art, but remained committed to realistic and therefore didactic art. On the sacralization of high culture see Laurence W. Levine, *Highbrow/Lowbrow: The Emergence of Cultural Hierarchy in America* (Cambridge, MA: Harvard, 1988).

25. Paul Tillich, *A Theology of Culture* (Oxford University Press, 1959); H. Richard Niebuhr, *Christ and Culture* (New York: Harper and Row, 1951).

26. "TV—a Giant for Good or Ill" *The Christian Century* 72 (February 2, 1955): 131.

27. Carolyn Marvin, *When Old Technologies Were New: Thinking about Electric Communication in the Late Nineteenth Century* (New York: Oxford University Press, 1988), pp. 124–128.

28. Susan Douglas, *Inventing American Broadcasting: 1899–1922* (Baltimore: John Hopkins University Press, 1987), pp. 311–312; Moore, *Selling God*, p. 232.

29. This assumption of audience passivity is shared by secular mass culture critics of this era as well. On the educational model of religious broadcasting see J. Harold Ellens, *Models of Religious Broadcasting* (Grand Rapids, MI: Eerdmans, 1974), pp. 95–123.

30. A. Gordon Nasby, "Television and the Church," *The Christian Century* 66 (February 2, 1949): 143.

31. J. Edward Carothers, "A Television Ministry," *The Christian Century* 66 (May 11, 1949): 591–592.

32. A. Gordon Nasby, "Television and the Church," *The Christian Century* 66 (February 2, 1949): 142–143.

33. Alton M. Motter, "Back to the Kefauver TV Show," *The Christian Century* 68 (May 9, 1951): 584.

34. Ibid.

35. On the evolution of the domestic hearth into the electronic hearth see Cecilia Tichi, *The Electronic Hearth: Creating an American Television Culture* (New York: Oxford University Press, 1991), pp. 42–61. Tichi convincingly argues that the preexistent image of the hearth was used by television networks, and advertisers to sell television to the American public. Although she traces the historical origins of the hearth, unfortunately Tichi ignores their religious dimension. Lynn Spigel in her book, *Make Room for TV: The Television and the Family Ideal in Postwar America* (Chicago: University of Chicago Press, 1992) argues that television transformed Victorian domestic ideology, but ignores domestic religion. On Victorian domestic religion see Colleen McDannell, *The Christian Home in Victorian America, 1840–1900* (Bloomington: Indiana University Press, 1986), pp. 77–107. On the ritual use of television today see Gregor Goethals, *The TV Ritual: Worship at the Video Altar* (Boston: Beacon Press, 1981).

36. McDannell, *The Christian Home*, p. 106.

37. Ibid., p. 79.

38. "Will Television Depend on Advertising?" *The Christian Century* 61 (October 25, 1944): 1221, emphasis mine.

39. See Moore on the gradual erosion of liberal Protestant prejudice against painting over the nineteenth century, p. 109. On the visual culture of Protestantism see David Morgan, "Introduction," in *Icons of American Protestantism: The Art*

of Warner Sallman, edited by David Morgan (New Haven: Yale University Press, 1996), pp. 4–18. On the liberal rejection of mass cultural images see. Promey, "Interchangeable Art," in *Icons*, pp. 150–180.

40. "Can't it Be Applied to Television?" *The Christian Century* 61 (November 1, 1944): 1245–1246; "One More Argument for Subscription TV." *The Christian Century* 72 (May 18, 1955): 589. In a similar vein TV manufacturers' advertisements were condemned for their explicit manipulation of children, see "TV Manufacturers Stir Up a Storm," *The Christian Century* 67 (December 6, 1950): 1444.

41. "TV Opportunity Is Fleeing." *The Christian Century* 67 (November 29, 1950): 1414.

42. A. Gordon Nasby, "Television and the Church," *The Christian Century* 66 (February 2, 1949): 142; Charles M. Crowe, "Television Needs Religion," *The Christian Century* 66 (August 10, 1949): 938; "TV Opportunity Is Fleeing," *The Christian Century* ; "Insist Religion Merit Public Service Time," *The Christian Century* 75 (March 19, 1958): 333–334.

43. On the sustained-time system see William Fore, *Television and Religion: The Shaping of Faith, Values and Culture* (Minneapolis: Augsburg, 1987), pp. 77–81; and Dennis Voskuil, "The Power of the Air: Evangelicals and the Rise of Religious Broadcasting," in *American Evangelicals and the Mass Media*, edited by Quentin J. Schultze (Grand Rapids, MI: Academie Books), pp. 83–84.

44. "Missouri Lutherans Produce TV Series," *The Christian Century* 69 (August 13, 1952): 916.

45. "How Effective Are the Mass Media?" *The Christian Century* 73 (August 29, 1956): 988.

46. "TV—a Giant for Good or Ill" *The Christian Century* 72 (February 2, 1955): 131; "Is Television Making a Nation of Hypochondriacs?" 72 (October 19, 1955): 1198; "Is Television a Fiasco?" *The Christian Century* 73 (October 17, 1956): 1188; "Television Arrives in Education," *The Christian Century* 75 (October 1, 1958): 1102; "Networks Miss a Good Bet," *The Christian Century* 75 (March 12, 1958): 301.

47. "Oklahoma Faith-Healer Draws a Following" *The Christian Century* 71 (June 29, 1955): 750. See also "TV—A Giant for Good or Ill," *The Christian Century* 72 (February 2, 1955); "What about Oral Roberts?" *The Christian Century* 73 (September 5, 1956): 1018–1021.

48. "Graham Clarifies the Issue," *The Christian Century* 75 (July 30, 1958): 870.

49. "What about Religious Doctrine on Television?" *The Christian Century* 68 (February 14, 1951): 196. See also guest writer A. Gordon Nasby, "Television and the Church," *The Christian Century* 66 (February 2, 1949): 143.

50. "What about Religious Doctrine on Television?" *The Christian Century* 68 (February 14, 1951): 196. Part of the agreement of sustained-time religious programming included the avoidance of creedal specificity. See Voskuil, "The Power of the Air," pp. 83–84.

51. "Bishop Cloys as Critic," *The Christian Century* 73 (December 5, 1956): 1413.

52. Moore, *Selling God*, p. 112. Catholic (Irish, German and Italian) immigrants were held responsible for the rise of permissiveness, while the Catholic elite was

held responsible for the rise of repressiveness. On *The Christian Century's* attitude to the Roman Catholic role in the censorship of moving pictures, see Moore, *Selling God*, pp. 227–231.

53. See, for example, during the years 1943 to 1946: "Notre Dame Would Censor Professor's Speeches," *The Christian Century* 60 (October 6, 1943): 1325–1326; "Radio Used to Attack Protestant Missions," *The Christian Century* 60 (October 6, 1943): 1123; "Where Can the Pope Go?" *The Christian Century* 60 (December 22, 1943): 1496–1497; Harry F. Ward, "Vatican Fascism," 61 (June 7, 1944): 693–695; "Public Money Diverted for Catholic Schools," *The Christian Century* 62 (January 24, 1945): 101; "Oppose Conscription on Moral Grounds," *The Christian Century* 62 (January 31, 1945): 131–132; "How the Catholic Church Supervised Movies," *The Christian Century* 62 (February 7, 1945);"Protestantism and Tolerance," *The Christian Century* 62 (February 14, 1945): 198–200; "Roman Catholic Church Never Sells Spiritual Blessings," *The Christian Century* 62 (March 7, 1945): 292; Charles M. Crowe, "So This is Good Will!" *The Christian Century* 62 (April 4, 1945): 427–429; Ralph W. Sockman, "Catholics and Protestants," *The Christian Century* 63 (May 15, 1945): 545–547; "Can the Home be Saved," *The Christian Century* 62 (February 21, 1945): 231; "Prelate Sees Catholicism Winning Japan," *The Christian Century* 63 (August 21, 1946): 1004–1005; "Denies Civil Power Over Marriage," *The Christian Century* 63 (July 17, 1946): 883–884; "Roman Catholicism and Religious Liberty," *The Christian Century* 63 (September 4, 1946): 1052; "Protestantism Coming Alive," *The Christian Century* 63 (October 23, 1946): 1267. For a more charitable view of *The Christian Century's* anti-Catholicism see Marc Tolouse, "*The Christian Century* and American Public Life," in *New Dimensions in American Religious History*, edited by Jay P. Dolan and James P. Wind, pp. 61–65. Grand Rapids, MI: Eerdmans, 1993.

54. "Censorship in Chicago," *The Christian Century* 74 (January 23, 1957): 102.

55. Ibid., p. 102.

56. Robert E. A. Lee, "Censorship: A Case History," *The Christian Century* 74 (February 6, 1957): 163.

57. "Easter on TV," *The Christian Century* 70 (March 25, 1953): 339. On critiques of the commercialization of Easter see Leigh Schmidt, *Consumer Rites: The Buying and Selling of American Holidays* (Princeton University Press, 1995): 234–243. According to Schmidt, the "televised antics" in 1952 was enough to put in motion reform efforts to rid Easter of commercialization (p. 239).

58. Schmidt, *Consumer Rites*, p. 239.

59. "All Aboard for Rainbow Land!" 72 (September 14, 1955): 1045.

60. "Give-Away Shows Raise Ethical Questions," 71 (February 24, 1954): 227.

61. "Turn the Dial," *The Christian Century* 75 (September 10, 1958): 1011.

62. "CBS Ousts Source of TV Corruption," *The Christian Century*, 76 (October 28, 1959): 1238.

63. Martin E. Marty, "Second-Chance Protestantism," *The Christian Century* 78 (June 21, 1961): 770–772.

64. "Yawn and Flip the TV Knob," *The Christian Century* 75 (October 22, 1958): 1198. Violence continued to be a problem for the editors even after 1960. See,

for example, "Murder by TV," *The Christian Century* 79 (April 18, 1962): 482, on the televised death of world champion boxer welterweight, Benny Paret.

65. "Paar Show a Measure of American Culture," *The Christian Century* 76 (September 23, 1959): 1076–1077.

66. "Yawn and Flip the TV Knob," *The Christian Century* 75 (October 22, 1958): 1198.

67. Ibid.

68. On alcohol advertising see, "Ban Liquor Drinking on Michigan TV?" *The Christian Century* 71 (March 24, 1954): 356; "Beer Consumption Declining," *The Christian Century* 72 (August 24, 1955): 964–965.

69. "What Should Be Done about TV Programs?" *The Christian Century* 69 (May 28, 1952): 637.

70. "Protestantism and Tolerance," *The Christian Century* 62 (February 14, 1945): 198.

71. On a television code see "How Far from Code to Control?" *The Christian Century* 73 (June 13, 1956): 716. On the need for network self-censorship see "Responsible Broadcasting in Racial Disturbances," *The Christian Century* 72 (August 17, 1955): 941. On the Catholic use of censorship see "TV Station Yields to Catholic Pressure," *The Christian Century* 74 (January 2, 1957): 4; "Censorship in Chicago," *The Christian Century* 74 (January 23, 1957): 102–103; Robert E. A. Lee, "Censorship: A Case History," *The Christian Century* 74 (February 6, 1957): 163–165; "Demand License Hearing on Chicago TV Station," 74 (February 20, 1957): 220; "Luther Film Makes Belated Television Debut," *The Christian Century* 74 (March 13, 1957): 317; "TV Censorship Case Enters New Phase," *The Christian Century* 74 (March 27, 1957): 379–380.

72. Swidler, "Culture in Action," p. 278.

73. McDannell argues that domestic piety was the private side of the "Righteous Empire" (*The Christian Home*, p. 49).

74. Tolouse, "*The Christian Century* and American Public Life."

75. See Martin E. Marty, *Under God Indivisible, 1941–1960: Modern American Religion, Vol. 3* (Chicago: University of Chicago Press, 1996), pp. 5–6, on the lack of "public women" in the mid-century.

76. Andreas Huyssen has argued that mass culture was gendered as feminine and inferior in the late nineteenth century. See Andreas Huyssen, "Mass Culture as Woman: Modernism's Other," in *After the Great Divide: Modernism, Mass Culture, Postmodernism* (Bloomington: Indiana University Press, 1986), pp. 44–62. On the gendering of the television audience see Spigel, *Make Room for TV*, particularly "Women's Work," pp. 73–98.

77. On the civil rights movement and the National Council of Churches see James Findlay, *Church People in the Struggle: The National Council of Churches and the Black Freedom Movement, 1950–1970* (New York: Oxford University Press, 1993).

78. Spigel, *Make Room for TV*.

79. Quoted in Tolouse, "*The Christian Century* and American Public Life,*"* p. 77 (original source): "Good-by to Gothic," *The Christian Century* (January 1, 1969): 4.

Chapter 3   Mainline Religious Broadcasting: A Failure?

1. Carolyn Marvin, *When Old Technologies Were New: Thinking about Electric Communication in the Late Nineteenth Century* (New York: Oxford University Press, 1988), p. 5.
2. On mainline religious broadcasting in the radio era see Ralph M. Jennings, "Policies and Practices of Selected National Religious Bodies as Related to Broadcasting in the Public Interest, 1920–1950," (Ph.D., New York University, 1968), pp. 10–263, and Harold Ellens, *Models of Religious Broadcasting* (Grand Rapids, MI: Eerdmans, 1974). For an account of evangelical broadcasting and radio see Tona J. Hangen, *Redeeming the Dial: Radio, Religion and Popular Culture in America* (Chapel Hill, NC: University of North Carolina Press, 2002).
3. The blandness of liberal Protestant programming would be the object of criticism by both the neo-orthodox or Christian realist wing of the mainstream (see Martin E. Marty, *The Improper Opinion: Mass Media and the Christian Faith* [Philadelphia: Westminster Press, 1961]) as well as by the neoevangelicals.
4. R. Laurence Moore, "Secularization: Religion and the Social Sciences," in *Between the Times: The Travails of the Protestant Establishment in America, 1900–1960*, edited by William R. Hutchison (New York: Cambridge University Press, 1989), pp. 233–252.
5. On the neo-orthodox position vis-à-vis the modernist position see Moore, "Secularization: Religion and the Social Sciences," pp. 245–248.
6. Ibid., p. 250.
7. For an insider's view of BFC history see William F. Fore, *A Short History of Religious Broadcasting*, RG 16, Box 3, Fol. 9 located in the National Council of Churches Archives at the Presbyterian Historical Society, Philadelphia (hereafter cited as PHS). On the NCC and the civil rights movement see James Findlay, *Church People in the Struggle: The National Council of Churches and the Black Freedom Movement, 1950–1970* (New York: Oxford University Press, 1993).
8. Technically this expanded their constituency as the Protestant Radio Commission had represented only sixteen denominations. Robbins W. Barstow (chairman of the editorial committee), and F. D. C., Donald C. Bolles, Luther Wesley Smith, and Norman E. Tompkins, eds. *Christian Faith in Action: Commemorative Volume, The Founding of the National Council of the Churches of Christ in America* (Central Department of Publication and Distribution National Council of the Churches of Christ in the United States of America, 1951), p. 44.
9. Barstow et al., *Christian Faith in Action*, p. 44.
10. Henry Knox Sherrill, "The Presidential Message," in *Christian Faith in Action*, p. 143.
11. On the founding of the NCC Marty notes: "Almost at once one could see the ironic situation of a council that would represent One Church in One Nation and One World, though it was organized against the Catholic one-fourth of

America, paying little attention at first to African-American denominations, being opposed by the anticonciliar fifth of the American population, and finding its own denominations riven over theology and economic alike" (Martin E. Marty, *Under God Indivisible, 1941–1960: Modern American Religion, Vol. 3* [Chicago: University of Chicago Press, 1996], p. 268). Robert Schneider suggests that the Mainline leaders may have seen the NCC as a vehicle for making the Protestant establishment more visible (Robert A. Schneider, "Voice of Many Waters: Church Federation in the Twentieth Century," in *Between the Times: The Travail of the Protestant Establishment in America, 1900–1960*, edited by William R. Hutchison [New York: Cambridge University Press, 1989], p. 117).

12. Marty claims this perspective to be a cynical interpretation of ecumenism (Marty, *Under God, Indivisible*, p. 248).

13. My understanding of Gramsci and his concept of hegemony relies greatly upon T. J. Lears interpretation, "The Concept of Cultural Hegemony: Problems and Possibilities," *American Historical Review* 90:3 (June 1985): 567–593. See also, T. J. Lears, "A Matter of Taste: Corporate Cultural Hegemony in a Mass-Consumption Society," in Lary May, ed., *Recasting America: Culture and Politics in the Age of the Cold War* (Chicago: University of Chicago Press, 1989), pp. 38–57. Historians of American religion have, for the most part, steered clear of using Gramsci's terms to describe the mainline Protestant leadership and its role in American public life. William Hutchison, for example, prefers the term "Protestant Establishment" (William Hutchison, "Introduction," in *Between the Times: The Travails of the Protestant Establishment in America, 1900–1960* [New York: Cambridge University Press, 1989], pp. 3–18). In my mind, Gramsci's terms are helpful in so far as they provide a framework for understanding how, despite the legal separation of church and state, American Protestant leaders continued to influence the direction of American life. Dating the decline of Protestant hegemony is a controversial historiographical point. Robert Handy suggested that "The Protestant era in American life had come to its end by the mid-thirties" (*A Christian America: Protestant Hopes and Historical Realities*, [London: Oxford University Press, 1971], p. 213). Others, such as Sydney Ahlstrom, have dated the end of Protestant dominance to 1960 with the election of John F. Kennedy as president (Sydney Ahlstrom, *A Religious History of the American People* [New Haven: Yale University Press, 1972], pp. 875, 1079).

14. Ahlstrom, *Religious History*, p. 901.

15. Compare Robert Wuthnow's thesis on the decline of denominationalism and the rise of special interest groups in the *Restructuring of American Religion: Society and Faith Since World War II* (Princeton, NJ: Princeton University Press, 1988), pp. 100–132.

16. Martin E. Marty, *Under God, Indivisible*, Chapter 16, p. 265, and pp. 248–273 on ecumenism. Marty claims that practical types would interpret NCC and ecumenism in general as strategic on behalf of establishment, while he claims for the participants it was fueled by an idealism. On anti-Catholicism, see also Wuthnow, *Restructuring American Religion*, pp. 73–80.

17. "The Convention Program," in *Christian Faith in Action*, pp. 47–66. See the description on p. 58, and the picture on the cover of the book.

18. Ralph W. Sockman, "This Nation under God," in *Christian Faith in Action*, p. 69.

19. Nevin C. Harner, "Religious Education—Foundation of the National Life," in *Christian Faith in Action*, p. 76.

20. Henry Knox Sherill, "The Presidential Message," p. 143, emphasis mine.

21. Will Herberg, *Protestant, Catholic, Jew* (Garden City, NY: Anchor, 1955).

22. The Federal Council was founded in 1908.

23. Jennings, "Policies and Practices," p. 22. Jennings quotes Eric Barnouw as stating that the Council was devised as a strategy to prevent possible government intervention. See Eric Barnouw, *A History of Broadcasting in the US: A Tower of Babel* (New York: Oxford University Press, 1973), p. 205.

24. Jennings, "Policies and Practices," p. 22.

25. Jennings claims that 1927 was a pivotal year in religious broadcasting, because of an incident with the Jehovah's Witnesses' leader Judge Rutherford, who originally petitioned for a better frequency for their radio station (WBBR). Part of their petition was based on the claim that they were unable to gain access to time on the broadcasting networks. NBC's president therefore invited the Judge to appear on NBC (during the usual scheduled time of the Greater New York Federation of Churches), who used the time to attack the Federal Council of Churches. This series of events, claims Jennings, led to the creation of these policies. See Jennings, "Policies and Practices," pp. 25–26, 29.

26. Jennings, "Policies and Practices," p. 29 (Original: *Advisory Council of the National Broadcasting Company, Committee Reports, The President's Report, Second Meeting, March, 1928* [New York: National Broadcasting Company, 1928], pp. 14–15).

27. "The idea of hegemony does not suggest that domination is achieved by manipulating the world view of the masses. Rather, it argues that in order for cultural leadership to be achieved, the dominant group has to engage in negotiations with opposing groups, classes and values—and that these negotiations must result in some *genuine* accommodation" (Graeme Turner, *British Cultural Studies: An Introduction* [Cambridge, MA: Unwin Hyman, 1990], p. 211). Obviously, to some extent, this is a retrospective interpretation. I think the Protestant, Catholic, Jew mentality was viewed within the liberal Protestant camp as the beginnings of a necessary pluralism. In other words, liberal Protestant leaders while not consciously articulating their establishment status or intent at preserving their status nonetheless acted in such a way, and a close examination of their discourse points to that kind of reading.

28. Obviously this suited both the Jewish leaders, who were fearful of all kinds of proselytism, particularly after World War II, and the mainline Protestant leaders, who were fearful of the effects of Catholic propaganda.

29. Jennings, "Policies and Practices," p. 486. Interestingly enough this tactic is not so different than that of the televangelists, with one main difference: the Federal Council did *not* solicit funds on the air, but relied on these preachers to raise funds in their congregations. Notably, Everett Parker objected to this "one

man" model and the potential "personality cult" that would be associated with this tactic (Ellens, p. 28).

30. Jennings, "Policies and Practices," p. 486.

31. Ibid., p. 194. Jennings claims that the committee "maintained close liaison with the liberal wing of the Federal Communications Commission, and supported such Commission innovations as the 'Blue Book.' " Ibid., p. 217.

32. Parker's first piece of research was on Chicago area broadcasting while he was a seminary student. Parker was truly a pioneer in religious media research and in communications in general. His interest in the audience, would prove to be forward-looking.

33. Jennings discusses the Federal Council's lack of strong reaction to the Blue Book ("Policies and Practices," pp. 172–175). In the Blue Book the Commission called upon networks to meet their obligations to the public. Noted specifically in this regard were: "sustaining features, local live presentations, public discussions and restraint in advertising" (Jennings, "Policies and Practices," p. 172).

34. Ibid., p. 228. While the new Protestant Radio Commission also included smaller organizations under its umbrella, the main merger was between the Federal Council and the Joint Committee.

35. Since 1922, Goodman had run the Greater New York Federation's Department of Religious Radio, which had been the main sponsor of Protestant broadcasting on WEAF, what would be one of NBC's New York stations. Ibid., p. 24.

36. Parker et al., *The Television-Radio Audience and Religion* (New York: Harper Brothers, 1955).

37. Of course, it was precisely this system that promoted antagonism on the part of evangelical broadcasters and prompted the creation of the NRB.

38. Jews and Catholics also benefited from this sustained-time system.

39. R. Laurence Moore, *Selling God: American Religion in the Marketplace of Culture* (New York: Oxford, 1994), pp. 231–235; Dennis N. Voskuil, "Reaching Out: Mainline Protestantism and the Media," in *Between the Times: The Travail of the Protestant Establishment, 1900–1960* (New York: Cambridge University Press, 1989), pp. 72–92; Dennis N. Voskuil, "The Power of the Air: Evangelicals and the Rise of Religious Broadcasting," in *American Evangelicals and the Mass Media*, edited by Quentin J. Schultze (Grand Rapids, MI: Zondervan, 1990), pp. 69–95.

40. Rev. Alton M. Motter, "Report on the Sixth Annual National Religious Radio Workshop," PHS, RG 16, Box 1, Fol. 2.

41. Ronald Bridges, "Report of the Executive Director to the Board of Managers," PHS, RG 16, Box 1, Fol. 3. This echoed Truman's comments on the bomb: "It is an awful responsibility which has come to us. We thank God that it has come to us instead of to our enemies and we pray that He may guide us to use it in His ways and for His purposes" (Paul Boyer, *By the Bomb's Early Light: American Thought and Culture at the Dawn of the Atomic Age* [Chapel Hill, NC: University of North Carolina Press, 1985], p. 6).

42. [Ronald Bridges], "General Report October 16, 1952 of the Broadcast and Film Commission of the National Council of Churches," p. 29, PHS, RG 16, Box 1, Fol. 4.

43. J. Edward Carothers, "A Television Ministry," *The Christian Century* 66 (May 11, 1949): 591.
44. [Ronald Bridges], "General Report to the Board of Managers, October 16, 1952," p. 28, PHS, RG 16, Box 1, Fol. 4, emphasis mine.
45. TV was like radio, in that it "represented the perfect blend of the public and private. The notion of a pubic church service carried into the home was wonderfully compatible with ideals of domesticity they had championed" The movies, on the other hand, had always been problematic because of the dangerous atmosphere of the movie house (e.g., it was dark, unescourted men and women sat together, etc.) (R. Laurence Moore, *Selling God*, p. 233; p. 221).
46. On the religious reception of the telegraph see Daniel J. Czitrom, *Media and the American Mind: From Morse to McLuhan* (Chapel Hill, NC: University of North Carolina Press, 1982), pp. 9–11.
47. [Ronald Bridges], "General Report to the Board of Managers, October 16, 1952, of the Broadcast and Film Commission of the National Council of Churches," p. 28, PHS, RG 16, Box 1, Fol. 4.
48. [Albert Crews], "Television," in the "Annual Report to the Board of Managers, March 6–7, 1956," p. 15, PHS, RG 16, Box 1, Fol. 5.
49. "Television Programming," Annual Report to the Board of General Managers, 1958, p. 15, PHS, RG 16, Box. 1, Fol. 6.
50. [Ronald Bridges], "General Report October 16, 1952 of the Broadcast and Film Commission of the National Council of Churches," p. 29, PHS, RG 16, Box 1, Fol. 4.
51. Crews et al., "Programs—Radio, Television, Films," in the General Report, October 2, 1951, p. 19 by Albert Crews, PHS, RG 16, Box 1, Fol. 3.
52. Ibid., p. 23.
53. Ibid., pp. 27–28.
54. Marjorie Hyer, ed., "Religious Radio and Television Newsletter, 1951," in the "General Report to the Board of Managers, 1951," PHS, RG 16, Box 1, Fol. 3. On the longer relationship between Protestants and advertising see R. Laurence Moore, *Selling God*, pp. 204–237.
55. J. Edward Carothers, "A Television Ministry," *The Christian Century* 66 (May 11, 1949): 591.
56. Rev. Alton M. Motter, "Report on the Sixth Annual National Religious Radio Workshop."
57. Crews et al., "Programs—Radio, Television and Films," in the "General Report, October 2, 1951, Broadcasting and Film Commission," by Albert Crews, p. 23, PHS, RG 16, Box 1, Fol. 3.
58. Ibid., p. 25.
59. Ibid., p. 28.
60. Ibid., p. 27.
61. Of these four shows only the Peales' show seems to have been aired long enough to be listed in *Penguin's Total Television: A Comprehensive Guide to Programming from 1948 to the Present* , edited by Alex McNeil (New York: Penguin Books, 1984). The other three probably never made it past the planning stages.

62. Ronald Bridges, "Three Year Report," in the "Annual Report of the Broadcast and Film Commission, March 2–3, 1954," p. 3, PHS, RG 16, Box 1, Fol. 4.

63. Franklin S. Mack, "Executive Director's Report," in the "Annual Report to the Board of Managers, March 6–7, 1956, BFC," p. 4, PHS, RG 16, Box 1, Fol. 5.

64. Ibid. See also Liston Pope, "Religion on the Air," *Christianity and Crisis* 15 (November 14, 1955):147–148.

65. Liston Pope, "Religion on the Air," *Christianity and Crisis* 15 (November 14, 1955): 147–148.

66. Ibid.

67. Parker et al., *Television-Radio Audience.* On the relationship between mainline Protestantism and the social sciences see R. Laurence Moore, "Secularization: Religion and the Social Sciences," pp. 233–252.

68. See, for example, Parker et al., *Television-Radio Audience*, p. 373. In contrast to the Frankfurt School, Parker et al. derided the use of "mass" to describe the audience. The audience, they claimed, was far more fragmented and intelligent to be described as one conglomerate, undifferentiated mass. Interestingly enough, the interest in the role of audience as meaning-makers recently reemerged in Cultural Studies as the concept of "resistance" became the watchword of new analyses. On the history of cultural studies, particularly its move away from the Frankfurt School theory of mass culture to a more Gramscian informed perspective see Patrick Brantlinger, *Crusoe's Footsteps: Cultural Studies in Britain and America* (London: Routledge, 1990).

69. While there has been much research on televangelism, even quite a substantial portion of that on the televangelist audience, there has been (to my knowledge) no other study that so carefully breaks down television viewing (nonreligious programming as well) practices according to class, and religion. The confessional at the beginning of the introduction is interesting, especially as the authors remind us of their bias intermittently, especially when looking at Fulton Sheen or his audience. See p. xvi for the framework of book (basically stresses ethical imperative, and ability of person to choose to live according to God's will, etc.).

70. Parker et al., *Television-Radio Audience*, p. 159.

71. Ibid., pp. 96, 143.

72. On Norman Vincent Peale see Carol V. R. George, *God's Salesman: Norman Vincent Peale and the Power of Positive Thinking* (New York: Oxford University Press, 1993). It is interesting that the therapeutic, even in these early days, had such a strong impact on the audience. Peale almost foreshadows all of the talk shows and self-help trends publicized on those talk shows.

73. Parker et al., *Television-Radio Audience*, p. 210.

74. Ibid., p. 411.

75. Ibid.

76. On the background of *The Authoritarian Personality* see Daniel Jay, *The Dialectical Imagination: A History of the Frankfurt School and the Institute of Social Research* (Boston: Little, Brown and Company, 1973), pp. 219–252. Five volumes would be published in this study.

77. Jay, *The Dialectical Imagination*, p. 243.

78. Ibid.
79. Parker et al., *Television-Radio Audience*, p. 251.
80. Ibid.
81. Ibid., p. 249.
82. On the background of *The Authoritarian Personality* see Daniel Jay, *The Dialectical Imagination*, pp. 219–252. The following statements were added:
    - "Most people who try to run their lives according to the teaching of the Bible find that Bible principles are not practical in real life."
    - "The minister (or priest or rabbi) should be the final authority on the way we should act and what we should believe."
    - "In order to obtain Divine assistance in life's crises, it is necessary to get it through your church (or priest, pastor or rabbi)."
    - "There is little hope of getting along with people of foreign countries that are not Christian."
    - "Sending missionaries to Communist China would help defeat communism and save our way of life."

    Parker et al., *Television-Radio Audience*, p. 249. See appendix E, pp. 441–451 for tables showing the results of the F-scale in New Haven.
83. Parker et al., *Television-Radio Audience*, p. 271.
84. Ibid., p. 373.
85. Ibid., p. 391.
86. Ibid., p. 390.
87. Ibid., p. 373.
88. Ibid., p. 397.
89. Ibid., p. 403.
90. Ibid., p. 409.
91. Ibid., p. 402.
92. Ibid., pp. 401–414.
93. Ibid., p. 408.
94. Horsfeld notes that E. Parker, the author of the study, "eventually withdrew his denomination's participation from religious programming because he felt that there were more important areas of ministry within television, particularly in the area of media reform." Peter G. Horsfeld, *Religious Television: The American Experience* (New York: Longman Inc., 1984), pp. 4–5.
95. Mack, "Annual Report, 1956," p. 4.
96. "Urgent and Confidential Memorandum to the Executive Committee from Ronald Bridges," June 12, 1953, p. 2, PHS, RG 16, Box 2, Fol. 28.
97. Ibid.
98. "Should Religious Broadcasts be Sponsored by Commercial Advertisers?" n.d. [1953?] n.a. [Ronald Bridges?], PHS, RG 16, Box 2, Fol. 28.
99. *What's Your Trouble* seems to have been aired only one year. In comparison to Fulton Sheen's 5 year primetime run, including the 1952 emmy for best outstanding personality, this was a complete failure (Alex MacNeil, *Total Television: A Comprehensive Guide to Programming From 1948 to the Present* [New York: Penguin Books, 1984], pp. 710, 372, 821).

100. "Advisory Policy Statement Concerning Religious Broadcasting," PHS, RG 16, Box 1, Fol. 24.
101. "Reactions to the National Council Advisory Policy Statement on Religious Broadcasting," in the "Annual Report to the Board of Managers, 1957," p. 96, PHS, RG 16, Box 1, Fol. 6.
102. Ibid., p. 98.
103. Ibid., p. 97.
104. "Reactions to the National Council Advisory Policy Statement on Religious Broadcasting," p. 97.
105. Ibid.
106. Ibid.
107. Ibid., p. 98. Did the BFC knowingly conspire to keep the evangelicals off the air? Mainline leaders have responded with a resounding "no," but the fact is that the BFC policy reflected in the Advisory Policy Statement, and if enacted, would have severely limited the number of evangelical broadcasters on the air. True, there may have been no "conspiracy" per se [e.g., they did not sit behind closed doors and think about how to put them out of business] but because the BFC operated under hegemonic assumptions, its positions, perhaps unknowingly or unselfconsciously, clearly elided any reference to the right of conservative Protestantism to determine its own destiny or even perhaps share responsibility for the Protestant destiny of the country. Moreover, the BFC's position was often reinforced by broadcasting policy, a fact that only served to reinforce the evangelical fear of conspiracy. Stewart Hoover and Douglas Wagner have suggested that the evangelical "conspiracy theory" is largely unwarranted as the NAE was marginalized for its desire to preach doctrine and not "broad truths." While this observation is factually correct, it ignores the fact that the "broad truths" policy was devised by the networks *in collaboration* with the mainline religious groups. It was in the interest of mainline Protestants to promote "broad truths" broadcasting precisely because it limited the chances of evangelicals, and left the mainline to define Protestant "broad truths" to the viewing public. "Broad truths" broadcasting ultimately served the interests of the mainline Protestant hegemony (See Stewart Hoover and Douglas Wagner, "History and Policy in American Broadcast Treatment of Religion," *Media, Culture and Society* 19: 7–27, specifically p. 22).
108. "Reactions to the National Council Advisory Policy Statement on Religious Broadcasting," p. 99.
109. Albert S. Crews, "Television Programming," in the "Annual Report to the Board of Managers, February 18–20, 1958," p. 16, RG 16, Box 1, Fol. 6.
110. "Report of Executive Director," Franklin S. Mack, in "Annual Report to the Board of Managers, March 4–6, 1957, BFC," p. 6, RG 16, Box 1, Fol. 6.
111. Malcolm Boyd, "The Crisis of the Mass Media," *Christianity and Crisis* 16 (April 16, 1956): 68.
112. Parker et al., *Television-Radio Audience*, pp. 412–413.

113. Wuthnow, *Producing the Sacred*, p. 84.
114. Mack, "Annual Report, 1958," pp. 75–77, PHS, RG 16, Box 1, Fol. 6. The Study Commission consisted of Dr. Saunders, Dr. Barry, Mrs. Wedel, Dr. Bachman, Dr. Pope, Dr. Saunders, Dr. Spike, Mr. Betts, and Mr. Sproul. The Mass Media Commission was chaired by Everett Parker, and included Charles Huschaw, Paul Slater, Harry Stacks, Murray Stedman, Mrs. Cynthia Wedel, and Rome Betts.
115. "Background Statement: The Church and Television and Radio Broadcasting," June 6–8, 1963, PHS, RG 16, Box 2, Fol. 18.
116. Ibid., p. 4.
117. Ibid.
118. Ibid., p. 5.
119. Ibid., p. 6.
120. Martin E. Marty also suggests that the proper approach is to attempt to shape existent secular programming. See *The Improper Opinion*, p. 141.
121. "Background Statement: The Church and Television and Radio Broadcasting," June 6–8, 1963, PHS, RG 16, Box 2, Fol. 18.
122. Ibid., p. 11.
123. Of course, we know now that it is precisely those groups who were less likely to adopt these modern strategies that were most likely to succeed on the modern technology of television.
124. "Study Commission on the Role of Radio, Television and Films in Religion," p. 3, RG 16, Box 1, Fol. 19.
125. Ibid., p. 9.
126. Ibid., p. 10.
127. *The Church and Television Broadcasting*, p. 8.2–1. RG 16, Box 2, Fol. 8.
128. Ibid., p. 8.2–3.
129. Ibid.
130. "Background Statement: The Church and Television and Radio Broadcasting," p. 3, RG 16, Box 2, Fol. 18.
131. Ibid., p. 4.
132. This shift is similar to the suburban jeremiads described in James Hudnut-Beumler, *Looking for God in the Suburbs: The Religion of the American Dream and its Critics, 1945–1960* (Brunswick, NJ: Rutgers University Press, 1994), pp. 109–174.
133. Ibid., p. 1177.
134. Ibid., p. 1179.
135. S. F. Mack, "Executive Director's Report: The Role of the National Council's BFC," in the "Annual Report, 1960," p. 7, PHS, RG 16, Box 1, Fol. 7.
136. Sally M. Promey, "Interchangeable Art: Warner Sallman and the Critics of Mass Culture," in *Icons of American Protestantism: The Art of Warner Sallman*, edited by David Morgan (New Haven: Yale University Press, 1996), pp. 167–173.

Chapter 4   "Preserving Our American Heritage": Television and the Construction of Evangelical Identity

1. "Preserving Our American Heritage" was the theme of the 15th Convention of the National Religious Broadcasters, February 5–6, 1958 (Billy Graham Center Archives [hereafter cited as BGCA] CN 209, Box 7, Fol. 3). Almost exactly the same formulation is used by the BFC to legitimate their stance toward paid-time TV: "the inclusion of the right kind and amount of religion in the broadcast schedule is essential to the preservation of our American heritage" (Reactions to the National Council's Advisory Policy Statement on Religious Broadcasting, p. 97, Presbyterian Historical Society [hereafter cited as PHS] RG 16, Box 1, Fol. 6).

2. Joel Carpenter, *Revive Us Again: The Reawakening of American Fundamentalism* (New York: Oxford University Press, 1997), pp. 150–151.

3. In contrast to their mainline counterparts.

4. Tona J. Hangen, *Redeeming the Dial: Radio, Religion and Popular Culture in America* (Chapel Hill, NC: University of North Carolina Press, 2002), Carpenter, *Revive Us Again.*

5. For the standard historical account see George Marsden, *Understanding Fundamentalism and Evangelicalism* (Grand Rapids, MI: Eerdmans, 1991); George M. Marsden, *Fundamentalism and American Culture: The Shaping of Twentieth Century Evangelicalism: 1870–1925* (New York: Oxford University Press, 1980). Joel Carpenter's *Revive Us Again*, 1997, complements Marsden's account.

6. Martin Riesebrodt, *Pious Passion: The Emergence of Modern Fundamentalism in the United States and Iran,* Translated by Don Reneau (Berkeley, CA: University of California Press, 1993), p. 33.

7. Ibid., p. 58.

8. As we noted in chapter 2, liberals also were upset by these changes but directed their efforts in a different manner.

9. Riesebrodt, *Pious Passion*, p. 87.

10. For a general history of this period of rebuilding see Carpenter, *Revive Us Again.* On one specific institution see George Marsden, *Reforming Fundamentalism: Fuller Seminary and the New Evangelicalism* (Grand Rapids, MI: Eerdmans, 1987).

11. Martin E. Marty, *Righteous Empire: The Protestant Experience in America* (New York: Dial Press, 1970), pp. 177–187.

12. Riesebrodt, *Pious Passion*, p. 87.

13. The neo-evangelical label was quickly exchanged simply for evangelical. In this book, the terms are interchangeable unless otherwise indicated.

14. Wuthnow notes that the evangelical movement began in major cities, with an educated leadership. He traces the most important leaps of economic and educational growth in the evangelical circles to the 1960s, but it is clear these

processes were already at work in the 1950s as well. By the early 1970s, evangelicals were far more likely to identify as being part of the middle class and to have attended college. For Wuthnow's account of the rise of the evangelical movement in the post–World War II period, see Robert Wuthnow, *The Restructuring of American Religion: Society and Faith since World War II* (Princeton, NJ: Princeton University Press, 1988), pp. 173–214. For an opposing view concerning the middle class status of evangelicalism see James Davison Hunter, *American Evangelicalism: Conservative Religion and the Quandary of Modernity* (New Brunswick, NJ: Rutgers University Press, 1983), pp. 53–55.

15. Wuthnow, *Restructuring American Religion*, p. 187.

16. Although it is plausible to argue that these particular leaders and the organizations they shaped have left an indelible mark on contemporary evangelicalism, it would be a mistake to suggest that this study would not be different if we focused on the Pentecostal or holiness wing of evangelicalism. On the historiographical debates concerning evangelicalism see Donald Dayton, and Robert K. Johnson, eds., *The Variety of American Evangelicalism* (Downers Grove, IL: Intervarsity Press, 1991); and Douglas Sweeney, "The Essential Evangelicalism Dialectic: The Historiography of the Early Neo-Evangelical Movement and the Observer-Participant Dilemma," *Church History* 60 (March 1991): 70–84.

17. On the use of radio and the creation of an evangelical identity see Quentin J. Schultze, "Evangelical Radio and the Rise of the Electronic Church, 1921–1948," *Journal of Broadcasting and the Electronic Media* 32 (Summer 1988): 289–306.

18. Evangelical leaders did not know this was a "heavy effects model" but that is the most apt description of their media model.

19. Elihu Katz, "On Conceptualizing Media Effects," in *Studies in Communication: A Research Annual*, edited by Thelma McCormack, (Greenwich, CT: JAI Press, 1980), p. 121. According to Katz, this was the predominant assumption of early empirical research in mass communications.

20. Martin E. Marty, "The Revival of Evangelicalism and Southern Religion," in *Varieties of Southern Evangelicalism*, edited by David E. Harrell, Jr. (Macon, GA: Mercer University Press, 1981), p. 9.

21. Schultze, "Evangelical Radio," and Quentin J. Schultze, "The Two Faces of Fundamentalist Higher Education," in *Fundamentalisms and Society: Reclaiming the Science, the Family and Education*, edited by Martin E. Marty and R. Scott Appleby (Chicago: University of Chicago Press, 1991), pp. 490–535. Considering their search for approval, it is perhaps not surprising that Pat Robertson, Jerry Falwell, and Oral Roberts all founded universities.

22. On the founding of the NAE, see James DeForest Murch, *Cooperation without Compromise: A History of the National Association of Evangelicals* (Grand Rapids, MI: Eerdmans, 1956). See also Carpenter *Revive Us Again*, pp. 141–160.

23. On evangelical radio see Carpenter *Revive Us Again*, pp. 124–140; Hangen, *Redeeming the Dial*, Schultze, "Evangelical Radio," Murch, *Cooperation without Compromise*, see the titles of chapters 2 and 3; and Dennis N. Voskuil. "The Power of the Air: Evangelicals and the Rise of Religious Broadcasting," in *American Evangelicals and the Mass Media*, edited by Quentin J. Schultze (Grand Rapids, MI: Academie Books, 1990), pp. 69–95.

24. Murch, *Cooperation without Compromise*, p. 53. Separatism was a major issue in the early neoevangelical movement. See Carpenter, *Revive Us Again*, pp. 33–88 and Marsden, *Reforming Fundamentalism*, pp. 46–52.

25. "Evangelical Action! A Report of the Organization of the National Association of Evangelicals for United Action," in *A New Coalition: Early Documents of the National Association of Evangelicals*, edited by Joel A. Carpenter (New York: Garland Publishing, [1942] 1988), p. vi.

26. Ibid., p. vi.

27. "United . . . We Stand: A Report of the Constitutional Convention of the National Association of Evangelicals," in *A New Coalition: Early Documents of the National Association of Evangelicals*, edited by Joel Carpenter (New York: Garland, [1943] 1988).

28. Murch, *Cooperation without Compromise*, pp. 58–59.

29. Ibid., p. 52.

30. For an example of anti-ACCC rhetoric, which was actually quite mild, see Stephen W. Paine, "Principle vs. Practice in ACCC Membership" *United Evangelical Action* (July 15, 1951): 4–5, 8.

31. Murch, *Cooperation without Compromise*, pp. 24–25.

32. Ibid., p. 26.

33. Murch, *Cooperation without Compromise*, pp. 19–31, use of virus on p. 30; James DeForest Murch, "Adventuring in United Evangelical Action," *United Evangelical Action* 5 (1946): 5–8; James DeForest Murch, "On Winning America," *United Evangelical Action* 5 (1946): pp. 8–9; James DeForest Murch, "Why United Evangelical Action is Imperative," *United Evangelical Action* 5 (1946): 3–4; James DeForest Murch, "A Study in Christian Co-operation in America," *United Evangelical Action* 5 (1946): 3–4; James DeForest Murch, "How Federative Action Began in America," *United Evangelical Action* 5 (1946): 7–8; James DeForest Murch, "Why Evangelicals Cannot Co-operate in the FCCCA," *United Evangelical Action* 5 (1946): 5–7; James DeForest Murch, "The Proposed National Council of Churches," *United Evangelical Action* 5 (1946): 6–8.

34. James DeForest Murch, "Why Evangelicals Cannot Co-operate in the FCCCA," *United Evangelical Action* 5 (1946): 5–7 (p. 5).

35. James DeForest Murch, "The Proposed National Council of Churches," *United Evangelical Action* 5 (1946): 6–8 (p. 7).

36. Ibid.

37. "Editorial: Federal Council Caught 'Red-Handed'." *United Evangelical Action*, March 1, 1950, 9, 29.

38. Martin E. Marty, *Modern American Religion: The Noise of Conflict, 1919–1941*, Vol. 2 (Chicago: University of Chicago, 1991); and Leo P. Ribuffo, *The Old Christian Right: The Protestant Far Right from the Great Depression to the Cold War* (Philadelphia, PA: Temple University Press, 1983).

39. William Ward Ayer, "Evangelical Christianity Endangered by Its Fragmentized Condition," in "Evangelical Action! A Report of the Organization of the National Association of Evangelicals for United Action," pp. 41–47. Of course, these were internal documents, speeches given at conventions before evangelicals.

40. Interestingly enough, the metaphor of the virus could have easily been applied to the media as well—an enemy which had tangible effects—but it was not.

41. Rutherford L. Decker, "The Holy Spirit Works through the NAE," *United Evangelical Action* 1952 (1952): 13–14, 16; 5–6, 14–16; 4–6.

42. Frederick Curtis Fowler, "Render Unto Caesar and Unto God," *United Evangelical Action* 11 (1952): 11. See also for comparison, Verne P. Kaub, "The NCC at Denver," *United Evangelical Action* 11 (1952): 3–7, 16 which contains a very mild report of the NCC convention in Denver. Of course, DeForest Murch's attacks on the NCC remained quite vehement, especially his accusation that it was a "super-church."

43. Marsden, *Reforming Fundamentalism*, p. 162.

44. Ibid., p. 160.

45. John G. Merritt, "Christianity Today," in *Religious Periodicals of the United States*, edited by Charles H. Lippy (New York: Greenwood Press, 1986), p. 136. Originally cited from Carl F. H. Henry, memorandum, n.d., BGCA, coll. 8, box 15, folder 11.

46. Much, *Cooperation without Compromise*, p. 29.

47. Ibid., p. 32.

48. Ibid., p. 33. On Wuthnow's thesis see *The Restructuring of American Religion*.

49. See Murch's account in James DeForest Murch, "How Federative Action Began in America," *United Evangelical Action* 5 (1946): 8.

50. "United . . . We Stand," in *A New Coalition*, edited by Joel Carpenter.

51. James DeForest Murch, "A Study in Christian Co-operation in America," *United Evangelical Action* 5 (1946): 3–4, p. 3.

52. Murch, *Cooperation without Compromise*, p. 55. These are 6 of the 8 listed fields of cooperative endeavor in the first call for the St. Louis Conference. The other two: include the preservation of separation of church and state, and surprisingly "the united efforts of evangelical churches within local communities."

53. Ibid., p. 36.

54. Murch, *Cooperation without Compromise*, pp. 73–81.

55. Schultze, "Evangelical Radio."

56. The policies of NBC and CBS differed slightly, and Mutual continued to sell time until 1943. NBC used the Federal Council of Churches as the program producer; while CBS set up a program and invited mainline to use that time (Schultze, "Evangelical Radio and the Rise of the Electronic Church, 1921–1948").

57. See Voskuil, "The Power of the Air"; and Schultze, "Evangelical Radio."

58. Mark Ward Sr., *Air of Salvation: The Story of Christian Broadcasting* (Grand Rapids, MI: Baker Books, 1994), p. 67.

59. Ibid., pp. 69–70. Murch, *Cooperation without Compromise*, p. 80.

60. The NAE Commission on Radio was supposed to concentrate on gaining sustaining time for their members, while the NRB was supposed to concentrate on commercial time.

61. National Religious Broadcasters Association Constitution and Bylaws Pamphlet, BGCA, CN 209, Box 7, Fol. 3 n.d. [1953?].

62. On the origins of the broad truths policy see chapter 3 above. See also Stewart Hoover, and Douglas Warner, "History and Policy in American Broadcast Treatment of Religion," *Media, Culture and Society* 19 (1997): 7–27.

63. James DeForest Murch, "NAE Comes of Age," *United Evangelical Action* 7 (1948): 19.

64. "NAE Convention Resolutions," *United Evangelical Action* (May 1, 1952): 8.

65. "National Religious Broadcasters Report," *United Evangelical Action* (May 1, 1952): 36.

66. Ibid., p. 37.

67. James DeForest Murch, "Religious Freedom?" *United Evangelical Action* (May 11, 1953): 10.

68. Ibid.

69. Ibid.

70. There is some irony here because mainline Protestants likewise viewed fundamentalists.

71. See, for example, H. H. Savage, "United Evangelical Action: Presidential Address at the Chicago Convention," *United Evangelical Action* (May 1, 1955): 151–154, 159, where he defines four Satanic ideologies: communism, Catholicism, compromise, and criticism. "The most valuable asset to the welfare of our country at the present time is the prevailing prayer of Bible-believing Christians, who are willing to put forth the necessary effort to fight the good fight of faith" (p. 151). Notably, Savage's speech is more moderate in tone. While remaining critical of liberals, Catholics and seculars the discourse is far less polemical. Nowhere does he use adjectives such as octopus, virus, cancer, etc.

72. See above chapter 3, pp. 54–57, for the mainline approach.

73. See the Statement of Faith of the National Religious Broadcasters, Appendix A, p. 20, in the National Religious Broadcasters Consitution and Bylaws, pamphlet, BGCA, CN 209, Box 7, Fol. 3.

74. Franklin S. Mack, "Executive Director's Report," in the "Annual Report to the Board of Managers, March 6–7, 1956, BFC," p. 4, PHS, R.G. 16, Box 1, Fol. 5.

75. On the issue of church/state conflict and religious broadcasting see Marcus Cohn, "Religion and the FCC," *The Reporter* (January 14, 1965); Kenneth Cox, "The FCC, the Constitution and Religious Broadcasting Programming," *The George Washington Law Review* 34:2 (December 1965); and Lee Loevinger, "Religious Liberty and Broadcasting," in *George Washington Law Review* 33 (1965): 631.

76. "The BFC recognizes that it is vital to religious freedom that diverse religious positions have a right to be heard."

77. "Advisory Policy Statement Concerning Religious Broadcasting," PHS, RG 16, Box 1, Fol. 24.

78. Harold Fellows quoted in "Radio-TV Industry Replies to NCC Attack," *Radio-Tele-Gram: Official Newsletter of the National Religious Broadcasters Inc.* , October–December 1956, p. 2. BGCA, CN 209, Box 7, Fol. 2.

79. "Radio-TV Industry Replies to NCC Attack," *Radio-Tele-Gram: Official Newsletter of the National Religious Broadcasters Inc.*, October–December 1956, p. 2. BGCA, CN 209, Box 7, Fol. 2.

80. Eugene Bertermann, "Basic Principles in Religious Broadcasting," presented at the 14th annual meeting of the NRB, January 30–31, 1957, p. 26. BGCA, CN209, Box 7, Fol. 2.

81. Eugene Bertermann, "Basic Principles in Religious Broadcasting," presented at the 14th annual meeting of the NRB, January 30–31, 1957, p. 16. BGCA, CN 209, Box 7, Fol. 2; Code of Ethics of the National Religious Broadcasters, Appendix B, p. 21. in the National Religious Broadcasters Constitution and Bylaws, pamphlet, BGCA, CN 209, Box 7, Folder 3. See also "Broadcast Probe," *Christianity Today* 1 (February 4, 1957): 30. The NRB estimated that hundreds of evangelical programs were dropped at local levels as a result.

82. *Reactions to the National Council's Advisory Policy Statement on Religious Broadcasting*, p. 98, PHS, RG 16, Box 1, Fol. 6.

83. Ibid., p. 96.

84. Ibid., p. 97.

85. Ibid., p. 98.

86. Ibid., p. 99.

87. "The recurrent temptation seems to be to go it alone, to do as much as possible denominationally and only as much as necessary together" (S. Franklin Mack, "1958: Year of Decision," *Board of Managers Minutes*, p. 4. PHS, RG 16, Box 1, Fol. 24).

88. Martin E. Marty, "Second Chance Protestantism," *The Christian Century* 78 (June 21, 1961): 770–772.

89. The size of the NRB conventions, the number of exhibitors, the number of congressman attending the breakfasts at the convention, the thickness of the in-house publication, all increased over this period.

90. Robert Wuthnow, "Religious Discourse as Public Discourse," *Communication Research* 15 (June 1988): 318–388.

91. Ibid., p. 331.

92. Thomas C. Berg, "'Proclaiming Together?' Convergence and Divergence in Mainline and Evangelical Evangelism, 1945–1967," *Religion and American Culture* 5 (Winter 1995): 49–76. Berg suggests that there were moments of convergence, particularly as regards evangelism. Mark Silk, "The Rise of the 'New Evangelicalism': Shock and Adjustment," in *Between the Times: The Travail of the Protestant Establishment in America, 1900–1960*, edited by William R. Hutchison (New York: Cambridge, 1989), pp. 278–299. Silk suggests that there was potential for a moment of convergence, based on desire to preserve the Protestant establishment, although it did not acutalize. Martin E. Marty, *Modern American Religion, Vol. 3: Under God, Indivisible, 1941–1960* (Chicago: University of Chicago Press, 1996). Marty refers to these moments of consensus as the centrifugal forces of the 1950s, which operated at large in post–World War II America, not just in religion.

93. Thomas C. Berg, "Proclaiming Together?"; Martin E. Marty, *Under God, Indivisible*; Silk, "The Rise of the 'New Evangelicalism.'"

94. Marty, *Under God, Indivisible*, p. 201.

95. On the appointment of the ambassador to the Vatican see Marty, *Under God, Indivisible*, pp. 198–204.

96. Silk, "The Rise of the 'New Evangelicalism,'" p. 297.

97. As cited in Silk, "The Rise of the 'New Evangelicalism,'" p. 286. Original, *Christianity and Crisis* 16 (March 5, 1956): 18.

98. Marty, *Under God, Indivisible*, p. 278. Also note that Berg's argument is precisely the opposite—that evangelism offered a moment of cooperation.

Chapter 5   "The Age of Space Requires Space Age Teaching Tools": Technology on Evangelical Terms

1. Everett Mendelsohn, "Religious Fundamentalism and the Sciences" in *Fundamentalisms and Society: Reclaiming the Sciences, the Family, and Education*, edited by Martin E. Marty and R. Scott Appleby (Chicago: University of Chicago Press, 1993), p. 23.

2. James Gilbert, *Redeeming Culture: American Religion in an Age of Science* (Chicago: University of Chicago Press, 1997). Gilbert emphasizes that the definitions of "science" and "religion" are unstable and change over time.

3. Conservative Protestants rejected evolution in so far as it contradicted the biblical story of creation. While liberal Protestants were able to accept and even embrace forms of evolutionary theory, conservative Protestants viewed evolution as one of the main causes of World Wars I and II (Ferenc Morton Szasz, *The Divided Mind of Protestant America, 1880–1930* [Alabama: University of Alabama, 1982]).

4. Frederick Gregory distinguishes between three main kinds of Protestant responses to Darwin: the orthodox (conservatives) who rejected any scientific development which clashed with religious belief, a more moderate group which hoped to create harmony between science and religion partially by adapting Christian theology and partially by forcing science to admit that religion has a role in the natural world and a smaller tradition which wished to separate science and religion (Frederick Gregory. "The Impact of Darwinian Evolution on Protestant Theology," in *God and Nature: Historical Essays on the Encounter Between Christianity and Science*, edited by David C. Lindberg and Ronald L. Numbers [Berkeley, CA: University of California Press, 1986], pp. 369–390) .

5. On the distinction between liberals and modernists see William R. Hutchison, *The Modernist Impulse in American Protestantism* (Cambridge, MA: Harvard University Press, 1976), pp. 2–4.

6. Theodore Dwight Bozeman, *Protestants in an Age of Science: The Baconian Ideal and Antebellum American Religious Thought* (Chapel Hill, NC: University of North Carolina Press, 1977). Bozeman studies the Presbyterian example, but claims that Baconianism pervaded intellectual life in America, and was much more influential than previously thought.

    Bacon's arguments concerning the harmony of science and religion were well received by English puritans in the seventeenth century, but by the eighteenth century the Enlightenment strongly called into question this assumption. Bozeman's study shows that Baconianism persisted in the American context throughout the nineteenth and in the case of fundamentalists into the twentieth century.

   On the relationship between Protestantism and science see George Becker, "Pietism's Confrontation with Enlightenment Rationalism: An Examination of the Relation Between Ascetic Protestantism and Science," *Journal for the Scientific Study of Religion* 30 (1991): 139–158.

7. The American Heritage Dictionary, 3rd Edition, currently defines science as "The observation, description, experimental investigation, and *theoretical explanation* of phenomena" (New York: Houghton Mifflin, p. 1616).

8. Ian G. Barbour, *Religion and Science: Historical and Contemporary Issues* (San Francisco: Harper San Francisco, 1997), p. 11.

9. Paul Jerome Croce, *Science and Religion in the Era of William James: Eclipse of Certainty, 1820–1880.* Vol. 1 (Chapel Hill, NC: University of North Carolina Press, 1995), pp. 90. pp. 87–110; Gilbert, *Redeeming Culture*, p. 30; Nathan O. Hatch, *The Democratization of American Christianity* (New Haven, CT: Yale University Press, 1989).

10. Bozeman, *Protestants in an Age of Science*, pp. 132–144.

11. Croce, *Science and Religion in the Era of William James*, p. 88. This is Croce's main thesis.

12. Szasz, *Divided Mind of Protestant America*, pp. 129–130. On William J. Bryan see also Gilbert, *Redeeming Culture*, pp. 23–37.

13. George M. Marsden, *Fundamentalism and American Culture: The Shaping of Twentieth Century Evangelicalism: 1870–1925* (New York: Oxford University Press, 1980), pp. 212–221.

14. Ibid., pp. 212–213.

15. Ibid., p. 214.

16. Bozeman, *Protestants in an Age of Science*, p. 43. More importantly Bozeman notes that the proponents of Baconianism were Protestant (p. xii).

17. George M. Marsden, *Fundamentalism and American Culture*; George Marsden, "The Evangelical Love Affair with Enlightenment Science," in *Understanding Fundamentalism and Evangelicalism* (Grand Rapids, MI: Eerdmans, 1991), pp. 122–152; Mark A. Noll, *The Scandal of the Evangelical Mind* (Grand Rapids, MI: Eerdmans, 1994). See also David A. Hollinger, *Science, Jews, and Secular Culture: Studies in Mid-Twentieth Century American Intellectual History* (Princeton, NJ: Princeton, 1996), particularly pp. 31–32 on the problematic use of postmodern theory by evangelical scholars. One might question why such parity would be intellectually necessary, except for the evangelical belief-system of the scholars in question. In other words, while it is insightful to note that evangelicals believed that they had a scientific method for reading the Bible, and to note how they used that belief rhetorically in their fight against modernism, one does not need to cede epistemological validity to such a position. While Noll remains critical of the fundamentalist wedding with Baconianism and takes pains to show all the ways in which fundamentalists were innovators as they attempted to preserve the old-time religion, he also believes that the fundamentalist social critique of science is fundamentally correct (p. 186). Gilbert takes a similar, if more religiously neutral stance, when he

argues that W. J. Bryan operated from an alternative definition of science (pp. 23–35).

18. Indeed, one could argue that they themselves embody that instinct in adopting the latest kinds of critique.

19. Of course, in this regard they differed little from their religious studies academic counterparts. See Gilbert, *Redeeming Culture*, pp. 253–272.

20. Gilbert suggests that science was extremely high in prestige in the post–World War II era (Gilbert, *Redeeming Culture*, p. 5).

21. The Amish are an obvious comparison, but even they have made accommodations to modern communications technologies. Even so-called "separatist fundamentalists," such as those represented at Bob Jones University, are technologically friendly.

22. George Marsden, "Preachers of Paradox: Fundamentalist Politics in Historical Perspective," in George Marsden, *Understanding Fundamentalism and Evangelicalism* (Grand Rapids, MI: Eerdmans, 1991), pp. 119–120.

23. David Hollinger notes that throughout the 1940s Americans believed science and democracy to be expressions of each other (*Science, Jews and Secular Culture*, p. 158).

24. Editorial, "Dare We Renew the Controversy? II: The Fundamentalist Reduction," *Christianity Today* (June 24, 1957): 23–26.

25. Ibid., p. 25.

26. Editorial, "Science and the Bible," *Christianity Today* (September 1, 1958): 220–221. Here Henry seems to have anticipated Marsden's argument concerning science and fundamentalism.

27. Ibid., p. 21.

28. Editorial, "Declaration of Principles," *Christianity Today* (October 14, 1957): 20.

29. Ibid., p. 22.

30. "Christianity Today takes cognizance of the dissolving effect of modern scientific theory upon religion"; Editorial, "Why Christianity Today?" *Christianity Today* (October 15, 1956): 20–21.

31. James DeForest Murch, *Cooperation without Compromise: A History of the National Association of Evangelicals* (Grand Rapids, MI: Eerdmans, 1956). Of course, liberal Christianity was the direct result of this new scientism according to Murch (p. 21).

32. Ibid. See also the footnote on p. 28, where Murch defines fundamentalism and notes that "Many times they were dogmatic beyond evidence or were intractable of disposition, or were obnoxiously anti-cultural, anti-scientific and anti-educational."

33. Editorial, "Science and the Bible," *Christianity Today* (September 1, 1958): 20–22.

34. David H. C. Read, "Sputnik and the Angels," *Christianity Today* (December 9, 1957): 10.

35. This tactic should be contrasted to the liberal Protestant approach which was far more techno-phobic.

36. On Ritschl and Otto's attitudes toward science and religion see Gregory, "The Impact of Darwinian Evolution on Protestant Theology," pp. 386–387.

37. "NAE Reaffirms Strong Anti-Communist Stand," *Christianity Today* (May 9, 1960). In 1960 the NAE passed resolutions including: opposition to election of

any Roman Catholic to Presidency; deploring communist infiltration of churches, approval of Bible reading in public schools, to preserve the "right" to purchase radio and television time; opposition to recognition of Red China; and a warning of dangers "to faith and freedom implicit in the United Nations and related world groups."

38. George Washington Robnett, "Communism a Threat to America's Churches," *United Evangelical Action* (August 1, 1949); Editorial, "The Second Call," *Christianity Today* (April 27, 1962); Edward J. Carnell, "Can Billy Graham Slay the Beast?" *Christianity Today* (May 13, 1957): 4 . In addition, the NAE published their own study guide to communism. See the series of articles entitled "The Christian Answer to Communism," in *United Evangelical Action 1960–1961*.

39. Richard W. Gray, "God, America and Sputnik," *Christianity Today* (December 1957): 16.

40. Ibid., p. 17.

41. David H. C. Read, "Sputnik and the Angels," *Christianity Today* (December 9, 1957): 9–11.

42. Editorial, "God and Satellites and Modern Unbelief," *Christianity Today* (February 16, 1959): 22.

43. Editorial, "Advance of Science and Decline of Morality," *Christianity Today* (December 9, 1957): 21.

44. "Chief Concerns of Prominent Christian Mothers," *Christianity Today* (April 27, 1959): 27–28.

45. It also provoked suggestions as to the potential role of the church in such a disaster. See, for example, James Deforest Murch, "The Church and Civil Defense," *Christianity Today* (December 22, 1958): 15–17, where he suggests that church buildings (if not destroyed) could serve as shelters for radioactive fallout. The churches were likewise seen to have an important role in propaganda in preaching the evils of atheism and materialism.

46. They certainly rejected postmillennialism almost completely as it was considered to be almost synonymous with the social gospel. On premillennialism in the U.S. see Timothy P. Weber, *Living in the Shadow of the Second Coming: American Premillennialism, 1875–1982*. Enlarged edition (Chicago: University of Chicago Press, 1987).

47. Editorial, "God's Countdown: 1960," *Christianity Today* (December 1960): 2281.

48. Ibid., p. 231; Eutychus, "Atomic Alphabet," *Christianity Today* (January 5, 1959): 16.

49. Ralph T. Overman, "Will Science Destroy the World?" *Christianity Today* (May 25, 1959): 3–5.

50. Editor, "Space Age Teaching Tools," *Christianity Today* (August 31, 1959): 7–8.

51. Ibid., p. 7.

52. Ibid.

53. Ibid. (emphasis mine).

54. Editorial, "The Bible and Modern Man," *Christianity Today* (November 21, 1960): 156.

55. Dr. Ockenga, "The Space Age: NAE Convention Report," *United Evangelical Action* (May 15, 1958): 148.

56. Edward John Carnell, *Television: Servant or Master?* (Grand Rapids, MI: W. B. Eerdmans Publishing, 1950), p. 116.

57. It is important to note that evangelical leaders believed that their potential listening and viewing audience was huge. The possibility of low program ratings was not considered.

58. Edward John Carnell, *Television: Servant or Master?* (Grand Rapids, MI: W. B. Eerdmans Publishing, 1950).

59. Carnell was in many ways not a typical evangelical leader. He was educated at Harvard, wrote a dissertation on Reinhold Neibuhr, and later committed suicide. Rudolph Nelson, *The Making and Unmaking of an Evangelical Mind: The Case of Edward Carnell* (New York: Cambridge, 1987); George Marsden, *Reforming Fundamentalism: Fuller Seminary and the New Evangelicalism* (Grand Rapids, MI: Eerdmans, 1987).

60. Rudolph L. Nelson, "Fundamentalism at Harvard: The Case of Edward John Carnell," in *Historical Articles on Protestantism in American Religious Life*, edited by Martin E. Marty (Munich: K.G. Saur, 1993), pp. 228–247.

61. Carnell, *Television: Servant or Master*, p. 23.

62. Ibid., p. 35.

63. Ibid., pp. 35–39. See also Mimi White, *Tele-Advising: Therapeutic Discourse in American Television* (Chapel Hill, NC: University of North Carolina, 1992); and Jane Shattuc, *The Talking Cure: TV Talk Shows and Women* (New York: Routledge, 1997). One cannot help but think while reading Carnell's description of TV as a panacea for the troubled soul, that he might be referring to his own soul.

64. Carnell, *Television: Servant or Master*, p. 39.

65. Ibid., pp. 88–89.

66. Almost the opposite of the kinds of programs that the BFC produced!

67. Carnell, *Television: Servant or Master* p. 91.

68. Here clearly Carnell misunderstood the persuasive and deceptive power of the television. His underlying assumption was clearly — what you see is what you get. How would Carnell have understood Jim and Tammy Bakker?

69. Carnell, *Television: Servant or Master*, p. 108.

70. Ibid., pp. 125–131.

71. Ibid., p. 147.

72. Ibid., p. 116.

73. Ibid., p. 187.

74. Ibid.

75. Eutychus, "Big Smoke," *Christianity Today* (November 9, 1959): 15.

76. L. Nelson Bell, "A Layman and His Faith: The Bible and Sex Education," *Christianity Today* (June 8, 1959): 19.

77. Ibid.

78. J. Edgar Hoover, "What does the Future Hold?" *Christianity Today* (June 19, 1961): 802.

79. Carnell, *Television: Servant or Master*, p. 143.

80. Ibid., pp. 142–144.

81. Ibid., p. 153.

82. Editorial, *Christianity Today* (November 12, 1956): 23.

83. "TV-Movie Moral Laxity Stirs Protestant Ire," *Christianity Today* 4 (1959): 71, quoting Robert W. Spike, p. 71.

84. Ralph A. Cannon, and Glenn D. Everett, "Sex and Smut on the Newsstands," *Christianity Today* (February 1, 1958): 5–8.

85. Editorial, "The Press and Sex Morality," *Christianity Today* (January 30, 1961): 360–362.

86. Carnell, *Television: Servant or Master*, p. 161.

87. Joseph Martin Dawson, "The Problem of Censorship," *Christianity Today*, June 22, 1959, pp. 15–16.

88. Editorial, "The Fall of an Idol: Some Deceptions that Remain," *Christianity Today* (November 23, 1959): 150–151.

89. "TV-Movie Moral Laxity Stirs Protestant Ire," *Christianity Today* 4 (1959): 71.

90. "The Minister in the Mirror," *Christianity Today* (April 25, 1960): 621.

91. Ibid.

92. "Profaning God's Name on Sunday Television," *Christianity Today* (March 2, 1959): 23.

93. Interestingly enough, this was irrelevant to the success or failure of televangelism.

94. Eutychus, "All in Color," *Christianity Today* (April 11, 1960): 576.

95. Otto A. Piper, "Christians in a Secular World," *Christianity Today* (June 6, 1960): 731–732.

96. Editorial, "The Church and Public Relations," *Christianity Today* (April 14, 1958): 20–22. This is a particularly interesting quote in light of the contemporary mega-church phenomenon.

97. Eutychus, "All in Color," p. 576.

98. Ibid.

99. Carnell, *Television: Servant or Master*, p. 129.

100. It is interesting that this discourse concerning the end of the book era which recently has become more popular again with the rise of use of the internet is actually 40 years old.

101. Eutychus, "Sacred Electronics," *Christianity Today* (January 21, 1957): 18.

102. Ibid.

Chapter 6   Protestants and the Television: The Paradox Reassessed

1. Some scholars argue that we no longer live in an era of mass communications. See Steve H. Chaffee and Miriam J. Metzger, "The End of Mass Communication?" *Mass Communication & Society*, 4:4 (2001): 365–379.

2. Recent works on religion and the internet include: Stewart Hoover, Lynn S. Clark and Lee Rainie, "Faith Online: 64% of Wired Americans Have Used the Internet for Spiritual or Religious Information," *Pew Internet and American Life Project* (April 7, 2004). http://www.pewinternet.org/pdfs/PIP_Faith_

Online_2004.pdf; Heidi Campbell, *Exploring Religious Community Online: We are One in the Network* (New York: Peter Lang, 2005); Morten T. Højsgaard and Margit Warburg, eds., *Religion and Cyberspace* (New York: Routledge, 2005).

3. "Nearly Half of all Americans are Tuning into Christian Radio," News release for the NRB, March 22, 2005, downloaded from www.nrb.org, May 2006.

4. Annual Report 2005, The Communication Commission of the National Council of Churches of Christ, downloaded from http://www.ncccusa.org/communication/comcomreport2005.htm, May 2006.

5. "The Church and the Media: An NCC Policy Guide," downloaded from http://www.ncccusa.org/about/comcompolicies.html, May 2006.

6. Ibid.

7. ("Global Communication for Justice: A Policy Statement Approved by the General Board of the National Council of the Churches of Christ in the USA," November 11, 1993, downloaded from http://www.ncccusa.org May 2006.)

8. See p. 1, ch. 2, where I discuss the original Elvis editorial.

9. "The Church and the Media: An NCC Policy Guide," downloaded from http://www.ncccusa.org/about/comcompolicies.html, May 2006.

10. During the calendar year 2005, the NCC website hit an all-time high for page views, 958,940—just short of its 1 million goal, but 50% higher than the 639,866 hits in 2003.

11. Joshua Meyrowitz, "Multiple Media Literacies." *Journal of Communication* 48:1 (1998): 96–108.

12. Fore, Horsfield, and Marty as noted in chapter one all suggest that the nature of television limits the kinds of messages one can transmit. This is an important observation about the ways in which our notion of television has limited the kinds of messages that can successfully be transmitted (success being measured by the number of viewers, or their appreciation of the message?), but it attributes far too much importance to the technology itself, rather than its users.

13. Herbert J. Gans, *Popular Culture and High Culture: An Analysis and Evaluation of Taste* (New York: Basic Books, 1974), p. 7.

14. Martin E. Marty, "The New Establishment," *The Christian Century* 75 (October 12, 1958): 1176.

Bibliography

Archival Collections

Presbyterian Historical Society, Philadelphia, PA
National Council of Churches of Christ Archives
Broadcast and Film Commission Collection
Billy Graham Center Archives, Wheaton, IL
National Religious Broadcasters Collection

Articles Cited from *The Christian Century* (by Author Name)

"All Aboard for Rainbow Land!" (September 14, 1955): 1045.
"Ban Liquor Drinking on Michigan TV?" (March 24, 1954): 356.
"Bishop Cloys as Critic" (December 5, 1956): 1413.
"Can the Home be Saved?" (February 21, 1945): 231.
"Can't It be Applied to Television?" (November 1, 1944): 1245–1246.
"CBS Ousts Source of TV Corruption" (October 28, 1959): 1238.
"Censorship in Chicago" (February 6, 1957): 163.
"Denies Civil Power over Marriage" (October 16, 1946): 1236–1237.
"Easter on TV" (March 25, 1953): 339.
"Give Away Shows Raise Ethical Questions" (February 24, 1954): 227.
"Graham Clarifies the Issue" (July 30, 1958): 870.
"How Effective are the Mass Media?" (August 29, 1956): 988.
"How Far From Code to Control?" (June 13, 1956): 716.
"How the Catholic Church Supervises the Movies" (February 7, 1945): 164–165.
"Insist Religion Merit Public Service Time" (March 19, 1958): 333–334.
"Is Television Making a Nation of Hypochondriacs?" (October 19, 1955): 1198.

"Luther Film Makes Belated Television Debut" (March 13, 1957): 317.

"Missouri Lutherans Produce TV Series" (August 13, 1952): 916.

"Murder by TV" (April 18, 1962): 482.

"Networks Miss a Good Bet" (March 12, 1958): 301.

"Notre Dame Would Censor Professor's Speeches" (November 17, 1943): 1325–1326.

"Oklahoma Faith-Healer Draws a Following" (June 29, 1955): 750.

"One More Argument for Subscription TV" (May 18, 1955): 589.

"Oppose Conscription on Moral Grounds" (January 31, 1945): 131–132.

"Paar Show a Measure of American Culture" (September 23, 1959): 1076–1077.

"Prelate Sees Catholicism Winning Japan" (August 21, 1946): 1004–1005.

"Protestantism and Tolerance" (February 14, 1945): 198–200.

"Protestantism Coming Alive" (October 23, 1946): 1267.

"Public Money Diverted for Catholic Schools" (January 24, 1945): 101.

"Radio Used to Attack Protestant Missions" (October 6, 1943): 1123.

"Responsible Broadcasting in Racial Disturbances" (August 17, 1955): 941.

"Roman Catholic Church Never Sells Spiritual Blessings" (March 7, 1945): 292.

"Roman Catholicism and Religious Liberty" (September 4, 1946): 1052.

"Television Manufacturers Stir Up a Storm" (December 6, 1950): 1444.

"Turn the Dial" (September 10, 1958): 1011.

"TV—A Giant for Good or Ill" (February 2, 1955): 131.

"TV Opportunity Is Fleeing" (November 29, 1950): 1414.

"TV Station Yields to Catholic Pressure" (January 2, 1957): 4.

"What about Oral Roberts" (September 5, 1956): 1018–1021.

"What about Religious Doctrine on Television?" (February 14, 1951): 196.

"What a Twisted Scale of Values!" (May 25, 1960): 630.

"What Should Be Done About TV Programs?" (May 28, 1952): 637.

"Where Can the Pope Go?" (December 22, 1943): 1496–1497.

"Will Television Depend on Advertising?" (October 25, 1944): 1221.

"Yawn and Flip the TV Knob" (October 22, 1958): 1198.

Articles Cited from *The Christian Century* (by Author Name)

Carothers, J. Edward. "A Television Ministry" (May 11, 1949): 591–592.

Crowe, Charles M. "So This Is Good Will" (April 4, 1945): 427–429.

———. "Television Needs Religion" (August 10, 1949): 938–939.

Fey, Harold. "Can Catholicism Win America" (April 3, 1944): 1378–1380.

Lee, Robert E. A. "Censorship: A Case History" (February 6, 1957): 163.

Morrison, Charles Clayton. "Can Protestantism Win America" (April 3, 1946): 425–427.

———. "Protestantism and Commercialized Entertainment" (April 3, 1946): 425–427.

Motter, Alton M. "Back to the Kefauver TV Show" (May 9, 1951): 584–585.

Nasby, A. Gordon. "Television and the Church" (February 2, 1949): 142–413.

Sockman, Ralph W. "Catholics and Protestants" (May 2, 1945): 545–546.

Articles Cited from Christianity and Crisis

Boyd, Malcolm. "The Crisis of the Mass Media." *Christianity and Crisis* (16 April 1956): 68.

Pope, Liston. "Religion on the Air." *Christianity and Crisis* (15 November 1955): 147–148.

Articles Cited from United Evangelical Action

"Editorial: Federal Council Caught 'Red-Handed'" (March 1, 1950): 9, 29.

Fowler, Frederick Curtis. "Render Unto Caesar and Unto God" (May 1, 1952): 9–12, 18.

Kaub, Verne P. "The NCC at Denver" (February 1, 1953): 3–7, 16.

Murch, James DeForest. "Adventuring in *United Evangelical Action*" (October 1946): 5–8.

———. "America's Vatican Envoy Must Be Recalled Now" (March 15, 1946): 5–6.

———. "The Christian Citizen's Duty" (August 1, 1952): 6.

———. "Current Moves for World Christian Co-operation" (November 15, 1946): 4–7.

———. "Fundamental Principles in Papal-US Relations" (March 1, 1946).

———. "How Federative Action Began in America" (September 1, 1946): 7–8.

———. "NAE Comes of Age" (May 15, 1948): 3–6, 15–23.

———. "On Winning America" (July 15, 1946): 8–9.

Murch, James DeForest. "Papal-American Relations Prove Bitter Venture" (February 15, 1946): 7–8.

———. "The Proposed National Council of Churches" (October 1, 1946): 6–8.

———. "Religious Freedom?" (May 11, 1953): 10.

———. "A Study in Christian Co-operation in America" (August 15, 1946): 3–4.

———. "The Supreme Court Speaks" 7 (1948): 8–9.

———. "Trends in Protestantism." (March 1, 1958): 7.

———. "Why Evangelicals Cannot Co-operate in the FCCCA" (September 15, 1946): 5–7.

———. "Why *United Evangelical Action* Is Imperative" (August 1, 1946): 3–4.

"NAE Convention Resolutions" (May 1, 1952): 8.

"National Religious Broadcasters Report" (May 1, 1952): 36–37.

Ockenga, Dr. "The Space Age: NAE Convention Report" (May 15, 1958): 148.

Paine, Stephen W. "Principle vs. Practice in ACCC Membership" (July 15, 1951): 4–5, 8.

Robnett, George Washington. "Communism a Threat to America's Churches" (August 1, 1949).

Savage, H. H. "United Evangelical Action: Presidential Address at the Chicago Convention" (May 1, 1955): 151–154, 159.

Articles Cited from *Christianity Today* (by Article Name)

"Chief Concerns of Prominent Christian Mothers" (April 27, 1959): 27–28.

"NAE Reaffirms Strong Anti-Communist Stand" (May 9, 1960).

"TV-Movie Moral Laxity Stirs Protestant Ire" (October 26, 1959): 71.

Articles Cited from *Christianity Today* (by Author Name)

Bell, L. Nelson. "A Layman and His Faith: The Bible and Sex Education" (June 8, 1959): 19.

Cannon, Ralph A., and Glenn D. Everett. "Sex and Smut on the Newsstands" (February 1, 1958): 5–8.

Carnell, Edward J. "Can Billy Graham Slay the Beast?" (May 13, 1957): 4.

Dawson, Joseph Martin. "The Problem of Censorship" (June 22, 1959): 15–16.

Editorial. "Advance of Science and Decline of Morality" (December 9, 1957): 21.

———. "The Bible and Modern Man" (November 21, 1960): 156–157.

———. "The Church and Public Relations" (April 14, 1958): 20–22.

———. "Dare We Renew the Controversy? II: The Fundamentalist Reduction" (June 24, 1957): 23–26.

———. "Declaration of Principles" (October 14, 1957): 20–22.

———. "The Fall of an Idol: Some Deceptions that Remain" (November 23, 1959): 150–151.

———. "God and Satellites and Modern Unbelief" (February 16, 1959): 22.

———. "God's Countdown: 1960" (December 1960): 228–231.

———. "Profaning God's Name on Sunday Television" (March 2, 1959): 23.

———. "Science and the Bible" (September 1, 1958): 20–22.

———. "Space Age Teaching Tools" (August 31, 1959): 7–8.

———. "The Second Call" (April 27, 1962).

———. "Why Christianity Today?" (October 15, 1956): 20–21.

Eutychus. "All in Color" (April 11, 1960): 576.

———. "Atomic Alphabet" (January 5, 1959): 16.

———. "Big Smoke" (November 9, 1959): 15.

———. "Like It Means Nothing" (March 2, 1959): 24.

———. "Sacred Electronics" (January 21, 1957): 18.

Gray, Richard W. "God, America and Sputnik" (December 9, 1957): 15–17.

Hoover, J. Edgar. "The Challenge of the Future" (May 26, 1958).

———. "Communism: The Bitter Enemy of Religion" (June 22, 1959): 3–5.

———. "What does the Future Hold?" (June 19, 1961): 802.

Murch, James Deforest. "The Church and Civil Defense" (December 22, 1958): 15–17.

Overman, Ralph T. "Will Science Destroy the World?" (May 25, 1959): 3–5.

Piper, Otto A. "Christians in a Secular World" (June 6, 1960): 731–734.

Read, David H. C. "Sputnik and the Angels" (December 9, 1957): 9–11.

Books and Articles

Ahlstrom, Sydney. *A Religious History of the American People*. New Haven, CT: Yale University Press, 1972.

Alexander, Bobby Chris. *Televangelism Reconsidered: A Ritual in Search of Human Community*. Atlanta, GA: Scholars Press, 1994.

Armstrong, Ben. *The Electric Church*. Nashville, TN: Thomas Nelson Publishers Inc., 1979.

Bachman, John W. *The Church in the World of Radio-Television*. New York: National Board of Young Christian's Associations, 1960.

Barbour, Ian G. *Religion and Science: Historical and Contemporary Issues*. San Francisco: Harper San Francisco, 1997.

Barnouw, Eric. *A History of Broadcasting in the US: A Tower of Babel*. New York: Oxford University Press, 1973.

Barstow, Robbins W., Luther Wesley Smith, and Norman E. Tompkins, eds. *Christian Faith in Action: Commemorative Volume, The Founding of the National Council of the Churches of Christ in America*: Central Department of Publication and Distribution National Council of the Churches of Christ in the United States of America, 1951.

Becker, George. "Pietism's Confrontation with Enlightenment Rationalism: An Examination of the Relation Between Ascetic Protestantism and Science." *Journal for the Scientific Study of Religion* 30.2 (1991): 139–158.

Becker, Howard. *Art Worlds*. Berkeley: University of California Press, 1982.

Berger, Peter L. "The Descularization of the World: A Global View," in *The Desecularization of the World: Resurgent Religion and World Politics*. Edited by Peter L. Berger, pp. 3–18. Grand Rapids, MI: Eerdmans, 1999.

Bjiker, Wiebe J. *Of Bicycles, Bakelites, and Bulbs: Toward a Theory of Sociotechnical Change* (Cambridge, MA: MIT Press, 1997).

Bourdieu, Pierre. *Distinction: A Social Critique of the Judgment of Taste*. Cambridge: Harvard University Press, 1984.

Boyer, Paul. *By the Bomb's Early Light: American Thought and Culture at the Dawn of the Atomic Age*. Chapel Hill: University of North Carolina, 1985.

Bozeman, Theodore Dwight. *Protestants in an Age of Science: The Baconian Ideal and Antebellum American Religious Thought*. Chapel Hill, NC: University of North Carolina Press, 1977.

Brantlinger, Patrick. *Crusoe's Footsteps: Cultural Studies in Britain and America*. London: Routledge, 1990.

Bruce, Steve. *Pray TV: Televangelism in America*. London: Routledge, 1990.

Campbell, Heidi. *Exploring Religious Community Online: We are One in the Network*. New York: Peter Lang, 2005.

Carpenter, Joel. *Revive Us Again: The Reawakening of American Fundamentalism* (New York: Oxford University Press, 1997).

Carpenter, Joel, ed. "Evangelical Action! A Report of the Organization of the National Association of Evangelicals for United Action." *A New Coalition: Early Documents of the National Association of Evangelicals*. New York: Garland Publishing, [1942] 1988.

————, ed. "United . . . We Stand: A Report of the Constitutional Convention of the National Association of Evangelicals." *A New Coalition: Early Documents of the National Association of Evangelicals.* New York: Garland, [1943] 1988.

Carey, James. *Communication as Culture: Essays on Media and Society.* Boston: Unwin Hyman, 1988.

Carnell, Edward John. *Television: Servant or Master?* Grand Rapids, MI: W. B. Eerdmans Publishing, 1950.

Croce, Paul Jerome. *Science and Religion in the Era of William James: Eclipse of Certainty, 1820–1880.* Vol. 1. Chapel Hill, NC: University of North Carolina Press, 1995.

Czitrom, Daniel J. *Media and the American Mind: From Morse to McLuhan.* Chapel Hill: University of North Carolina, 1982.

Dayan, Daniel. "The Peculiar Public of Television," *Media, Culture and Society* 23 (2001): 743–65.

Dayton, Donald, and Robert K. Johnston, eds. *The Variety of American Evangelicalism.* Downers Grove, IL: Intervarsity Press, 1991.

Delloff, Linda-Marie. "'God as Artist': Aesthetic Theory in *The Christian Century* 1908–1955." Ph.D., University of Chicago, 1985.

Dennis, Everette E., and Ellen Wartella, eds. *American Communication Research: The Remembered History.* Mahwah, NJ: Lawrence Erlbaum, 1996.

DiMaggio, Paul. "Cultural Boundaries and Structural Change: The Extension of the High Culture Model to Theater, Opera, and Dance, 1900–1940," in *Cultivating Differences: Symbolic Boundaries and the Making of Inequality,* edited by Michele Lamont and Marcel Fournier, pp. 21–57. Chicago: University of Chicago Press, 1992.

Dobbelaere, Karl. "Secularization: A Multi-Dimensional Concept." *Current Sociology* 29:2 (March 1981): 3–153.

Douglas, Susan J. *Inventing American Broadcasting: 1899–1922.* Baltimore: John Hopkins University, 1987.

Edwards, Mark. *Printing, Propaganda, and Martin Luther.* Berkeley, CA: University of California Press, 1994.

Eisenstein, Elizabeth. *The Printing Press as an Agent of Change: Communicaitons and Cultural Transformations in Early-Modern Europe, Vol. 1.* London: Cambridge University Press, 1979.

Ellens, Harold. *Models of Religious Broadcasting.* Grand Rapids, MI: Eerdmans, 1974.

Findlay, James. *Church People in the Struggle: The National Council of Churches and the Black Freedom Movement, 1950–1970.* New York: Oxford University Press, 1993.

Finke, Roger and Rodney Stark. *The Churching of America 1776–1990: Winners and Losers in Our Religious Economy.* New Brunswick, NJ: Rutgers University Press, 1992.

Fore, William F. *Mythmakers: Gospel Culture and the Media.* NY: Friendship Press, 1990.

Fore, William F. *Television and Religion: The Shaping of Faith. Values, and Culture.* Minneapolis, MN: Augsburg, 1987.

Fox, Richard. *Reinhold Niebuhr: A Biography.* San Francisco: Harper and Row, 1988.

Frankl, Razelle. *Televangelism: The Marketing of Popular Religion.* Carbondale, IL: Southern Illinois University Press, 1987.

Gans, Harold J. *Popular Culture and High Culture: An Analysis and Evaluation of Taste.* New York: Basic Books, 1974.

George, Carol V. *God's Salesman: Norman Vincent Peale and the Power of Positive Thinking.* New York: Oxford University Press, 1993.

Gilbert, James. *Redeeming Culture: American Religion in an Age of Science.* Chicago: University of Chicago Press, 1997.

Goethals, Gregor T. *The TV Ritual: Worship at the Video Altar.* Boston: Beacon Press, 1981.

Gregory, Frederick. "The Impact of Darwinian Evolution on Protestant Theology." *God and Nature: Historical Essays on the Encounter Between Christianity and Science,* ed. David C. Lindberg and Ronald L. Numbers. Berkeley, CA: University of California Press, 1986. 369–390.

Griswold, Wendy. *Cultures and Societies in a Changing World.* Thousand Oaks, CA: Pine Forge Press, 1994.

Hadden, Jeffrey, and Anson Shupe. *Televangelism: Power and Politics on God's Frontier.* New York: Henry Holt and Co., 1988.

Hadden, Jeffrey K., and Charles Swann. *Primetime Preachers: The Rising Power of Televangelism.* Reading, ME: Addison Wesley Pub., 1981.

Handy, Robert. *A Christian America: Protestant Hopes and Historical Realities.* London: Oxford University Press, 1971.

Hangen, Tona. *Redeeming the Dial: Radio, Religion and Popular Culture in America.* Chapel Hill, NC: University of North Carolina Press, 2002.

Hatch, Nathan. *The Democratization of American Christianity.* New Haven, CT: Yale University Press, 1989.

Hendershot, Heather. *Shaking the World for Jesus: Media and Conservative Evangelical Culture.* Chicago: University of Chicago Press, 2004.

Herberg, Will. *Protestant, Catholic, Jew.* Garden City, NY: Anchor, 1955.

Højsgaard, Morten T., and Margit Warburg, eds. *Religion and Cyberspace.* New York: Routledge, 2005.

Hollinger, David A. *Science, Jews, and Secular Culture: Studies in Mid-Twentieth Century American Intellectual History.* Princeton, NJ: Princeton, 1996.

Hoover, Stewart M. *Mass Media Religion: The Social Sources of the Electronic Church*. Newbury Park, CA: Sage Publications, 1988.

Hoover, Stewart M. *The Electronic Giant: A Critique of the Telecommunications Revolution from a Christian Perspective*. Elgin, IL: Brethren Press, 1982.

———. "The Religious Television Audience: A Matter of Significance or Size?" *Review of Religious Research* 29(December 1987): 135–151.

Horsfield, Peter. *Religious Television: The American Experience*. New York: Longman Inc., 1984.

Hudnut-Beumler, James. *Looking for God in the Suburbs: The Religion of the American Dream and Its Critics, 1945–1965*. New Brunswick, NJ: Rutgers University Press, 1994.

Hutchison, William R. *The Modernist Impulse in American Protestantism*. Cambridge, MA: Harvard University Press, 1976.

———, ed. *Between the Times: The Travails of the Protestant Establishment in America 1900–1960*. New York: Cambridge University Press, 1989.

Huyssen, Andreas. *After the Great Divide: Modernism, Mass Culture, Postmodernism*. Bloomington: Indiana University Press, 1986.

Jay, Daniel. *The Dialectical Imagination: A History of the Frankfurt School and the Institute of Social Research*. Boston: Little, Brown and Company, 1973.

Jennings, Ralph M. "Policies and Practices of Selected National Religious Bodies as Related to Broadcasting in the Public Interest 1920–1950." Ph.D. New York University, 1968.

Katz, Elihu. "On Conceptualizing Media Effects." *Studies in Communication: A Research Annual*, ed. Thelma McCormack. Greenwich, CT: JAI Press, 1980. 119–141. Vol. 1.

Kelley, Dean. *Why Conservative Churches are Growing*. New York: Harper and Row, 1972.

Lears, T. J. Jackson. "The Concept of Cultural Hegemony: Problems and Possibilities." *American Historical Review* 90.3 (June 1985): 567–593.

———. "A Matter of Taste: Corporate Cultural Hegemony in a Mass-Consumption Society." *Recasting America: Culture and Politics in the Age of the Cold War*, ed. Lary May, pp. 38–57. Chicago: University of Chicago Press, 1989.

———. "From Salvation to Self-Realization: Advertising and the Theraputic Roots of the Consumer Culture, 1880–1930." *The Culture of Consumption: Critical Essays in American History, 1880–1980*, ed. Richard Wrightman Fox and T. J. Jackson Lears. New York: Pantheon Books, 1983.

Lambert, Frank. *"Pedlar in Divinity": George Whitefield and the Transatlantic Revivals, 1737–1770*. Princeton, NJ: Princeton University Press, 1994.

Lamont, Michele, and Anette Lareau. "Cultural Capital: Allusions, Gaps, and Glissandos in Recent Theoretical Developments." *Sociological Theory* 6 (Fall 1988): 153–168.

Levine, Lawrence. *Highbrow/Lowbrow: The Emergence of Cultural Hierarchy in America.* Cambridge: Harvard University Press, 1988.

Liebman, Robert C., and Robert Wuthnow, eds., *The New Christian Right: Mobilization and Legitimation.* New York: Aldine Publishing, 1983.

Lippy, Charles H., ed. *Religious Periodicals in the United States: Academic and Scholarly Journals.* Westport, CT: Greenwood Press, 1986.

MacNeil, Alex. *Total Television: A Comprehensive Guide to Programming from 1948 to the Present.* New York: Penguin Books, 1984.

Marsden, George M., ed. *Evangelicalism and Modern America.* Grand Rapids, MI: Eerdmans, 1984.

———. "The Evangelical Love Affair with Enlightenment Science." *Understanding Fundamentalism and Evangelicalism.* Grand Rapids, MI: Eerdmans, 1991. 122–152.

———. *Reforming Fundamentalism: Fuller Seminary and the New Evangelicalism.* Grand Rapids, MI: Eerdmans, 1987.

———. *Understanding Fundamentalism and Evangelicalism.* Grand Rapids, MI: Eerdmans, 1991.

Martin, William. *With God On Our Side: The Rise of the Religious Right in America.* New York: Broadway Books, 1996.

Marty, Martin E. *The Improper Opinion: Mass Media and the Christian Faith.* Philadelphia: Westminster Press, 1961.

———. *Modern American Religion, Vol. 1: The Irony of It All.* Chicago: University of Chicago Press, 1986.

———. *Modern American Religion, Vol. 2: The Noise of Conflict, 1919–1941.* Chicago: University of Chicago, 1991.

———. *Modern American Religion, Vol. 3: Under God, Indivisible 1941–1960.* Chicago: University of Chicago Press, 1996.

———. "Protestantism and Capitalism: Print Culture and Individualism." *Communications in American Religious History,* ed. Leonard I. Sweet. Grand Rapids, MI: Eerdmans, 1993. 91–107.

———. "The Revival of Evangelical and Southern Religion." *Varieties of Southern Evangelicalism,* ed. Jr. David E. Harell. Macon, GA: Mercer University Press, 1981.

———. *Righteous Empire: The Protestant Experience in America.* New York: Dial Press, 1970.

Marvin, Carolyn. *When Old Technologies Were New: Thinking About Electric Communication in the Late Nineteenth Century.* New York: Oxford University Press, 1988.

McDannell, Colleen. *The Christian Home in Victorian America 1840–1900*. Bloomington: Indiana University Press, 1986.

McLoughlin, William. *Revivals, Awakenings, and Reform*. Chicago: University of Chicago Press, 1978.

Mendelsohn, Everett. "Religious Fundamentalism and the Sciences." *Fundamentalisms and Society: Reclaiming the Sciences, the Family, and Education*, ed. Martin E. Marty and R. Scott Appleby. Chicago: University of Chicago Press, 1993. 23–41. Vol. 2.

Merritt, John G. "Christianity Today." *Religious Periodicals of the United States*, ed. Charles H. Lippy. New York: Greenwood Press, 1986. 134–140.

Meyrowitz, Joshua. "Medium Theory," in *Communication Theory Today*, edited by David Crowley and David Mitchell, pp. 50–77. Stanford, CA: Stanford University Press, 1994.

———. "Multiple Media Literacies." *Journal of Communication* 48.1 (1998): 96–108.

Moore, R. Laurence. *Religious Outsiders and the Making of Americans*. New York: Oxford University Press, 1986.

———. "Secularization: Religion and Social Sciences." *Between the Times: The Travails of the Protestant Establishment in America, 1900–1960*, ed. William R. Hutchison. New York: Cambridge University Press, 1989. 233–252.

———. *Selling God: American Religion in the Marketplace of Culture*. New York: Oxford, 1994.

Morgan, David, ed. *Icons of American Protestantism: The Art of Warner Sallman*. New Haven, CT: Yale University Press, 1996.

Murch, James DeForest. *Cooperation without Compromise: A History of the National Association of Evangelicals*. Grand Rapids, MI: Eerdmans, 1956.

Nelson, Rudolph L. *The Making and Unmaking of an Evangelical Mind: The Case of Edward Carnell*. New York: Cambridge, 1987.

———. "Fundamentalism at Harvard: The Case of Edward John Carnell." *Historical Articles on Protestantism in American Religious Life*, ed. Martin E. Marty. Munich: K.G. Saur, 1993. 228–247. Vol. 10. 14 vols.

Niebuhr, H. Richard. *Christ and Culture*. New York: Harper and Row, 1951.

Noll, Mark A. *The Scandal of the Evangelical Mind*. Grand Rapids, MI: Eerdmans, 1994.

Oudshoorn, Nelly and Trevor Pinch. *How Users Matter: The Co-Construction of Users and Technology*. Cambridge, MA: MIT Press, 2003.

Ozment, Steve. *Protestants: The Birth of a Revolution*. New York: Doubleday, 1991.

Parker, Everett C., David W. Barry, and Dallas W. Smythe. *The Television-Radio Audience and Religion*. New York: Harper Brothers, 1955.

Peck, Janice. *The Gods of Televangelism: The Crisis of Meaning and the Appeal of Religious TV*. Cresskill, NJ: Hampton Press, 1993.

Postman, Neil. *Amusing Ourselves to Death: Public Discourse in the Age of Show Business*. New York: Penguin Books, 1985.

Promey, Sally M. "Interchangeable Art: Warner Sallman and the Critics of Mass Culture." *Icons of American Protestantism: The Art of Warner Sallman*, ed. David Morgan. New Haven, CT: Yale University Press, 1996. 167–173.

Ribak, Rivka, and Michele Rosenthal, "From the Field Phone to the Mobile Phone: A Cultural Biography of the Telephone in Kibbutz Y," *New Media and Society* 8(4): 553–574.

Ribuffo, Leo. *The Old Christian Right: The Protestant Far Right from the Great Depression to the Cold War*. Philadelphia: Temple University Press, 1983.

Riesebrodt, Martin. *Pious Passion: The Emergence of Modern Fundamentalism in the United States and Iran*. Trans. Don Reneau. Berkeley, CA: University of California Press, 1993.

Rogers, Everett M. *A History of Communication Study: A Biographical Approach*. New York: The Free Press, 1997.

Roof, Wade Clark and William McKinney. *American Mainline Religion: Its Changing Shape and Future*. New Brunswick, NJ: Rutgers University Press, 1987.

Ross, Andrew. *No Respect: Intellectuals and Popular Culture*. New York: Routledge, 1989.

Schmidt, Leigh Eric. *Consumer Rites: The Buying and Selling of American Holidays*. Princeton, NJ: Princeton University Press, 1995.

Schultze, Quentin J., ed. *American Evangelicals and the Media*. Grand Rapids, MI: Zondervan, 1990.

———. *Televangelism and American Culture: The Business of Popular Culture*. Grand Rapids, MI: Baker Book House, 1991.

———. "The Two Faces of Fundamentalist Higher Education." *Fundamentalisms and Society: Reclaiming the Science, the Family and Education*, ed. Martin E. Marty and R. Scott Appleby. Chicago: University of Chicago Press, 1991. 490–535. Vol. 2. 5 vols.

Scribner, Robert W. "Oral Culture and the Diffusion of Reformation Ideas." *History of European Ideas* 5 (1984): 237–256.

Shattuc, Jane. *The Talking Cure: TV Talk Shows and Women*. New York: Routledge, 1997.

Silk, Mark. *Unsecular Media: Making News of Religion in America*. Urbana, IL: University of Illinois Press, 1995.

Smith, Christian. *American Evangelicalism: Embattled and Thriving.* Chicago, IL: University of Chicago Press, 1998.

Sockman, Ralph W. "Catholics and Protestants." *The Christian Century* (May 2, 1945): 545–546.

Spigel, Lynn. *Make Room for TV: Television and the Family Ideal in Postwar America.* Chicago: University of Chicago Press, 1992.

————. *Welcome to the Dreamhouse: Popular Media and Postwar Suburbs.* Durham, NC: Duke University Press, 2001.

Stout, Daniel A., and Judith M. Buddenbaum, eds. *Religion and Mass Media: Audiences and Adaptations.* Thousand Oaks, CA: Sage, 1996.

Sweet, Leonard I, ed. *Communication and Change in American Religious History.* Grand Rapids, MI: Eerdmans, 1993.

Swidler, Ann. "Culture in Action: Symbols and Strategies." *American Sociological Review* 51.2 (April 1986): 273–286.

Szasz, Ferenc Morton. *The Divided Mind of Protestant America, 1880–1930.* University, Alabama: University of Alabama, 1982.

Tichi, Cecilia. *Electronic Hearth: Creating an American Television Culture.* New York: Oxford University Press, 1991.

Tillich, Paul. *A Theology of Culture.* New York: Oxford University Press, 1959.

Tolouse, Marc. "*The Christian Century* and American Public Life," in *New Dimensions in American Religious History*, edited by Jay P. Dolan and James P. Wind, pp. 44–82. Grand Rapids, MI: Eerdmans, 1993.

Turner, Graeme. *British Cultural Studies: An Introduction.* Cambridge, MA: Unwin Hyman, 1990.

Umble, Diane Zimmerman. "The Amish and the Telephone: Resistance and Reconstruction." *Consuming Technologies: Media and Information in Domestic Spaces*, ed. Roger Silverstone and Eric Hirsch. London: Routledge, 1992. 183–195.

————. *Holding the Line: The Telephone in Old Order Mennonite and Amish Life.* Baltimore, MD: John Hopkins University Press, 1996.

Voskuil, Dennis N. "The Power of the Air: Evangelicals and the Rise of Religious Broadcasting," in *American Evangelicals and the Mass Media*, edited by Quentin J. Schultze, pp. 69–95. Grand Rapids, MI: Academie Books, 1990.

Wallis, Jim. *God's Politics: Why The Right Gets It Wrong and the Left Doesn't Get It: A New Vision for Faith and Politics in America.* San Francisco: HarperSanFrancisco, 2005.

Ward, Mark Sr. *Air of Salvation: The Story of Christian Broadcasting.* Grand Rapids, MI: Baker Books, 1994.

Weber, Timothy P. *Living in the Shadow of the Second Coming: American Premillennialism, 1875–1982*. Enlarged edition. Chicago: University of Chicago Press, 1987.

White, Mimi. *Tele-Advising: Therapeutic Discourse in American Television*. Chapel Hill, NC: University of North Carolina, 1992.

Williams, Raymond. *Television: Technology and Cultural Form*. [1974] Reprint Hanover, NH: Wesleyan University Press, 1992.

Wuthnow, Robert. *Producing the Sacred: An Essay on Public Religion*. Urbana, IL: University of Illinois Press, 1994.

———. "Religion and Television: The Public and the Private." *American Evangelicals and the Mass Media*, ed. Quentin J. Schultze. Grand Rapids, MI: Zondervan, 1990. 199–214.

———. *The Restructuring of American Religion: Society and Faith Since World War II*. Princeton, NJ: Princeton University Press, 1988.

———. "The Social Significance of Religious Television." *Review of Religious Research* 29 (December 1987): 97–210.

Index

(Please note that page numbers in *italics* indicate end notes.)